MUSIC OF OUR DAY
ESSENTIALS AND PROPHECIES

MUSIC OF OUR DAY

Essentials and Prophecies

by

LAZARE SAMINSKY

NEW ENLARGED
EDITION

Essay Index Reprint Series

BOOKS FOR LIBRARIES PRESS
FREEPORT, NEW YORK

First Published 1939
Reprinted 1970

STANDARD BOOK NUMBER:
8369-1682-4

LIBRARY OF CONGRESS CATALOG CARD NUMBER:
78-117838

PRINTED IN THE UNITED STATES OF AMERICA

THIS *writer dislikes exhausting a subject in discourse as much as he would shun doing so in a sonata. As soon as the kernel of a thing is held up to the light, it is easy to see the rest. This book has no desire to race the arrow telling off seconds, to record minutely changes in the body of modern music since the first edition. As a matter of fact, nothing has changed; only processes before described have been aggravated.*

The shifts in this new edition are only additions —a new introductory essay, new chapters on Sibelius, on North and Latin America, on French and English composers, and on the Composer versus Critic. Only one chapter, that on the Russian Ballet, is revised; the rest has been left intact.

Of course, the reader is always curious to have our own confession as to whether anything has shifted—in our viewpoint. With one who has set out to describe the true state of things this query is, I believe, beside the mark.

Is not the instinct of fact but a moment in our awareness when truth is filtering through one's mind?

The mind can be neither wrong nor right. Like sight or hearing, it either lets things through, or it does not. L. S.

CONTENTS

MUSIC OF OUR DAY
A PRELUDE TO RESURRECTION

"FOR some years they have lived on nothing but tactics, and now they have died of tactics."

What a British statesman said of his political enemies, might well explain many a thing now.[1]

*　　　*　　　*　　　*　　　*

A strange stillness hovers over the dreary lanes of today's music.

Some time ago we sat before the burning house waiting. Would the high wind die down? Was the frame strong enough to survive? We now lean over unrelieved debris.

The musical map before us is very much like a photograph of the moon. A glazed, seared surface dotted with extinct volcanoes. Ours are the three S's which have come very near to taking the place of the three B's, at any rate—to elbowing them out of much of their realm. By the side of dead giants

[1] Sir Henry Campbell-Bannerman, premier of England (1905-1908) and leader of the Liberal Party.

—a number of minor and local craters; they fumed so busily not long ago, and now are not eligible for even a listing.

Strauss, Schoenberg, Stravinsky! A rumbling is still heard in semi-cold craters; a queer piece is flung out, now and then, and rolls down the slope.

But nothing can be found in *Arabella* or the rest of Strauss' mellifluous inanities, nothing save tricks of a formerly glamorous craft. And it is clear that Schoenberg has died from carrying beyond art's endurance a perverse structural obsession, a technical strategy cruelly alien to the native order of song. As to Stravinsky, the greatest tactician of them all, his exit marks the exhaustion of a limited creative gift drawn out into a semblance of genius by studied invention. In his later works—violin concerto, last ballets—he offers us objects so stale and stiff and brittle in their dull deformity that they can not survive a showing. Stravinsky and all his spiritual kinsmen of today should confess as Oscar Wilde: "I am dying as I have lived, beyond my means."

What is there to say of the minor, and the ex-stars never meant by nature to shine as creators? What is there to report of promoters of fashions, composers by propaganda, figures kept in circulation by an incessant buzzing of manufactured novelty? These have not been able to live on even tactics; you would not call "life" the glint of a firecracker against the evening sky.

Survived have only men of one mind, one creed, precisely those who do not live on manoeuvre, shrewd use of dogma, or premeditated newness.

I cite Sibelius, Florent Schmitt, Prokofiev, Ernest Bloch and Roy Harris of our own exuberant States, Vaughan Williams, Shostakovitch.

Extinct volcanoes! You can not, however, speak so of Berlioz and Liszt, nor even of Ravel. And the reason for the fact explains the doom of our iconoclasts. The former are organic in spite of all their debilities of pith and style; our own image-breakers, episodic in spite of all their building theories so amply advertized.

The very term "music of our day" is full of absurd connotations. Firstly, "music of our day" is rarely music of *today*. Part is tentative, another dead, and much of the rest lives through galvanizing and artificial respiration. Stravinsky's music since *Sacre* and *Noces* lingers on in much the same way as that cute elderly belle: "all dressed up like a well-kept grave." The covering is new, trim and piously fashionable, yet there is not a drop of life in the body. We wonder about that odd and moving creation, Berg's *Wozzek*. How long will it last, with its gray atonal melopee corseted in so formal a frame? We wonder if the strange use of strict old classical forms will keep sharp new wine fresh. Hindemith's cubicles did not, in spite of all their polyphonic bustle.[2]

In fine, we "hear the noise of the mill, but do not see the flour." For a while we, at least, saw the miller. But now even that imposing or entertaining character busily handling his wheel, has faded out. Hindemith of the sturdy younger chamber music, of the delectable choruses to medieval German texts, of the dark appealing *Daemon*, receded into a grower of dross products of mechanical sculduggery. Such is his newest viola concerto *Der Schwanendreher*, or the piano sonata. The latter is placed by one eminent American writer, Pitts Sanborn, with precision and wit: "Little that strayed far from the cerebral and the adroit . . .

---

[2] In his vivacious book the gifted Constant Lambert speaks of Hindemith's "deadness and monotony of rhythm, and atonal jazzing up of Bach's sewing-machine counterpoint." *Music Ho!* (Faber and Faber, London, 1934).

an almost uncanny mastery of material . . . it takes more than wizardry to extract juice from sack-cloth and ashes." Even that strong creative gift of irrepressible freshness, Prokofiev of the delicious *Ugly Duckling* and the mighty fresco *We Are Seven,* has turned to subtle trivialities of the Classical Symphony, and worse, to the clever, penny-wise, mild pun of *Peter and the Wolf.*

In gaging the studied vivacity which Stravinsky and Hindemith try to pass off for life, one can not but recall the pointed word of Middleton Murray on one of his *bêtes noires:*

"His hypertrophy of style has a certain vitality; it is, however, but the vitality of a weed or mushroom that we can not call precisely spurious but which we certainly can not call real."

* *
*

The music of our day was badly born. Poorly prepared by an epoch of subtitans and deputy geniuses who have lived on not wholly decayed transitory forms. We still use devices bequeathed to us by the understudies of Berlioz and Liszt. We still knead the post-classical and post-romantic paste spiced with nationalist ginger.

Remember how Bach's art was prepared by the long pull of the flourishing polyphonic craft in the Netherlands and Italy; how Mozart's and Beethoven's organic, finished forms were slowly conditioned by Philip Emanuel Bach's and his giant sire's invention. Into these forms longing to be used, the titanic heirs poured their new moods and idioms, all the exuberance of creation. They set up art forms never to lose their hold on the human race.

As to the subtitans who have fathered our music since 1900, the Saint Saens', Griegs, Francks, Mahlers, D'Indys, Regers, Chaussons, Bruckners, they have settled upon us second-hand ideas and a watered technique to start a new life with. Decidedly, we were badly born.

Even Debussy's individualist tone-painting with its improvised, moody and random outline, and its restrained Gallic expressionism, even Debussy's exquisite creation has proved to be too unique and too unstable a soil to grow a lasting new craft. The weakened form-idiom left to us by the subtitans is, of course, traceable to the half rotted pith of the old program-poem of Berlioz and Liszt, but far more so to decay within the cell or structural brick of post-romantic music. Theatrical, literary, pictorial, theosophic heritage, even this was at first unable to losen the structural frame of new music. But the watered thought of the transitory period, the expressionist-impressionist improvisation, has managed to thin the whole structure. In Mahler's "symphonies of a thousand," even in the vast orchestral buildings of Scriabin, a creator of greatness, we find an ample show of this formal anaemia.

Is it a wonder that even the mightiest palladin of today's music and its most acute mind, Schoenberg, speaks with frank contempt of the helplessness of our present creator in integrated form-building?

"I always maintained that most of the composers of today are able to write only introductions—able only to place one thing next to another." [3]

* *
*

[3] "Schoenberg," a collection of articles edited by Merle Armitage (G. Schirmer, New York).

To endure and to become a generator of new art, a musical piece of our time must answer to properly balanced exigencies of attack and defense. Potency of idea, radius of reach, clarity of presentation (diction and form), the impetus and momentum enabling the new pattern of art to conquer or, at least, force attention, are the means of attack in a salient piece of new music. Points of defense lie in its ability to withstand resistance of the milieu, to convince, to grow in adaptability and yet keep its newness and substance undiluted, and therefore respected.

At the dawn of our revolution the impact of aggression seemed terrific. Strauss' *Salome,* Schoenberg's *Five Orchestral Pieces,* Stravinsky's *Sacre* seemed ideal engines of attack on behalf of new tonal concepts. They seemed installed forever as a permanent shaping force.

But look at the artillery now!

One of the most sagacious writers of today, Dr. Alfred Einstein, has measured the true worth of the present aggression when he said with finesse:

"Modern technique, with its complex wealth of harmonic and rhythmical devices, of contrapuntal and orchestral effects, allows the composer to make his choice and simulate a reasonable degree of intoxication." [4]

What intoxication? Where does the tonal fury of our grim aggressors come from, in attack and defense?

Certainly, there has been, so to speak, a *rhum* in the new musical speech that has helped to forward the impact of the present composer's attack. But drive of this kind alone cannot hold a position. It signifies only another return to the barbaric implement of ignition.

To be sure, self-incitement, and not the aims so imperiously heralded, is the true earmark of our "revolution." What has happened to music since 1900, is not a liberation of our tone-art from the extra-musical, not a return to classical self-sufficiency, not a rebuilding of our tonal speech from within on a universal basis. A mere widening of the means of ignition is all one can find.

Nothing else could have happened since absolute music, that is, absolute at its base, does not exist. There is some stimulant back of even the most objective pages of music. In the course of history

[4] Dr. Alfred Einstein: *A Short History of Music*, published by Alfred Knopf, New York, 1937.

the circle of igniters of tonal creation widens and contracts periodically. Of this circle, intoxication with a formal idea—that is what absolute music means—is only one sort of starter.

Program or verbal rhythm, a pictorial image or religious idea, can still stimulate the creation of a lasting, self-dependent form just as the savage rondo danced by the Indian around his totem molded his magnificent war chant, just as the demand of his parish made Bach write many of his strong-limbed cantatas.

Their sources do not disable in the least the æsthetic independence and absolute musical value of these chants.

To the long list of stimuli of musical creation our era has added the tortures of illness and childbirth (Strauss' *Death and Transfiguration* and the *Domestica*), a theosophist's bible (in Scriabin's *Divine Poem*), intoxication with modern machines (Honegger's *Pacific*), hyperprisms, sexual complexities, almost anything. Such intoxicants are as lawful a fuse for musical creation, and could be a source of great music as much as the "absolute," the musical impulse or the emotion behind Mozart's d-minor quartet or *Die Verborgenheit* of

xvi

Hugo Wolf or another immortal song of mankind.

The musical *fleurs du mal* of our day have been born in quite the same way. But their soil was meager and the creative spirit cramped.

* *

*

In the queer flow of our day's music, formerly furious, and now limp and dull, one may read, however, a new story of the basic pattern of musical creation.

The traditional realm of our old music—let us call it for convenience "music before 1900"—sprang from the emotional ego of man. Its form-design hailed from the rule of dramatic discourse and emotional climax.

On the contrary, our own revolutionary period centers its drive around the integrated body of sound. Its law is organic self-sufficiency of musical logic and structure. The parts of our structural mold are supposed to have no expressive or ieratic, sacred value; their only import must lie in being undiluted musical facts strictly related to the integrated body of sound.

In the twelfth century a Calabrese monk Joachino de Floris divided history into three parts: the Epoch of the Father (Judea and Rome), that of the Son (Christian Era), and the period to come, one of the Holy Ghost (the Kingdom of True Knowledge).

This idea, a distant forerunner of Hegel's dialectical trinity and Spengler's rotating cycles of civilization, sheds a certain light on the musical highway of our race. Our tonal history also might be cited as a rotation of three cycles:

a) ieratic or classical, that of æsthetic worship in a sphere closed to personal message;
b) antropomorphic or romantic, that of the cultivation of the inner individual life;
c) mystico-objective or philosophic, the expressing in music of man's communion with the universe [5]

Bach's Gigue in G-major from the French Suite or Mozart's *Juppiter* mirrors perfectly the mind of the first cycle; Schubert's second movement of the C-major symphony or Chopin's c-sharp minor pre-

[5] This point is fully developed in the first chapter of *this* book (Tonal Language of Our Time). It remains intact in the new edition.

lude typify the second; and *Parsifal* or Scriabin's *Divine Poem*—the third.

The excruciatingly long life of official romanticism, its lush rotting maturity in itself, called for a reaction and a successor. A secondary and modified romanticism, none other than the impressionist trend, set in, also a short-lived theosophical Scriabin period, and other, lesser ideologies.

In his highly valuable *Music since 1900* Nicolas Slonimsky, one of the sharpest musical minds in this country, describes this stretch of history with great accuracy:

"Extraordinary popularity of pictorial representational music—Birth of impressionistic opera—Neo-primitivistic tendencies as a reaction to the refinement of the impressionist palette—neoromanticism with philosophic implications in Germanic countries; musico-theosophic, neo-mystical tendencies in Slavic nations." [6]

This new process of personalizing and humanizing musical creation reached a breaking point after the first decade of our own centennium.

Again weary of their overripeness and individualistic fever, art and life demanded a reversal.

[6] Nicolas Slonimsky: *Music since 1900* (Norton).

The clamor was now for de-humanization, for the freeing of musical creation from literary emotions, personal vagaries, extraneous imagery, from all manner of connotation.

The feeling was right and the instinct true. But the peculiar interplays of world forces shaping our creative currents, were at that turning point inimical to right response. And the urge for de-humanization of art was misguided onto a wrong route.

Our musical concept we again crammed, but now with notions snatched from modern science, physics and mathematics instead of, as formerly, with the last cry of painting and literature. These new fancies were as artificial and lurid as the cramming with romanticism run to seed.

With the upheaval of the World War the natural sense of values and relationship underwent a complete distortion. New friendships and animosities among nations sprang up, singled out for special ballyhoo were composers and works and tendencies which would normally have had no chance for a life of any length. And the tremendous new war-industrial order of mass production affected mightily the musical creation of our day. Suddenly the normal small composer's world widened into a world-arena. The composer found himself bound to exaggerate his creative make-up, drift into a staccato of style and diction. But above all, did he live on the contriving of new things. The new musical industry did not have time for discovery; it threw itself on invention.

The composer of the post-War era pressed all motive into a hard, hooked metallic line, turned each element of rhythm into a hammer, and every expressive mark into a shriek. He merits the rebuke which Debussy addressed backward, to Gluck, and . . . in an open letter:

"You turn the French language into an accentuated language when it is, on the contrary, a language of fine shades." [7]

Music as well is mainly a language of fine shades. But in that gigantic tussle of beasts, the World War, and in its aftermath, who could remember that?

Our music craves de-personalization, to be sure, but of another kind, and not in the sense of acting as servant maid. *Gebrauchsmusik,* music for the

[7] See Edward Lockspeiser's excellent book on Debussy (Dutton), which, together with the new volume of Oscar Thompson and the superb older monograph of Léon Vallas, constitute three of the best source books on this master.

new masses, dance-song for all, and other red-hot utility fads of our day that scorn personal art, are detours of de-humanization.

Our music yearns for a return to the green earth.

A plane deeper than immediate and humdrum utility is before us. The return of music to the role of organ of mass-communion with the universe, the basic craving of the human race. Service in a temple-palace akin to the Mayan shrines which had no kitchen. A feast to serve the spirit, not the palate.

Music should be so. As supplement to our pantry art means nothing; it is as gratuitous and feeble as freedom of speech reserved only for the end of dinners. It is sometimes startling to hear a teacher of materialism speak of art. Lenin's words should be a lesson to his own flock. "The beautiful old things should be preserved, taken as an example and point of departure. . . . Why kneel before the new, as such, as if it were a God? . . . Nonsense and hypocrisy!"

These words exalt "art for art's sake." Neither could modern music be chided as an inane play detached from life's struggle. Like old music, it is a part of life in its deeper invisible layers; it can not help being so.

Creating artificial "cure-all's," *Gebrauchsmusik,* music for the new masses, etc., is not really a remedy. As a matter of fact, these nostrums are not a response to the new thought and needs of the people, but devices of economic policy aimed at capturing an illusory gigantic new market.

Let us cease banal shooting at the "ivory tower!" So much of the immortal music of our race has been born in ivory towers. So much of it seemed alien to the *then* living men and has become an expression of the ages. So much of it responds to the deepest craving of the human soul to live in harmony with the green earth, to know our place on it, to recede to the primeval sense of nature, to feel that that is important and real, and not our human quirks and petty drama.

Our music must get back to the broad real life of cosmos and to the faceless man, as the primeval artist sketched him in the Cromagnon caves. I mean a state of art where our earthly tempests, our insect busyness, our puny "humanities" fill as scant a place as the economy of the universe allots us.

Of course, music of our day has attempted certian de-humanization. But this has proved to be only literal and material, not æsthetical or creative. The return of our tonal creation to the green earth will be renovation at the base. Certainly all true discovery found in the best that new music has already brought forth, will of itself add to the upsurge of the new creative mind by touching the eternal soil of man's song.

For all else will have withered away, will have died of temporizing, not of revelation.

*   *   *   *   *

Touching the green earth may come about in countless ways—from communion with folklore to a grasping of the grandiose novel forms that will arise from the social realignment of a new humanity, something Mahler dreamed of.

"Folklorism" fought by such queer alliance as Heinrich Schenker and our own "neo-classicist" may be dead. Folk-melos lives and is an immortal force for renovation; a guardian of serenity and clarity; an eternal purifier of our over-heated blood-stream chocked with dead artifice.

Look at the pages of today's music that *are* living, see what they are and how they come to be.

Significant, beautiful and vital are the *Fantasia on a theme of Tallis* by Vaughan Williams, the opening page of the Sactification in Ernest Bloch's *Sacred Service,* Florent Schmitt's Psalm XLII Prokofiev's *Seven, they are Seven,* Sibelius' *Lemminkainen Sagas,* the spring-roundels from Stravinsky's *Sacre,* the Passacaglia in Roy Harris' *Quintet.* These leaves have sprung from the seeds of folk-melos, and are here to remind us of the eternal triumph of the earth, its song, its holy ghost. These pages are a prologue to resurrection.

With all my admiration for the spatious intellect and culture of Roger Sessions, I would not subscribe to his words that it is "all too easy for those incapable of meeting the creative problems of a period like our own to take refuge in a contempt for the present and its struggle."[8]

It is easier still to take doubtful modernity to one's bosom. Far easier to read into it a fertility not there; to mistake drive for genius, twist for invention, brazenness for courage of expression, vulgarity for popular utility. Easier still to mistake

[8] Roger Sessions in his article on Schenker's *Freier Satz* (Modern Music, March 1938).

the wane froth of today's music for creative discovery.

But there is certainly a sane kernel in the heart of our music. It is like a submarine chaser camouflaged for war. Throw off the drab, muddy set of covers, draw away the rotting canvas, and pert fresh guns are shining gamely ready to give a good account of themselves.

They were there all the time. Let us not despair!

PART I

THE TONAL LANGUAGE
OF OUR TIME

I

THE TONAL LANGUAGE OF OUR TIME
ITS TECHNICAL AND MORAL ASPECTS

HISTORY is a procession of mediocrity. The day's motto is flung by this favorite child of the weekdays, not by genius, not by a creator of feasts. History is bookkeeping of weekdays.

An alliance of the mediocrity of our day, a possessor of strong elbows, with the new musical dandy have set up the cult of wonder-child in composition. A host of sundry platitudes nests in this idolatry.

Today's composer is the man who is always better than his predecessor. We are less afraid of being a hundred years behind our time than one hour. That dangerous hour in which we may, God forbid, miss the birth of a new genius or arrive late for the christening.

We are not conscious of the fact that *la beauté de diable,* the beauty of youth, exists in creation, is a deceptive charm there as well. We are ready

3

to grant large and foolish credit to each attractive infant.

Even our new fashion, the delight in musical *plus quam perfectum,* a cherished grimace of to-day's dandy, is really but another manner of deny-ing "yesterday." Alfred de Vigny long since described this pose perfectly: *"C'est convenu dans chacque siècle qu'on va rire sur le costume de son père."* [1]

The new platitudes of viewpoint have indeed their new mouthpieces. "Yesterday" the proces-sion of mediocrity was recruited from romantic *pleurnicheurs,* from music's weeping willows. Understudies of Wagner, Tchaikovsky and Franck,—the Chaussons, the Bruckners, the Mah-lers and other epigones of the mighty were the "contemporaries." Now, behold a cortège of academicians of modernity, of *bruiteurs* and fail-ures whom the vague claim of modernity provides with their only hope to float a sorry while.

The pious attention of the city crowd is at-

[1] "It is taken for granted, in every period, that one will laugh at the dress of one's father." (Alfred de Vigny in *Saint Mars.*)

Dr. Hans Heinsheimer, the dynamic and gifted Viennese writer, points to the fact that "youth leaves the vanguard." Of course, for a Kurt Weil or a Clicquet Pleyel or another of those now glori-fied young men in a hurry, Schoenberg's or Stravinsky's tone-medium is already "the dress of one's father."

tracted by more resolute doctrines and proceedings than *Sehnsucht* and sighs of the old romantic weepers. Manifestoes acclaiming an art of direct action, brutal and labored tonal dynamism, are invoked; orchestration discovered in the fire brigade inventory is resorted to.

The word "stillborn" is stricken from art's vocabulary, but only the word. An old and forgotten "excavation," Mozart's g-minor quintet with two violas, is still vibrant with life, and it shines like an immortal day over the corpse of Stravinsky's *Octuor* or that of Schoenberg's woodwind quintet, the *fine-fleur* of our "progressive" music.

The history of musical creation is a range of cycles, often with a very weak continuity, sometimes with none. At times these cycles bequeath us organic types of art, types with a mighty spiritual stem and slated for a life eternal; at others they produce stillborns only to burden books and our memory.

One cycle enriches music with new æsthetic emotions, means and ideas. Another distorts its bequest or loses it. The classical epoch of Philip Emanuel Bach, Haydn and Beethoven has entirely

5

forgotten the harmonic invention of Monteverdi, Gesualdo and Marenzio; and Sebastian Bach is much more radical in the use of chromatic harmony than Beethoven.

Our own time has reached extraordinary heights of harmonic and orchestral mastery, but it has lost the gift of invention and of imagination in the spheres of melody, form and polyphony.

In reviewing the tonal language of our time it is not my aim to condemn or to bewail its shortcomings, its penury, but rather to find out exactly what part of our musical heritage is lost. Also, I shall not dwell particularly on our modern achievements; they are well known, and rather suffer from exaggerated publicity.

However, even establishing what was lost of our tonal heritage will play here but a subordinate rôle. My aim is the definition of our æsthetic longitude and latitude, and of our place in history. Its exact position we have long since lost.

My questions run as follows:

Where do we find ourselves, æsthetically, and historically?

What is the present waterway of our musical thought?

6

To which type of spirituality belongs the musical culture created today and what is its destiny?

* *
*

Nothing characterizes the music of our day better than its diseases as they sharpen the expression in so peculiar a way. These debilities are abuse of nourishment or underfeeding, the monotony of wealth or of penury. The æsthetic will and imagination of our day's composer—a city dweller, *par excellence*—suffer both from the putrefying luxury of tonal riches and from their unrelatedness. This is followed by a revulsion to tonal luxury and by greed for another extremity. A characteristic clinical picture!

The music of our time swings frantically from abuse of harmonic and orchestral color to conscious or instinctive rebarbarization.

Swamped by means, methods, proceedings or strangled by forced simplification, trying to stem the befuddling luxury with the device of *l'art dépouillé*, art stripped to the bone—our music has come to the point of sublimating the scarecrow.

7

Such a sublimation, for example, is the only meaning of Satie's pitiful creative grimace.

As yet, we are not fully conscious of the sins of our æsthetic aspect; or perhaps we dare not confess to those sins.

All the brave doctrines of our day cannot veil the fact that the composer of the modern era lives in exceptional servitude to two strong agents, the means and the market. Considering these in conjunction with the new history of our tonal language, we may come to define with precision the longitude and the latitude of our æsthetic position.

A) DOMINATION OF THE MEANS

"The sole content of music is the tonal arabesque." This old maxim of Hanslick should be thought of as the forgotten source of our modern doctrines of neoclassicism, objectivity and the doctrine of authonomous sonority, a new substitute for old emotion.

This path is one that leads to the domination, I might better say, to an orgy of means, methods and formulas of today; to the "objectivity" of Stravinsky and Hindemith; to the "barbarism" of

Bartok and Prokofiev; to the "hedonism," the doctrine of music-entertainment, of the younger
Frenchmen.

Domination of the means is not at all new; its
present chart, however, is curious and complex.

The route leads us through a furnace of contradicting ideologies, through the discolored and
decayed pseudo-classicism of Saint-Saëns, the
pseudo-impressionism of Ravel, the pseudo-romanticism of Richard Strauss.

Ravel is the spiritual child of Saint-Saëns. They
both have tried to galvanize the musical arabesque
of classical art, to replace emotion by *musical fact.*
They have essayed with one stroke to rebuild music
into a plastic art. But Ravel, with his sharp
artistic intelligence and his sense of modernity,
himself ripens in the post-Wagnerian and post-
Debyssian tempests. He realizes that the early
neoclassicism of Saint-Saëns is but a lifeless repro-
duction of old building schemes and skeletons, but
a repeating of dead ornamentation, not a resurrection of it. This awareness pushes Ravel, "the enemy
of the unforeseen," toward a consciously chosen
path of tonal chemistry and musical mechanics.

The three naïvely honest creative types of the

9

past, the improviser, the compiler and the composer, are now superseded by a new, formerly
unheard of generation of musical chemists and en-
gineers headed by Ravel and Stravinsky. Of
course, the improviser and the compiler have
rushed at once to occupy the new position of
vantage.

The very attitude that is the kernel of art-creed
for the honest and single-minded Ravel, forms but
one of the many superficial æsthetic positions of
the ever manœuvring Stravinsky. In their very
piety, the words of Ansermet concerning Stravinsky, describe the "new composer" faithfully.

*"On croit qu'il cherche des effects de couleurs
ou de comique ou de pittoresque, alors qu'il évalue
des volumes, des poids ou des densités."* [2]

This attitude of musical mechanician easily degenerates into pure fraud. We have heard the
quasi learned manifestoes in which creative failure
and conscious *charlatanerie* drape themselves so
greedily.

The comparatively better type of such a par-
asite and sophist in composition is thus described

[2] "One would think that he looks for effect of color, for the
comical or the picturesque whereas he is calculating the volumes,
the weight or the density." *Revue Pleyel*, March, 1925.

by Nicolas Slonimsky, the brilliant Boston musician and writer.

"He does not possess a degree of creative power which would entitle him to the dignity of an individual composer. He is an extraordinarily gifted man, eclectic in his tastes and just as vague in his musical expressions as in his general ideas. But, lacking in creative power, he has developed an acute sense for persuasive argument. He possesses the necessary literary technique to present his cause with seeming coherence. But the amazing hollowness of his fundamental concepts stand out all the more clearly. He battles in an empty air—and for a dialectician of his order it may be all he cares for." [3]

Exploiting absurd mutilations of Einstein's relativity badly understood, one of the pseudo-prophets of home-made radicalism, who filled a messianic position in New York some years ago, let an adept explain his great deeds in the following:

"If we project an imaginary sound-mass into space, we find that it appears as constantly changing volumes and combination of planes, that these

[3] *Boston Evening Transcript,* 3/1/30.

11

are animated by the rhythm, and that the substance of which they are composed, is the sonority. Might it then be possible to consider a musical composition as a succession of geometric sound-figures, as a resultant of volumes and planes whose successive projections would give birth to architectures of sound, whose logic would be given by the equilibrium of their sound vibrations and their forms?" The "works" of our new messiah are called "sound-geometry, the objectivation of music obtained by subordination of the melodic and harmonic element and by setting in motion his sound-groups like waves that change in shape and intensity."

With such concoction, transparently inaccurate to all who know something of the new physics and Einstein's relativity, one charms the civilized simpleton of today. We shall see further that these machinations hide also a method by which the modern engineer of composition is even freed from the very obligation to be a musician.

*   *

*

It is curious to see how melodic invention has been drying up, and how it has been replaced by the growth of tone-color manufactured methodically.

The real forefathers of the new tonal chemistry, Berlioz, Liszt and Rimski-Korsakov, had the ability for cultivation within only isolated domains of the musical universum. For instance, they let polyphony dry away, and disguised the resultant penury by a surplus of harmonic and orchestral invention. After them, Ravel and Stravinsky let the dimension of melody petrify.

The latter fact is very characteristic and it reveals the pathetic necessity for doctrines of "coolness" and "objectivity." Melody is a child of the human voice; in its river-bed flow emotion and dramatic conflict. Boris de Schloezer says very justly, though in no derogatory sense: *"Le conflit dramatique est absent de l'art de Ravel; sa musique sensuele est intelectuelle et amorale."* [4]

Berlioz, Liszt and Rimski-Korsakov abjured polyphony not because they felt it to be a child of the past; they simply were born without that gift. But knowing that a very important organ of musical speech was lost to them, they, the honest

---

[4] "The dramatic conflict is absent from Ravel's art; his sensuous music is intellectual and amoral."

souls, did not try to whitewash the death of polyphony, nor did they proclaim the abolition of it an achievement. But when Stravinsky abolishes melody, for which he has not the slightest gift, he issues an edict on the death of melody. Before the first performance of *Noces* in 1923 he heralded substitution of the sheer pressure of rhythm for melody and harmony. *A propòs* of this, when he first conceived the *Noces,* about or before 1917, this "reform" had not occurred to him. The insincerity and falsehood of Stravinsky's manifesto and longing for melody not given to him, appear later and in a stringent way, in his gaudy and dead *Oedipus.* As always unexpectedly, he undertook here to show the world that no less than another, he is blessed with an elemental and direct melodic endowment. He knows well that this gift is one of the indispensable traits of a great creator.

In laboratories of harmonic and orchestral color by the process of a new tonal chemistry, Ravel and Stravinsky have transformed the thematic and harmonic *pasticcio* of Saint-Saëns and Rimski-Korsakov, of Liszt and Wagner. They have created an immense arsenal of new tonal means. The dead

14

ornamentics, the neoclassic arabesque of Saint-Saëns, the narrow and frozen logic of Wagner's harmony, have all been remodelled in those new laboratories and whipped with somewhat primitive mechanicity into the *fait musical* of our day.

The much subtler formula of Schoenberg's *Farbenerlebnisse* emotionalizes the pure tonal proceeding, the sound-color *an und für sich*. Schoenberg's formula ingrains into the doctrine of simon-pure tone-color a new life, at least theoretically. But in Ravel's and Stravinsky's hands sound-color is distilled and dehumanized.

Thus the gates were thrown open to that savage pandemonium of means, to that wild superabundance of color, harmonic and orchestral, whose despotism gnaws out the æsthetic will and muscles from our creation and the clarity of art perspective from our imagination. Thus a false notion is arrived at, that by way of new technical resources one can transform an old *cliché* into new music. This tendency has substituted for renovation of the spirit of musical art, mere reform in musical dress. Hence the quick fading of our revolution.

A modern Russian composer, Roslavietz, says aptly that we live now in a state of impressionistic-expressionistic anarchy. Indeed, our stand is a naïve and crude synthesis of the past and the present, the milking of two mothers, "yesterday" and "today." It would be wrong to describe our present art as a search for an entirely new tonal logic, for entirely new ways of organizing sound. Also, we often mistake the activities of modern acoustics for those of modern music.

Having taken the "purged sonority" or the "musical fact" for the sole content of music, Ravel and also Stravinsky, a similar creative nature, though more tense, more brutally stubborn and less aristocratic than Ravel, have both systematized the manufacturing of musical newness. They have consecrated it according to Edgar Allan Poe's formula outlining originality as subject to study rather than to inspiration.

In its primitive form the system consisted of what young Schoenberg, so his friends say, used to improvise and to call *"Akkorde verbiegen."* He liked to play chains of most innocent piano chords and then alter notes in the chords in such a way as to get cruel and harsh dissonant successions. But then, indeed, he didn't think of attaching any dogma to the peaceful exercise.

16

It is true, however, that many remarkable technical ideas have been arrived at by this manner of willfully curling the traditional melodic, harmonic and rhythmic formulas. In the fourth of Schoenberg's "Six piano pieces" op. 19 the habitual melodic structure is reversed. Instead of varying the melodic motive while keeping the rhythm intact, Schoenberg leaves the melodic contour of the piece unaltered and changes its rhythmic structure with each bar. Another nine-bar piece of the same opus is, so to speak, an integral of eight microscopic variations emanating from a one-bar motive; together with the germ-motive it forms one unbroken melodic line. This is, indeed, a very extraordinary theme with variations of infinitesimal sort.[5]

However, while cultivating with tremendous energy a similar system of newness produced by disjointing old patterns, neither Ravel, nor Stravinsky has noticed that in fact, they had been caught in a tonal formula of degenerated romanticism. They are notably enslaved by the melodic, harmonic and rhythmic grotesque. Spiritually,

[5] The distinguished German writer-composer, Dr. Hugo Leichtentritt, has analyzed these Schoenberg pieces very admirably in *Modern Music*, Vol. V, 4.

modern jazz—it is opportune to say—is but a vulgar specimen of this same grotesque emphasizing of the humoristic or comic-elegiac element.

* *

*

It is easy to see that by its nature, the method of studied or manufactured originality leads us to the rule of *cliché* and stamped pattern just as swiftly and surely, as the abuse of the Dyonisian creative ways, as the outmoded cult of "inspiration."

One may take the table of polytonal harmonies of Milhaud [6] and use it to mix new harmonic color and thus extract some very sharp and whimsical shading. This naïve and primitive harmonic addition and multiplication is not much subtler and does not approach creation any more closely, than does the proceeding of a pharmacist who opens his powder drawers and mixes his drugs mechanically, according to a prescription.

It is quite evident that in such a case, the harmonic and rhythmic machinations are apt to lure the composer into subordinating his creative con-

[6] Darius Milhaud, "Polytonalité et atonalité," *La Revue Musicale,* February, 1923.

ception to technical newness. The system of harmonic arithmetic infuses into creation a queer mixture of mechanicalism and improvisation. It is a very manifest and facile form of composing by way of the least resistance. Emil Vuillermoz says very subtly: *"Le polytonalisme n'est pas un élément architechtural nouveau. C'est un revêtement, c'est un badigeon qui peut souvent récouvrir la plus traditionnelle des façades."* [7]

Indeed the spiritual undersoil of polytonality, as well as its origin and meaning are quite clear. The polytonal epidemics spring from our fatigue caused by the static dissonance of Wagner, Liszt and Debussy. Movement within a polytonal plan supplies any dissonant rubbish with a sort of entertaining animation and a mask of consequence. This is the reason why polytonal writing has become the key to a cheap and easily accessible polyphony of a well-known sort. In fact, polytonal counterpoint has grown to be the polyphony of amateurs, of unskilled understudies, of each failure in composition.

The following example of "contrapuntal poly-

[7] "Polytonality is not a new architectural element. It is only a change of dress, a new paint that often covers a most traditional façade." Emil Vuillermoz *Musiques d'aujourd'hui.*

tonality" from an American work has been presented without a smile.[8]

Such *acqua distillata* in polytonal counterpoint can indeed be manufactured and enjoyed by deaf-mutes. Whether you listen to this music or you simply look at the printed notes without trying to decipher the sound, the impression is precisely the same,—tonal and artistic blankness.

This music is typical of that new kind of composer liberated by clever sophism from the very obligation to be a musician.

There is nothing easier than to effect mechanical revolution, that of the tonal garment, in the sphere of orchestral writing. For example, one may take a commonplace orchestral *tutti*; put the usual registering topsy-turvy; replace the orchestral

[8] Henry Cowell: "New Terms for New Music," *Modern Music*, Vol. V, 4. Mr. Cowell is an ardent propagandist of such grave matter.

design given to instrumental registers in normal use by ones forced from tense and harsh registers never before exploited.

One may season the orchestra with rare sound lying at the confines of the uppermost and the lowest registers of the woodwind, or with sound brought to life by the new virtuosity of the performer. One may throw in newly discovered tone-color, such as the "laughing" trombones and clarinets, the howling and barking *cuivrés* of the trumpets, etc. In addition, *dynamize* sharply the orchestral design, transform every sustained harmony into a web of fast moving figures, taint the whole with heterophonic ornamentation and any new color of orchestral polychromy, apply also batteries of yet unemployed percussion, such as whistles, police-horns, etc., and we have before us the newest orchestral *tutti* of our day. It is achieved by the well-known method of "curling the orchestra," *Orchester verbiegen.*

For special scenic effects and action in my opera-ballet *The Plague's Gagliarda* (its first stage performance took place in New York, in February, 1925), I needed a battery of unusual percussion. I used a sort of xylophone formed of large dried

21

oyster shells loosely hung on a wire and attached to a wooden frame, a tambourine in the form of a metallic shaker filled with buckshot, etc. These "inventions" required indeed neither labor, nor genius. After the première Ernest Newman said humorously: "Mr. Saminsky uses chains in his orchestra; for *this* instrument he orchestrates admirably." There is, however, a serious side to this remark. Every apprentice orchestrates well for chains, sirens, fog-horns, slapsticks and the like "revolutionary" orchestra. But let him write one *individual sounding tutti* for the usual orchestra! Then only he passes the test of orchestral mastery.

* *

*

One of the numerous manifestoes from the keepers of Stravinsky's ideology, or rather phraseology, announced another new path chosen by the great musical engineer. It spoke of the manufacturing of "objects of musical utility."

A composer is thought of as a kind of preoccupied laborer surrounded by tonal retorts and gears. Stores of harmonic and orchestral color and of rhythmic building material are procured in

22

advance as munition for future utility. It is produced regardless of any æsthetic center and conception, with no creative need, with no dependence on something that may give meaning, instill inner life into the painstaking ants' labor. Very characteristic is this doctrine and well suited to the mind of the arch-slaves of method and proceeding.

I have already mentioned that the hunt for sonorities, for new harmonic, rhythmic and orchestral color, has degenerated into the domination of the grotesque, a mouldy remnant of old romanticism. In this respect the entire current is actually backward.

But in the "progressive" music of our time, in its tonal conception, we see a trait of even more elementary nature than the grotesque of decayed romanticism. I speak of the resurrection of *Tonmalerei* and sound-mimicking, of that definite and strong trait of contemporary musical rebarbarization.

No matter how magnificent are the formulas attached to Honegger's *Pacific*—the "kinetic rhythm" replacing the emotional rhythm, the "modern perception of time and motion," etc.,—that bright child of Honegger's fine talent is very

23

symptomatic of the evident prevailing degeneration.

The old *Tonmalerei* and program music sink into photographic realism and a motion-picture impressionism of our day.

The crude falsehood of this sort of realism is fired at by Jean Cocteau, and with excellent marksmanship, when he says: "Photography is not true to reality; it alters the values and perspective. Its eye of a cow registers stupidly what our eye corrects and then distributes according to necessity." [9]

Stravinsky, a brilliant and supremely intelligent artist, but an arch-slave of proceeding as well, has mainly a genius for tone-mimicking. The very appearance of Stravinsky in musical history, from *Petrushka* through the *Sacre* to *Noces,* is a symptom of the renaissance of savagery in music, savagery now miserable and naked, then gorgeously draped. All is a regress to sound-mimicry, but of a new kind.

The musical substance of Stravinsky's invention in nothing more than magnificent refabrication

[9] "La photographie est irréelle, change les valeurs et les perspectives. Son œil de vache enregistre stupidement ce que notre œil corrige et distribue ensuite selon les besoins de la cause." Jean Cocteau: *Le secret professionel.*

and dynamizing of his native, formerly loved pattern, the basic design of Rimski-Korsakov's *Kastcheï* and *Cocq d'or*.

On this woof he works his pastiche with the same admirable art as Ravel transforms on his loom the "lessons" from Saint-Saëns and Mozart.[10]

No matter how violently Stravinsky burns his former standard, no matter how diligently he now works on new woofs taken from Bach, Handel and Verdi, as in his piano concerto, in *Oedipus*, etc., *Petrushka*, *Sacre*, *Rossignol*, and in a certain measure *Noces* will remain the most valuable of his contributions. Perhaps, they are the only ones to be taken into account when estimating Stravinsky.

As in Ravel's talent, the diapason of Stravinsky's melodic invention is exceedingly narrow. This weakness as well as his other limitations, spiritual or purely æsthetic, he camouflages by his miraculous gift for tonal scenery.

The imagination of Stravinsky perceives things and presents them musically in terms of noises immanent to those things, eternally present in

[10] In the magnificent article of Roland Manuel *"L'esthétique de l'imposture"* in the Ravel issue of the *Revue Musicale*, Ravel's art is analyzed with merciless lucidity.

them. He is curiously and characteristically deaf to the *inner* music of things—to their spiritual pulse. Let us recall the sharp and cold glitter of the *kermesses* from *Petrushka,* the spring-roundels from the *Sacre,* the Chinese march from the *Rossignol,* those glowing pages of tone-decor. In the creating anew of the inborn noises of things, of their resonance and physical boiling, lies the whole of Stravinsky's talent, magnificent of its kind.

He is the father of the rebarbarization in music. He has transformed music into a collection of qualified noises, but fascinatingly colored, irresistible. He has reduced melody to the primitive, inarticulate refrain of a Zulu and has converted the orchestra into a gigantic rattle, the toy and mouthpiece of the new savage.

But in the new music the conception of sound-mimicking has unfolded a very vast and variegated gamut, from the inferior kind embodied in Honegger's *Pacific,* a type now degenerated into pure *bruitisme,* often charlatan in character, to the highest and most spiritual sort as presented by Schoenberg's *Fünf Orchesterstücke*—that wonderful tonal shadow of a dematerialized gong.

26

* *
*

B) TAMING THE PROCEEDING

In the raging pandemonium of means, in the maze of harmonic, rhythmic and orchestral systems with peaks of polyharmony, polyrhythmics and polychromatics, in such a tempest the shaky bark of composition has begun to drift pathetically. To use the image of Paul Valéry, "the ship has pitched and tossed too long; the stoutest lamps are fully overturned." [11]

Our new composition has lost its rudder. We are to subdue and to unburden the musical proceeding, then to systematize and to justify the residue of the accepted technical formula by some philosophy.

The attempts to systematize and to synthesize the tonal means, necessary for the taming, are well known.

In the sphere of harmony the internecine war of doctrines and formulas is not solely a distressed scouting for the harmonic position of the day. It is also manifestly an attempt to master the raging

[11] Paul Valéry: "Intellectual Crisis," letter published in the *London Athenæum* in 1919.

27

harmonic elements and to recapture the drifting rudder.

Above the well-known though often misinterpreted formulas of polytonality, chromatic tonality and atonality, I would place *synthetic* tonality. I name thus the all-embracing, mathematically complete, range of the natural scale emitted by a resounding body, that is the *whole* range of feasible overtones. Some of these overtones form the roots of Scriabin's and Debussy's harmony; the latter employ, however, a minimum part of that scale.

The use of notes quasi-foreign to a given harmony, the employing of the so-called *"notes de coté"* (side notes) and of unresolved appogiaturas —one of the basic elements of the new tonal language—and the free play of inner pedals as well, is really an anticipation of the coming utilizing of all the notes of the natural scale.

André Schaeffner, the brilliant French musicologist, speaks with rare clarity of the eternal and salubrious rôle of the natural scale, of its being the source of tonal order and a bulwark against tonal disintegration:

"One escapes the vertigo of rapid harmonic decay and one discerns a principle of tonic conservation as opposed to that destructive work, for both currents have their origin in nature, in the phenomenon of resonance. The ever growing scale of harmonics is capable of inspiring chord-formations more and more complex, and it leans at the outset, by virtue of its first and most intense harmonics, on the very foundation of tonality as well. Nature which comprises all possible sound-combinations, indicates in a most expressive manner the way to escape both atonality and pure noise." [12]

Joseph Yasser, the outstanding New York musician and savant, has evolved his own tonal synthesis, the supra-diatonic scale of the future, which covers the old tonal systems and the new, such as polytonality, atonality, etc. In his monograph "The Future of Tonality" [13] Yasser shows with illuminating logic the necessity of a coming tonal order which is to be the synthesis of tonality and atonality

[12] André Schaeffner: "Evolution harmonique et fixité tonale dans la musique contemporaine" (see the very valuable special issue of *Journal de Psychologie*, 1926, Editions Felix Alcan, Paris).

[13] Special supplement to Volume VIII, 1 of *Modern Music*. The American Library of Musicology has published Yasser's extraordinary book "A Theory of Evolving Tonality," where the past harmonic language of humanity and its anticipated future are reviewed with amazing clarity and competence.

in just the same way, as the tonality of the seventeenth, eighteenth and nineteenth centuries was the synthesis of the pentatonic scale (or of its Medieval, Celtic or Oriental ramification) and of its antithesis, the heptatonic scale. Yasser names the latter *"infra-atonality."* [14]

In my *Lehryahre* I, too, applied myself to the search of a universal tonal synthesis and a universal nomenclature. I then invented the names *fri-dur* and *fri-moll* for tonalities that admit, with unlimited freedom, any feasible harmony on any step of the scale and yet gravitate to a definite tonic, major-like (*fri-dur*) or minor-like (*fri-moll*). Thus I designated my first a symphony in E-fri-moll, and my second a symphony in H-fri-dur.

Here it is *à propos* to say that the harmony of Schoenberg's *Fünf Orchesterstücke* which has

[14] The formation of infra-atonality and atonality, an antithesis respectively of the pentatonic and diatonic scale-order, has been achieved by the transubstantiation of the non-basic, casual or, so to speak, the passing notes of the pentatonic and diatonic scales into the basic and independent notes of the heptatonic and duodecuple scales. Yasser's supra-diatonic scale, that of the future, is the synthesis of tonality and atonality: a gamut, in which the casual chromatic steps of the diatonic scale-order become through their independence in the atonal scale-order, basic links of a new, supra-diatonic chain.

30

revolutionized the composer's technique of our time as much as Debussy's *Iberia* and *La Mer* and Stravinsky's *Sacre,* is, however, not the specimen of atonal thought that it is taken to be by many. That extraordinary creation of Schoenberg captivates one as might the tonal magic of a spiritualized and infinitely tender gong. One senses a progression of all the harmonic color of the synthetic tonality, a phantastic play of most irrational overtones.

It will be well to establish here the true meaning of atonality, which in my opinion would be more correctly named "extratonality." I would also say that it is fallacious to deem atonality an organized tone-system, and to think of the latest works of Schoenberg as specimens of atonality. He himself said they were not.

Atonality or extratonality is solely the absence of gravitation to any harmonic or melodic center, to a chord or a note.

However, the new tonal conception of Schoenberg, the system of *series,* establishes a center of gravitation of his own cast, and individual for each given composition. This center is created by any melodic or harmonic formation of notes within

the twelve tones or the so-called chromatic tonality.[15] But is it quite evident, that owing to the
purely utilitary and temporary rôle, and to the
historically artificial birth of the chromatic tem-
pered scale, it would be erroneous to consider the
twelve-note system a scale or mode in the same
sense, as tonality born from the natural scale.

I wish to say also that one must differentiate
between the above mathematical definition of
atonality and what æsthetic atonality means. The
latter is a misty sensation produced by lack of
harmonic color in certain sound progressions.

We perceive as atonal certain harmonic progressions when indistinct modulations follow each
other with a speed approaching the limit. Our
ear can then distinguish one sound color from
another just as little as the eye is able to detect
shades in a speedily rotated disc with sectors of
different coloring.

Atonality of this sort is really the white color
of music. Its mathematical definition may be set
as the effect of numberless and indistinct elements
of modulation, that is, cadenceless changes of

[15] According to Schoenberg himself "a system of twelve notes
between which no relationship exists other than their relation to one
another." It is clear then that this is not a system at all.

tonalities, superimposed or taken consecutively at great speed. It is clear then that atonality is sometimes only an individual and ultimate case of polytonality, linear or vertical.

* *

*

Another series of formulas endeavors to subjugate and to unify the ocean of orchestral color.

The old principles inherited from the nineteenth century still hold their sway over modern orchestra. They are notably the organ-like planning of orchestral sonority, the pedalization of orchestral design by way of sustained background, the evenness and balance in all registers and a rigorously calculated doubling. Such is the general order of orchestral sonority in many of Richard Strauss' and in some of Rimski-Korsakov's *tutti,* and even in Ravel's *La Valse.*

Emil Vuillermoz says about Ravel's orchestra: "Without renouncing the silky softness of Debussy's orchestral velvet, the tissue of Ravel's strings is more luminous and crisp. It is in every instant stiffened with metallic embroidery in an

33

unforeseen manner." [16] These words most evidently pertain to the orchestra of *Daphnis*, not to that of *La Valse*. But, indeed, the undiluted orchestral color idea and an evading of superimposition is also an early twentieth century bequest, that of Rimski-Korsakov and Debussy.[17]

The technical principles of the new orchestra tend to an abolition of the orchestral pedal, to an economy and individualizing of the orchestral color, design and voice. This individualization is brought to its height in Schoenberg's *Piérrot Lunaire*, in Stravinsky's *Histoire du Soldat*, in Arthur Bliss' adorable *Rout*, in Von Webern's *Five Orchestral Pieces*, also the subtlest specimens of American jazz.

The most salient features of the new orchestra include a dynamizing of its sustained notes and chords and a dematerializing of the orchestral web. The new orchestra tries to liberate itself from the hypnotic power of orchestral grouping and to establish an independence, an equality and nonrelativity of the instruments. The composer of

[16] Emil Vuillermoz: *Musique d'aujourd'hui.*

[17] In his book *Die Neue Instrumentation* the well-known Viennese composer and savant, Dr. Egon Wellesz, holds that underlining of melodic and rhythmic profile and preservation of unmixed color are the fundamental traits of the nineteenth-century orchestra.

our time considers mainly the definite and absolute tonal shade of the instrumental registers. This is why he favors the chamber orchestra and often contents himself with a most limited ensemble, with a seemingly gaudy and incongruent, motley choice of instruments of sharply differing timbres, often of absolutely polar quality.

Ansermet has defined well that selective reasoning in the new orchestra which I have named "non-relativity":

"Stravinsky utilizes instruments of a frank character, instruments considered not for their tonal intensity, but for the absolute quality of their timbre. The timbre of the contrabass, for example, with its deaf and penetrating sound, is in itself something neither strong, nor weak, nor expressive. But it may take on each of these qualities in turn, in accordance with the handling of the timbre. These qualities do not depend on the timbres which surround them, and they will remain well pronounced even by the side of a trombone piercing a kettle-drum note or that of a violin singing a light air."

Very manifestly, here is an exposition of the instrumental idea of *Histoire du Soldat*.

Remarkable are the conceptions of Georges Migot concerning the *"construction polylinéaire,"* the play of sounding belts of varying depth and of "sound-intensities" that will replace in the new orchestra the play of registers. Migot's *"independance lineaire"* is to take the place of the authonomy of harmonies. Such ideas as these, interestingly applied by Migot to his own compositions, belong to the above described new tonal order. He formulates his scheme of a new orchestral polyphony with rare precision: "Polyphony is not necessarily fugato: but every real polyphony consists of free counterpoints or of the superimposition of several sound-lines. These can be independent not only in motive, rhythmic cells and order, but also in their sound-intensities." [18]

The new orchestration repudiates the alluring tone-shading, sweetened magic of the romantic and impressionist orchestra. In its search for sonorities of acute individuality and of sharply defined intensity, the new orchestration revels in abuse of all the stringent, merciless sound-color which it extracts from the orchestra with painstak-

[18] Georges Migot: "Appogiatures resolues et non resolues," in *Cahiers de la Douce France.*

ing labor. The new orchestration often amounts to patronizing all the step-children of the orchestra, in sheer spite against the old, venerable father. And, of course, all the "composers" whom the doctrine of objectivism has freed from the initial duty of musicianship, the composers who orchestrate beautifully for slapsticks, automobile chains, sirens, telephone keyboards, brooms, etc., have immediately rushed to claim the new tonal treasury displayed by the percussion. But in their ignorance and inability to grasp the real meaning of rhythm, they know no difference between the potentialities of noise and those of resounding percussion.

Georges Migot establishes the meaning and the confines in the use of percussion with fine clarity: "For the rhythms themselves the timbre plays a major rôle, as far as expression is concerned; without a difference in the timbre of the percussion, it would prove impossible to notice the polyrhythmics. . . . Without the resonance of the percussion, the rhythms would be left *outside* of music. . . . When the percussion is considered in the polyphony at all, it owes its musical rôle to the resonance. This rôle may be heightened to a degree necessitating a substantial change in orchestral writing." [19]

One of the most remarkable modern experiments in simplification and dematerializing of the orchestra is the true instrumental synthesis achieved in Schoenberg's *Piérrot Lunaire*.

In his *Fünf Orchesterstücke* Schoenberg embodies his scheme of synthetic harmony (twelve-tone harmony, he calls it) in a practical tonal synthesis, harmonic and orchestral. In this orchestral compound Schoenberg dematerializes all the sonorities and the potentialities of the old organ-like and pedal-infested orchestra to the extent of a real atomization. Only Von Webern's *Fife Orchestra Pieces* have managed to reach the limits of infinitesimal tone-dust more closely.

But in *Piérrot Lunaire* we find the highest and the most utterly individual expression of a practical synthesis of orchestral sound-color. Here Schoenberg condenses all the varieties of the orchestral color of his peculiar tonal world into one telling, deep gray spectre which, blended with the directness and iron logic of that extraordinary music, lends *Piérrot Lunaire* its singular might.

[19] Georges Migot, *ibidem*.

Schoenberg has succeeded in getting that miraculous monochromatic instrumental ensemble which Stravinsky fails to obtain in his thin, futile *Apollo*.

The admirable artistry of Schoenberg triumphs, in its struggle with both, the tyranny of means and the simplification of an elementary order, in the same way as does the genius of Mozart in the g-minor quintet with two violas, as does the mastery of El Greco in the portrait of Luigi Cornaro. In all we find a sublimated simplicity, a thrilling condensation of design and color. These flow unavoidably from the æsthetic and emotional center of the work. It is only logical on Schoenberg's part to maintain, as he does in one of his latest public statements, that ultimately the orchestral sonority will result not from "orchestration" but from the spontaneous movement and the interaction of the orchestral voices.[20]

* *

*

The palette of rhythmic colors, by its very nature mathematically neat and discernible, lends

[20] Dr. Erwin Stein, "Idées d'Arnold Schoenberg." *La Revue Musicale*, November, 1930.

itself better than anything else to systematization by modern æsthetics. Perhaps, solely in the rhythmic sphere the composer of our day feels himself a master, not a victim.[21]

Without exaggerating the value of American jazz, one must admit that it has done more than enrich our rhythmic conceptions. It has originated a crystal-clear kind of rhythmic synthesis which unites both the old and newly discovered rhythmic formations. Jazz has shown that synthetic rhythm embraces not only straight polyrhythmic structures. Typical of the new rhythm, it assimilates the displacement of the main accents to the subordinate times and even to their subdivisions.

* *
*

However, as we shall see further on, all these syntheses and generalizations are but external, superficial attempts to subdue the means and to

[21] It is characteristic that the useful but somewhat naïve book, the first steps of a gifted musicologist, *New Musical Resources* by Henry Cowell, presents all the new tonal means, but systematizes only the rhythmic acquisitions with assurance. In Copland's vivacious article "Jazz Structure and Its Influence" (*Modern Music*, January, 1927), the essence of the new rhythm is set forth with still greater clarity.

realize in some way, if only technically, our æsthetic status. This striving is intensified by a dark feeling of dependence on other forces, those of a moral and social order which are also juggling with our creation. To a description of them I am now coming.

* *

*

c) DOMINATION OF THE MARKET AND OF THE DOCTRINE

No one will deny the fact that even in the age of triumphant individualism in music, at the end of the eighteenth and all through the nineteenth century, the composer was dependent on a certain market and worked for it.

This dependence was slight, however. The composition attuned itself to a very narrow circle of aristocrats,—art-patrons, and the musical intelligentsia. What lessened the burden of adjustment still more, was the fact that the composer's spiritual leaning and his art views were, as a rule, of the same order as those of his clientele. Also, that *patronate*, the European aristocracy and the bourgeois intelligentsia of the eighteenth and nineteenth centuries, was a cultural stratum *par*

41

excellence. Thus the creator was left a spiritual freedom unknown to our industrial era.

Noting the tastes and viewpoints of Haydn and Esterhazi, of Beethoven and Prince Lobkowitz, of Wagner and Pauline Metternich, on the one hand, and of Strauss and Stravinsky and that pleasure-mad modern city *demos* for whom they work, on the other, one is appalled at the variance.

The market dictating to the composer of our day is a machine of incredible pressure. The labor, the electrified ambition and tendencies of the musical creator are all addressed to the immense city mass. Along the lines of its taste that of the composer's ranges itself; its whim and interest he tries to ignite, at whatever the cost. The civilized *demos* of the city, in alliance with the hypnotizing *mondain,* holds the creator of our day in a spiritual and material bondage undreamt of in the days of Monteverdi, organist and choir-master of Saint Mark's, servant of the Serenissime Republic of Venice,[22] unthought of by Couperin,

[22] It is inspiring to read *Monteverdi* by Henri Prunières, the eminent French musicologist, who describes so emphatically Monteverdi's authority, independence and absolute freedom in pursuit of his creative ideals, before which Monteverdi's patrons, the Venitian rulers and the mighty *procuratori* of St. Mark, bowed in reverence.

organist and official composer to King Louis XIV
or by Haydn, the humble Kapellmeister of Prince
Esterhazi. None of these composers by office and
appointment ever suspected what material and
spiritual serfdom might mean.

The yoke of the market and its conquest have
transformed the composer into a musical pyrotechnician, into a master of fireworks storing up
unceasingly new entertainment for the modern
barbarian. As a matter of fact, it is the latter's
whim which the new doctrines with the cheap and
pleasing revolutions of tonal dress, like fashionable
tailors, tend to serve.

The æsthetic demand of the past is replaced by
exigencies of a physiological order. The recent
day exacts from creation accessibility and entertainment. Creation has been pressed into a narrow
cage, the æsthetics of pleasure. Music is forced to
clear away all intellectual rigging, everything that
requires spiritual effort, anything barring the way
to physiological pleasure.

The imperative of "art stripped to the bone"
is a camouflage. There is an unconscious self-
accommodation to the intellectual and cultural
level of the city crowd, that nervous and fatigued

lover of light mental food. The motto of *l'art dépouillé* is naught but the ultimatum of machine-made art, of mass production looking to the street.

Hindemith's opera *Neues zum Tage* is a shining exhibit of a brilliant creative gift caught in the stream of mass production for the city mob, and degraded and mutilated by fashionable dogma. In *Neues zum Tage* we have neo-classicism, new polyphony, and "return to Bach" at any cost plus a strange and deadly tedious cabaret capriccio that is used in operatic writing. Neither the manufactured pastiche, nor the old classic polyphony set in motion at desperate speed, nor the dead grotesque with its sad, forced gayety, nor the master-tricks of orchestral writing applied to a purely cabaret stage "conception," are means as jocund or convincing or even as entertaining as is really good cabaret. One would never believe this music to be by the same Hindemith who wrote the fine string trio, the cello sonata, the *Marien-Lieder* and the adorable choruses to medieval texts.

The pressure of the market has disintegrated the orchestra, that fidel organ of the language and the spirituality of the time. Formerly a generator of tonal *chiaroscuro* and color, the orchestra is now

44

transformed into a gigantic rattle, entertainer of the modern caravansary. The new orchestra can do nothing more than rattle, giggle, make faces, grit its teeth, and play the devil generally.

Rossignol is full of it. The oddly hilarious opening bars of the Chinese march are but gigantic sneezes of the orchestra. Of course, they are executed admirably.

In the finale of Milhaud's amusing orchestral *Serenade* one finds the quaint joke of a lazily innocent major scale played pianissimo by a shy trumpet, at the end of a perfect musical pandemonium. This trick, as simple, ingenious and impossible of repetition as Columbus' egg, merely galvanizes one with zoological laughter; its effect does not reach beyond that.

Indeed the new orchestra of our day has learned to raise havoc, and its hysterical pranks are at times irresistible. But it has lost all capacity to mirror anything, even the most elementary and normal human emotion. When Stravinsky turns with fatigue from his loose orchestral dynamism to the "neoclassic" script of *Oedipus* and *Apollo,* his orchestra loses all trace of force, of conviction, even of sheer technical inventiveness.

Through the frankly physiological imposition of accessibility and entertainment, the yoke of the market has altered the very essence of new musical thought. It has made unavoidable the stressed contagion and exaggerated imagery that form the source of the new grotesque. From this flows the cinematographic romanticism and cinematographic impressionism that is embodied in Honegger's *Pacific*, in Gershwin's *Rhapsody in Blue*, in Stravinsky's *Histoire du Soldat*. They must be so classified, in spite of the high technical culture of one, the tonal attractiveness of the other, the harmonic and rhythmic stir of the third.

The new creation swings spasmodically from "cyclopism" to "lilliputianism" in musical language and imagery. The distinguished American writer on music, Lawrence Gilman, applies the latter eloquent term to the elusive forms and sonorities of the Schoenbergian school.

Another American musician of eminence, Carl Engel, places the lilliputian tonal thought very aptly:

"The smaller form is always the favorite during an interregnum. It lends itself better to tenta-

46

tive methods. . . . In the age of 'columnists' the essay has given way to the paragraph, the epic to the epigram. Music, too, has become paragraphic and epigrammatic."[23]

The bridge of entertainment and hyperbolism stretches between pieces mentally and emotionally polar. It forms the link between Stravinsky's *Histoire du Soldat,* that absurdly inflated dramatic scheme of a sorry human mannikin whose every feeling is condensed into a marche-grotesque, and the rarefied tonal thought of Von Webern's *Five Orchestral Pieces,* where according to Lawrence Gilman's ingenious word "the music is simplified nearly out of existence."

Between the pantagruelesque animal lyrics and dance of the sailors in Georges Auric's ballet *Les Matelots* and the spicily microscopic "symphonies" and "quartets" of Milhaud, is thrown the bridge of physiological art, of the æsthetics of pleasure, stripped of the last vestige of spirituality.

This entertaining cortège of new musical shadows impresses one as would a calculated *reductio*

---

[23] Carl Engel: *Discord Mingled,* Alfred A. Knopf, publisher, New York.

ad absurdum of the procession-scheme in *Cocq d'or*. Monstrous and rough-hewn giants of every sort and fantastically crooked dwarfs from out the netherworld follow each other with a bedevilling and insured effect.

The pressure of the market has also brought about the overgrowth of rhythmic invention and through this—the sickly hypertrophy of dance music. It is the sports' mania of our day that has created an exaggerated response to rhythm, that element of musical emotion which is the link between music and sport. The short-lived but intense domination of jazz and of provokingly rhythmic music in general, has been the unmistakable by-product of a football era.

The picture of the degeneration of modern dance and its music,—*Les Matelots* is a typical specimen of such,—shows with crystalline clarity how the football and dance manias of the modern barbarian, with his commercial mass production of art objects, have adapted and degraded most wholesome revolutionary ideas. Adapted, exploited their lowest potentialities and left mountains of empty shell.

The jazz movement manifestly began as a natural and useful reaction against musical "Ptolemaism." [24]

Failing a better thing, jazz became the heir to the Russian musical influence in Europe. In turn, in a more elementary and rougher way, jazz afforded Europe a restful change from a Ptolemaic tonal existence, from a tonal life which has made Europe stale and sour. Jazz has struck from the European mind that frozen idea that the whole being of world music and its destination are fully fixed in the petrified terms and habits of the civilized musician or of the civilized pedant of West Europe. Jazz has strangled the notion that musical history rotates around our library shelves.

However, originating in a wholesome reaction against musical Ptolemaism, jazz, that musical manifesto of the civilized savage, has immediately done away with immeasurable inner possibilities, spiritual and æsthetic. It has turned to a more accessible road: it has vulgarized the reform. Moving along the path of direct action, which is

[24] In his great book *Untergang des Abendlands,* Oswald Spengler speaks of our history as Ptolemaic, when he finds the prejudices of the old Ptolemaic astronomy in our habitual European viewpoint. He means the conceiving of the West European man as the presumed center of world-events around which great cultures move in turns.

in fact physiological action, we have substituted physiological obsession for æsthetic impression; sports' dynamism for spiritual dynamism.[25] Thus we have speedily reached the characteristic stage of the rhythmic and dancing debauch of our day, and just as quickly we have grown fatigued and been disgusted by it.

The music-hall and football classicism of the *Matelots* is a finished product of the disintegration of the rhythm and melody of dance into the rhythm and melody of sport. Æsthetic emotion degenerates into a physiological one. The latter is indeed legitimate in its own sphere; but it deceives, smacks of impostorship when pretending to the place and meaning of the former.

In the same by-ways of our music we easily trace a corrosion, a vulgarization due to another important modern principle, that of laconism and order in musical speech. Let me mention here, that the principle was hinted long ago in Richard

[25] The words uttered quite gravely by Stravinsky's Leporello, Mr. Artur Vincent Lourié, form an amusingly just verdict. "The music of *Noces* is so constructed as to prevent the hearing of the music itself. No matter how many times one may hear this composition, one is unable to perceive it, so strongly is the listener held under the constant physical influence of rhythm." (*Modern Music*, Volume VII, 1.)

Avenarius' formula, "thinking conformed to the least expense of energy."

The principle of laconism was also immediately adapted to the commercial policy of accessibility and insured success, a course pursued under the veil of doctrine. That principle of economy and order in tonal utterance was, of course, reconstructed at once into the formula of conscious simplification or "barbarism." This dogma openly repudiates the tradition of mastery and artistry, as bourgeois preciosity. In its final form it has taken on the shape of the *art dépouillé* theory, that of art denuded to essentials. However, this dogmatic scaffolding has not been needed by real masterpieces of today, such as Prokofiev's *Shout*. But it has supplied the *raison d'être* or rather been an excuse for compositions whose simplification or conscious barbarism derives not from creation of elemental strength, but from a meager, exhausted imagination. Such is the case of Stravinsky's piano-sonata, that eminent and over-explained stillborn.

* *

*

51

The conquest of the market has produced many "creative" phenomena which would have amused us had they not been so pathetic. Casella has said very well concerning Stravinsky: "Formerly the most personal and national composer of his country, the metamorphosis of late years has finally made him European and impersonal." [26] I would say, the great caravansary of Europe has almost played an even more wicked trick on Stravinsky, who is, however, a benevolent, a willing victim of his time. We were about to place in the same rank with Bach and Mozart, with Moussorgski and Wagner, a man whose talent is perhaps not so much of a musical as of a merely tonal order.

The artistic path of Stravinsky is a phenomenon of exceptional glitter. And he himself is so manifestly a compression of all the æsthetic and moral essence of the art of our day, that we must not pass by the methods created by him for the conquest of the market. Among these methods, a peculiar publicity *preceding* the first appearance of a new work and an exploitation of scandal are the most picturesque and effective. The first success of

[26] In his youthful and ardent book on Stravinsky Domenico de Paoli, one of the leading young musicians of Italy, strives to show that the real Stravinsky is cosmopolitan or possibly "Mediterranean."

Sacre, certainly the most brilliant of Stravinsky's works in its decorative magnificence and invention, was essentially a *succès de scandale.* Very significantly, it followed closely the clamorous days of Marinetti, Russolo and other *bruiteurs* (1909-1913). One might suspect that from them Stravinsky, the great observer, gleaned something.

The success of *Sacre,* or rather the very special character of its success, has corrupted the composer of our day. From it, perhaps for the first time, the composer, as such, has learned to fully exploit scandal as a bridge to mass recognition. It was the pandemonium created by *Sacre* that laid the foundation for a triumph of sensationalism. This opened gates to a policy of scandal in composition.

The rest of Stravinsky's spiritual and, so to speak, moral history is but the story of a fight to retain the electric, never to be repeated, success of *Sacre.* It is a history of nostalgic longing for another *succès de scandale.* With each new work he strives to create a precedent, a new path and a new manner. The performances of these works are preceded by edicts proclaiming, commenting on, glorifying the new fashion. This proves to be one of the mightiest weapons of publicity; it has helped Stravinsky and it has helped the great tailors of our day as well, to conquer the city host.

Manœuvres, such as this, have moved into the foremost rank a number of small personalities who live on the crumbs from Stravinsky's table; escorts, not worthy to unfasten his shoe, yet just as clever in handling the new machinery of *réclame*.

How many of these manifestoes have we not been listening to of late! Day before yesterday—it was burial of emotion and a replacement by the pressure of rhythm and movement; yesterday—a return to Bach. Last night we observed Hellenic musical contortions, listened to the edict announcing another change of tonal dress necessitated by a voyage to the land of Oedipus and Apollo. To-morrow, perhaps, it will be "come ye, this be the last embrace" or an æsthetic marriage to the Zulu.

The subtle French musician and writer, Artur Hoërée, says amusingly and rightly concerning the untiring manœuvres of Stravinsky: "There is to-day a snobbish and a most seductive mania which consists in discovering finality in each of Stravinsky's experiments. He has invented everything; he has overthrown, renovated and reconstructed everything; he has subjugated his own self. He has shaken the tyranny of the metric bar, saved harmony, counterpoint and orchestration from debacle, recaptured lost melody and, like a new Siegfried, destroyed the monster of romanticism."

However, one must notice that Stravinsky, though in lesser degree than Scriabin—has been not a little upset in his normal creative position by apostles and lieutenants who have helped to invent a suitable ideology.

It is quite possible that Scriabin, had he followed his æsthetic and creative instinct alone, would have become the great initiator, a triumphant builder of one of the most original art eras. But unfortunately, Scriabin was ejected from the purely musical and his native element not only by a strength-sapping literary fancy of his own, but also by the phraseology of his apostles and by their demagogic theosophy. This same thing has happened to Stravinsky. An entire retinue of theoreticians and proselytes fastened themselves on him, among them the great captain of international art-industry, Diaghileff, an important factor in Stravinsky's tortuous psychology. These councilors explained Stravinsky's own ways to himself so well, that he, a master-decorator and stylizer, began to mumble something about volumes, weights and objects (a remote after-ringing of Einstein's theories) and undertook to handle Apollo, Oedipus, etc. A master of color *par excellence,* he has undertaken to transform his art into a sort of sculpture, for example, as in the *Symphonies pour les instruments à vent.* He has ventured to replace the neat and definite functions of the sonata-form by curlicues of a freshly invented "dialectic method." How characteristic this typical commercial unscrupulousness, this interminable manœuvring is, can be seen from Stravinsky's words quoted by Boris de Schloezer: *"Mon idée vient de la musique et non la musique de cette idée."* [27] The real situation is quite the reverse of his statement. Since *Sacre* and *Rossignol* Stravinsky has had but one design, to evolve and to build his music from and around a new technical thought, or better said, a technical sensation.

It is curious, however, that none of his doctrines —manifestoes, have lived longer than needed, each in its respective turn, to excite the market. But all

[27] "My idea comes from the music, not my music from the idea." Boris de Schloezer in *Stravinsky.*

his tenets together have kept the prophet floating very comfortably on the gold-yielding waves of manufactured composition.

Stravinsky could well shield himself behind Oscar Wilde's paradox, that sonorous apology for pose and grimace: "Insincerity is merely a method by which we can multiply our personality." Very manifestly, this dictum plays on slipping falsity into the place of the fundamental convention lying at the root of any art.

But one word replaced in Wilde's aphorism, and a true formula is shaped: "*Art* is merely a method by which we can multiply our personality." This traces the furrow between the "artistic" and the "artificial," between creation and manufacturing. Is it not true, that a clear difference exists between the intuitive multiplication of our personality *pro arte* and the artificial fashioning of mere pretense commercially useful?

Thus it is clear that our quarrel with Stravinsky has nothing to do with imposition. Every living composer *imposes his music* on his contemporaries and must do so as *nobody needs a contemporary*. In their lifetime Beethoven and Wagner most peremptorily imposed their works on a resisting humanity, forced it to accept their creation, forced public taste to accommodate itself and to form new manuals of harmony.

But let us cast aside the smaller economics of modern doctrines with their ethical lining. Let us take those dogmas seriously and measure the dialectic power of their central point, objectivism.

* *

*

D) THE OBJECTIVIST DOGMA

Beloved of these days, objectivist or neoclassicist dogma, establishes the cult of musical fact (*fait musical*). This cult strives "to build rather than to express."

Creation is freed from all trace of personal and emotional accent, in fact from any extra-musical stimulus, accent and impulse. These are replaced by pure pressure of tonal lines, by an effect from their combinations, intensity and velocity.

This postulate embraces all the achievements of modern musical thought, that is, impersonality or rather superindividualism, and dynamism in its expressive aspect, and in its tonal aspect—a free and impassive, so to speak, display of harmonic,

58

rhythmic and orchestral combinations, a free poly-harmony, polyrhythmics and polychromatics.

But let me say at once that the term "neoclassicism" is a misnomer. The very fastening of an unemotional quality on old classical music is, to say the least, an exaggeration; it should be taken with a grain of salt.

Furthermore, it is not difficult to uncork the philosophical disarray underlying the objectivist dogma. As to the practice of "objectivism," this has indeed little to do with the old classical cultivation of the tonal arabesque, really spontaneous and apersonal to the root.

The main and the crudest fault in both the theorem of objectivism and its practice, is a confusing of the personal ego with the æsthetic ego, a confusing of the will-originating, acting center of the personality with its creative center. The classical canon of æsthetics sees in every process of art-creation an overpowering of the will-bearing or acting ego, whereby the energy of the æsthetic, creative ego is released. This is the principle of play.

But music fashioned through the command of "objectivity" or forced into such a category, does not embrace the giving up of will coercion, that is, of personal interference. In fact, the case of Stravinsky presents just the reverse. His is a case of deliberate, willfully enforced materialization of a doctrine *preceding* creation.

As a matter of fact, every work of his after *Sacre du Printemps* and even *Sacre* itself, embodies pure interference, namely, the deliberate enforcement of a doctrine. It is individualism of the first water; it strangles the æsthetic impulse of a creator and incarnates accent and impulse eminently personal. Pertaining to this Charles Koechlin has said, and with excellent judgment, that the ruthlessness with which Stravinsky and other neoclassicists erase emotion, their very destructiveness, is also emotionalism, but of a negative and polar kind.

Such "Shivaism," sadistic destructiveness as that of Stravinsky's, avidly adopted by the petty officers of modern music as a means to effortless composition, is, indeed, sheer expressionism and romanticism turned upside down. In spite of its dogma and a quasi-impersonal exterior, the cerebral, stillborn grotesque is a sharp and degenerate offal of romanticism. It embodies a definitely individualistic or rather, a despotic conception.

The recent artistic position of Stravinsky which has to be explained as an example of æsthetic objectivity, might justly be called technical despotism.

* *
*

The theorem of objectivity shelters also the unnoticed sin of nominalism. It is a recidive of the old Aristotelian and medieval philosophers' teaching that only individual things are a reality; that the very meaning of words, *i.e.* names of things, in themselves forestall reality. We ascribe to a given music qualities suggested by some label deliberately placed on it by ourselves, following the well-known medieval *mode de penser: "opium facit dormire quare in eo virtus dormitiva est."* [28]

Objective or absolute music keeps clear of impulse and elements foreign to a purely tonal domain; it discards any idiom of an emotional, literary or descriptive nature. This conception of objectivity embraces not only the confusion just described but also another philosophical error.

What does it mean: elements foreign to music?

[28] "Opium makes one sleep because it contains a sleeping power."

Strictly speaking, these do not exist. The already listed "non-absolute" elements,—the word, description, program, never have been the inward, the integral part of the musical fact. They have served sometimes as associations, but mainly as *Anregung* for musical thought, as an igniting fuse. But, of course, it has invariably proved to be an æsthetic and not an emotional inciter.

The legitimacy and intramusicality of any æsthetic ignition are beyond dispute. Musical creation flows unavoidably from within the *æsthetic ego*. The being of music is necessarily and always of æsthetic order, it is never individual or emotional *per se*. In this sense all music is objective, independent of whether it has been incited by emotion, by a program or by rhythm and movement.

As a minor issue of this, one can easily explain the doom of realistic or rather, veristic barbarism, the doom of the new tone-mimicry resurrected by Stravinsky in *Petroushka* and *Sacre* and by Honegger in *Pacific;* works which can not survive in spite of their brightness.

This new tone-painting strives, naïvely and unnaturally, to substitute literal reality for the æsthetic substratum of music, truthful because of the basic convention of it, proper to any art. One might accuse this new version of tone-mimicking of being photographic and nonreal because it changes values and perspectives, to requote an excellent analysis of Cocteau.

Let us observe that the new striving for melody and for eighteenth-century style points to our awareness of the crash of realistic objectivity.

The creed of objectivism is nothing but an apology for our fear of emotion, as antagonist to order in musical creation. This is why the doctrine is so overworked. It has grown to be a legal title for "icy" composers, a vindication for their existence. It serves composers deprived of emotion and of dramatic instinct. In fact, by them was the creed invented.

In one of his fascinating books Dr. Isaac Goldberg recalls Remy de Gourmont's sagacious dictum that Flaubert's objectivity was his way of being subjective. Dr. Goldberg adds delightfully: "Our composers who consider themselves 'beyond emotion' can as easily mean below it as above." [29]

---

[29] Dr. Isaac Goldberg: *George Gershwin, Study in American Music*, published by Simon and Schuster, New York.

* *

*

Stravinsky's *Histoire du Soldat* is thought to be one of the most brilliant examples of objective art. It is thought to reach by way of rhythm and movement the same expressive result, that old music has attained or has tried to attain by drawing on emotional and descriptive resources. But actually *The Soldier* explodes all such legends: that of emotion as an enemy of order, and that of the neoclassic rule as heir to dramatico-impressionistic chaos.

Together with *Petroushka*, the most dramatic of Stravinsky's works, and perhaps the best organized, although far weaker in its descriptive power than *Sacre*, *Histoire du Soldat* exemplifies just the opposite thesis. *The Soldier* is a marvelous specimen of the "affective" form; its unity flows from the emotion and conflict that has given birth to the form. The dramatic emotion embodied in *The Soldier* is the subsistence of a creature-grotesque whose aimlessness and futility is crystallized into one strangely clear and spiritually hollow formula. This weird march-two-step, now artificially gay or wistful, now absurd or savage, then human and poignant, portrays a queer, forlorn soul.

It passes the wit of man to see why just this composition is considered the leading specimen of new objectivity. If *The Soldier's* appearance points to anything, it is rather to a return to humanization, to a reinstalling of emotion.

*　*
*

Paul Valery deems characteristic the pandemonium of theoretical dialects in the Babel Tower of modern art. His definition of a *modern era,* I would claim it for any era stamped by deification of "today," is simplicity itself.

"What precisely characterizes a *modern* epoch is the free coexistence in all cultivated minds of the most dissimilar ideas, the most contradictory principles of life and knowledge." [30]

However, the symbiosis of both, the most polar modern dogmas and the most diversified compositions equalized by one and the same doctrine, remounts in our own ultra-industrial and ultra-commercial days to a very manifest source. I say

[30] Paul Valéry, "Intellectual crisis," letters to the *London Athenæum,* April and May, 1919.

this not by way of moralizing but by way of an analysis of the existing order.

We have already seen that the coexistence of dissimilar ideas serves towards a vindication of the means and the market. This does lend unity of a certain sort to the whole picture of our creative modernity.

Really, what have they in common, the Bachian grimace of Stravinsky's dead piano concerto, that wry mirror of old masters, and the circus "neoclassicism" of Auric's *Matelots?* The latter's rickety and playful spiritual father, Satie's *Parade,* and the music-hall'esque "neoclassical" polyphony of Hindemith's *Neues zum Tage?* What have these writers in common that should force their music inside the same paling, objective art?

Nothing in common, indeed, but the dogma and the legal title sought out by the modern mechanician and salesman of composition: a title which must with a stroke legalize and camouflage the vindication of the means and of the market.

The meaning of all noise, the intention of the purely verbal fight with individualism is, as I have already shown, to facilitate our accommodation to the taste of the "hundred-eyed blind one," and to minimize to the last degree the creative obligation of the new composer.

The Stravinsky phalanx of imitators pretentiously mark with the label of objectivity all their grotesque fabrications, whether sharply chromatic and involved, or diatonically discolored and dismantled to the skeleton. Their pretension is lashed solely by the trade value and industrial usefulness of the new slogan. That falsity, substitution of rhythm and movement for emotional and musical content, has all but emancipated the new composer from any need of professional skill. This self-grant is responsible for the open road to mass production and a replacing of composition by fabrication, by something accessible to all humbugs in music.

Through the drive of fashion and demand, men of talent and imagination, those like Hindemith, Krenek, Milhaud, have been sucked into the whirl of music manufacturing.

Of course, I am far from insisting that the modern musician is conscious of *all* of these enticements, that each is willfully a tradesman. He is, as a rule, a victim of a temporary industrial and cultural order which a creator weak in art morals and spiritually limited, such as Stravinsky, cannot resist.

At his side is to be found the proud figure of Schoenberg, the other great builder of modernity, and just as definite a representative of technical despotism. There is true consolation in the sight of a powerful character contemptuously evading the path laid by the trade directive of modern city art.

* *
*

E) OUR ÆSTHETICAL POSITION

The entire chain of preceding facts and reasoning leads us to the finding of the longitude and latitude of our æsthetic position.

The ideology of our day is an evident *reductio ad absurdum* of the æsthetics of our fathers. To-day, in the keep and on the pay of the means and the market, some points of the old aesthetics have been put to new use. They have degenerated into a white-washing of the new masters.

Virulent lordship of the proceeding and abuse of the moulded grotesque have transfigured the pseudo-romanticism of Strauss and pseudo-impressionism of Debussy's epigons into romanticism and impressionism of a cinematographic breed. This is the second level, so to speak, in the debasement of romanticism.

The jazz-grotesque drift of recent days has been one of the varieties of that new impressionism of the poster. A typical example is *Johny spielt auf*, opera by Krenek, a peculiar and wiry talent likely to create sturdy works if he—as well as Hindemith and Milhaud—will but tear himself away from the grind of music fabrication.

The market, with its lordly imperatives born of the sports' and the dance manias, has transfigured the pseudo-classicism of Saint-Saëns, Reger and Ravel into the music-hall classicism of Hindemith's *Neues zum Tage*, Auric's *Matelots*, etc.

* *

*

Both the technical aspect and the direction of our tonal speech are clear.

We have scarcely begun to leave behind us the initial, shallow watercourse of the tonal revolution, namely the *etymological* enrichment of our musical language.[31] We scarcely begin to abandon the

---

[31] I use the term *etymology* for all material changes within the tonal means, melodic, harmonic or rhythmic, and the term *syntax* for the interrelation of the tonal units.

stage of the purely etymological reform of our tonal vocabulary, of its cases, tenses and structure. Strauss and Stravinsky, the great growers of new musical resources, are the parents of this shallow, inexpensive revolution of the tonal garment, so agreeable to the consumer.

However, we begin to resist the yoke of the proceeding. We already know its menace and now strive to force it back to its proper place. We near a new technical organization of our tonal wealth and strive to overpower its verbal and etymological luxury, a crazed multifold of color.

We now stand at the gate of an indwelling revolution, one in our musical syntax.

We already sense its breeze, a noticeable tremor at the very basis of the spiritual girders of our speech. Derangements already manifest in the music of Debussy, Scriabin and Schoenberg, the true revolutionaries and leaders, augurate a crisis. But in spite of their vision and initiative we have as yet no tangible points. We can only guess at the ground idiom of the coming reform. We do know, however, that it will compel an entire *inner* reorganization of our speech; it will result in a new musical syntax.

Our present stage immediately precedes a full syntactic reform of our tonal language. This is the reason why our tongue is little sure of itself, is hysterical in its fling from one "manner" to another and inarticulate, in spite of all its impetus and insolence.

The cycle of etymological individualism, the cycle of small tonal invention, of, so to speak, bourgeois reform in music, is over. We find ourselves on the eve of *syntactic individualism.*

Schoenberg's effort is to create a new foundation for tonal order in today's musical parlance, which is mozaic, cellular, built on musical aphorism. His effort is a true anticipation of the coming syntactic individualism. Schoenberg has rejected the former firm basis of tonal gravitation. He has repudiated both the old tonics of traditional modes and the new ground of polytonality, atonality and what I have formulated formerly as synthetic tonality. Then he establishes instead the new principle of *series.* This order is enacted by individual and extratonal formulas, each fundamentally related to one particular composition, to its structural or gravitational tendency.

Johann Mathias Hauer, the singularly interesting and independent Viennese composer, has shaped his own system which adjoins Schoenberg's *series* rather closely. Within the twelve sounds' tonality Hauer establishes forty-four *tropuses*, a sort of chromatic hexachords with altering steps. These *tropuses* contain all feasible ways of melodic gravitation and millions of thematic variations: they actually embrace the whole melodic universum.

These concepts are so elastic, that they close the door to no tonal potentiality. But just because of their elasticity they contain no forecast, save a general and instinctive anticipation of the approaching order, that of syntactic individualism.

However, at a closer glimpse into a less noticed aspect of the modern theory and practice of "objectivism" and "neoclassicism," we shall discover a significant sign pointing to the coming tonal speech. It may serve in predicting some traits of the latter.

"Neoclassicism" and "objectivism" as well as the newly-annexed "return to melody" will prove to be, after a careful examination, symptoms of a camouflaged turn to tonal gravitation and of an evident turn to diatonism. I have in mind, however, neither the modulationless, absolute diatonism of the Renaissance, nor Wagner's chromaticized diatonic tonality. I speak of a new, relative diatonism, which admits *any* harmony on each step of the scale but gravitates to some basic diatonic configuration, harmonic or melodic.

In essence, Schoenberg's formula, too, endeavors to re-establish the principle of harmony-form. I name thus every harmonic complex that possesses formative power, the capacity to cement tonal structure.[32]

And strangest of all, this is the old and tried bulwark of tonal order that was lost in the disintegration of the gravitational centers, crudely and inexactly named "tonics,"—lost as a result of a sharp etymological reform.

But the turn to camouflaged diatony is nothing

[32] How significant it is to find in such a radical harmonic system, as that of Hauer's, germs of a strangely new diatonic order. Of Hauer's harmony Dr. Paul Pisk, who is with Berg and Von Webern, the most gifted and virile representative of the Schoenberg school, speaks thus: "In Hauer's polyphony parts of the *tropus* (three or four tones) are used as accompanying harmonies. It is characteristic that these accompanying chords frequently assume the form of triads and that even within the *tropus* there appear sequences with a leading-tone or cadencing activity. The impression of atonality is consequently weakened and through the concluding triads particularly dear to Hauer, an all too clear reference to tonality is re-established."

Dr. Paul Pisk: "The Tonal Era draws to a close" (*Modern Music*, March, 1926.)

more than the longing for that wisely apportioned monotony of tone-color, harmonic and orchestral, for that monotony of rhythm and form that in old music had the gift of evoking a hypnotic sense of unity in the tonal structure.

Dr. Alfred Einstein describes excellently the hypnotic power of *ostinato,* so much abused in our day of search for new cement for the form.

"A common means of binding together a movement is the ostinato bass motif; it hammers itself into the ear, ever gaining more melodic independence and importance; it permits other ostinato motives to be built up above it and lends itself to rhythmic definiteness." [33]

We are longing to reacquire the secret of a new and fresh euphony and form, an alloy of new eutonics, eurhythmics and euchromatics.

The striving for this leads us still, like new-born, blind puppies, into the swamp of "neoclassic" lanes, into the neoscarlattian pastiche of Stravinsky, into Hindemith's labored rush and muddle of a forced figured style which would simulate Bach's polyphonic energy. We are seeking to make

[33] Dr. Alfred Einstein: "The Newer Counterpoint," *Modern Music,* Volume VI, 1.

our own the creative secret of Beethoven who knew
that the reiterating of an inwardly potent formula
can evoke irresistible tonal and formal obsession.

We would learn the secret by which Wagner
managed to make a unity of the vast web of his
music drama, that fitful ocean of music seemingly
decimated and dissolved by the word and by legend,
by decorative ideas and by the theatre. Desperately we need the knowledge by which Wagner
succeeded, with the aid of the simplest formal proceedings, to force an immensity of elements into
a pure musical channel and to leave a great hypnotic sense of entity. Indeed, Wagner's mighty
illusion of unity deployed over a chaotic tonal
amalgam corroded by home-made literature and
philosophy, is only accentuated, not created by the
application of symphonic proceedings to opera: by
the use of monothematism, of quasi-development,
of transitional methods drawn from an expansion
of the leit-motive.

We yearn to recapture that mysterious skill by
which Scriabin was able, with a wisely inoculated
monotony of rhythm, as in *Flammes sombres* and
Ninth sonata, and with brightly illuminated harmonic buttresses and tonal shafts, to unify struc-

tures of a most capricious order, reeking with detail and ornamentation, his *Prometheus,* for instance.

Desperate, we would cure ourselves of the new form of musical hydrophobia, we would eradicate the fear of white color in music, the dread of c-major and of simple tonal formulas, harmonic or rhythmic. This mania was born from the dread of musical "yesterday," from resistance to emotion and to the dress of our fathers, as much as it is from the harmonic laxity of the recent day.

The turn to a new diatonism is the first sign of our coming cure from the dread of c-major.

* *

*

This anxiety of the modern creator rises from still deeper water than an inborn æsthetic thirst for oneness in multiformity, for æsthetic and formal monism.

After epochs of artificial and speculative composition, we invariably aspire to return to music born from our racial springs and from its mother eterne, the human voice. We revert to music flowing in its native canyon, that of the natural scale.

The indwelling, natural tonal firmament of our musical art is as unalterable and unavoidable as is the megacosm, the great universe itself. Thence everything returns, all elements, after vagaries, tempests and transmutations. From the many harmonic "systems" music is bound to revert to its native tonal and racial essence. But making use of all the natural resources interacting within the new and manifold racial idioms which have lately appeared on the arena of history, will *now* lead to the cultivation of riches hidden in the modal dissonance.[34] I mean, in combinations originating in the higher overtones. But this new and developed modal dissonance will be also dynamic. Dynamism will be the main difference in the foundation of the coming music and that of the pre-Bachian era with its belated heirs, the Russian "Mighty Handful" and Debussy. The pre-Bachian epoch was one of modal and static consonance; that of the Russians and Debussy—of modal and static dissonance.

After a six- or seven-centuries' old process of accumulation of sound, from the two part organum

[34] Of course, I use here the term of "dissonance" in its purely working and popular meaning, not in the highest theoretical sense.

77

up to the six- and seven-part tissue of Wagner and Scriabin, and the most complex tonal scaffoldings of Schoenberg, music will change to, has already begun to adopt, a process of harmonic and polyphonic unburdening.

From harmony and polyphony multiplied we shall turn to harmony and polyphony rarefied. But the rarefication will be new and fresh, spiritually tense and sharpened. Except for common source, the new structure will have no affinity with the rarefied sound-tissues of the organum or with the thinned web of some of the Oriental folk-songs.

Owing to the same causes we shall witness the death of the modern substitute for polyphony. The germs of this death are actually traceable to the general trend of mid-European polyphony as molded by Johann Sebastian Bach's iron hand. Bach touched off the disintegration of the early Middle Ages' counterpoint, just as he dealt a lethal blow to modal harmony. The divine ease, individuality and human warmth of such polyphony as is contained in the great psalm of Palestrina *Sicut Cervus,* yields place to mechanicity, apersonality and arid instrumentalism in the post-Bachian polyphonic culture.

Only Mozart's unsurpassed imagination managed to discover voices of individual appeal within even the simplest harmonic frames, such as the opening choral measures in the *Lacrimosa* of his *Requiem*.

Beethoven has finally substituted for polyphony a pale echo of the fugal style, and Wagner—a dense paste of the so-called harmonic counterpoint, really clusters of harmonic embellishments. Stravinsky adds a new kind of falsified counterpoint through the cultivation of orchestral dynamism.

But our own obvious, easily fabricated polytonal amalgam melted at random, will cease to be. We shall see the end of our pseudo-polyphony consisting of artificial harmonic counterpoint and labored orchestral voice-movement. This would-be polyphony of the present day will wilt to be replaced by a new and a true polyphony. The latter will come with the birth of a new tonal vision, with a new aural sense, and will annihilate our contrapuntal calculation, our counterpoint for the eye.

This new polyphony will come to light within the modal and dynamic dissonance, already poten-

79

tial in the natural scale element. The human voice, now fastidious and wise with the experience of two centuries of melodic individualism, will again seize its natural rôle. It will again be the font of our music, new and with a new syntax.

*　*

*

Our impending general tonal syntax or even the sheer harmonic perspective, may have something of the nature of Yasser's supra-diatonic harmony, or possibly follow along the line of Schoenberg's *series* applied not to the chromatic medium, but to a new and modalized diatonic essence. I mean by this, an element of which the gravitational tonal basis would breathe the air of modal dissonance, instead of Schoenberg's twelve-note configurations.

An analysis of the oldest folk-airs has shown that our modes are perhaps only débris from or mutilations of the ancient scales.[35] It is evident that the future harmonic syntax will preclude neither Schoenberg's, nor Yasser's tonal potentialities. Synthetic modes of a large trunk are mani-

[35] See "Music of the Russian Orient," supplement to the essay "New Russians and their *Alma Mater*" in this book.

festly the natural medium of any crystallized tonal speech of mankind. To these large natural river-beds, the tonal stream ever seeks a return.

In a broad amplitude, in an all-embracing synthesis, æsthetical and racial, the new tonal language will be *universal*, not international, not that longed for by the "objective" and "neoclassic" parlance of the present day, with their imitation of the international classical tonal esperanto of the eighteenth century. Universal, not international will be our new tonal syntax. For it will flow from eternal and submerged, common racial springs. To this synthesis all races, of East and of West, will yield the germ of their speech and musical riches.

The reappearance of racial art claiming its dormant rights; the new tonal allurement and the unexhausted, elemental potency of the veritable, unknown Orient, cradle of modal music and of that flowing from the natural scale, loom as indirect symptoms of the rebirth of natural polyphony. I mean, polyphony of a rarefied tonal formation and of dynamic and modal dissonant vein.

This is an unavoidable tribute to the tone-vision

of the common ancestors of our Hindu-German race. The future path of Western musical culture is prearranged in the ancient racial mind. Thus joy and fertility that has long since left our music, will be restored. Without new streams of racial art, without the ever-green bloom from racial roots, without cross-fertilization with fresh and aggressive musical elements, such as neo-Celtic, neo-Italian, Hebraic, neo-American, Hungarian, Spanish, our music would be doomed to sundown, to but melancholy perspective of "extensive possibilities." [36]

Marvelous are those flare-ups of a renaissance appearing from an Eastern racial direction just in this era of marasmus and death, in an age of visible petrification in Western European music! Possibly, the new Russian, Hungarian, Hebrew, Spanish and other vibrant and living streams of the Eastern flood now pouring its cutting waters into the new music of the West, have as their mission the stamping out of creative Ptolemaism ingrained in the Western musical mass-mind. This

[36] In *Untergang des Abendlands* Spengler describes admirably these sole possibilities left to a dying culture that is degenerating into civilization.

new and triumphant cortège of the musical East, augurates a real return to our common racial spring, heralds a reunion of the musical creeds, a tonal merging of the Orient and the Occident.

II

THE HISTORICAL AND THE PROPHETIC
ASPECT OF OUR TONAL LANGUAGE

I HAVE made clear our day's æsthetic position and the æsthetic aspect of our tonal speech. In the coming chapter I hope to answer the following queries:

Where do we now find ourselves, historically and spiritually?

In which of the ever-rotating and periodically returning culture-cycles do we belong?

What is the spiritual position of the latest musical era?

* *

*

The outward, purely tonal enrichment of musical speech is a function of three quantities: the natural scale, space, in its geographical sense, and time, in its historical meaning.[37] The incor-

[37] Mathematics defines *function* as a quantity whose value depends upon that of another quantity.

porating of a growing number of natural scale steps into the tonal web amounts to a purely numeric enrichment. Such is the historical ascension from monody and organum to polytonics, to the distinctly visible, mathematical complication of harmony.

As a function of space, the growth of the tonal language, its deepening and enrichment, depend on a geographic flow of musical wealth. As a function of time the growth hinges on the alterations in the spiritual forces which direct great movements of culture.

In turning to the geographic flow of tonal wealth and to its action on world music, one looks down the following vista.

The exchange of musical values between the great branches of humanity is strikingly similar to the basic physical phenomena of nature. Processes to be likened to radiation, to diffusion and osmosis, that is, transfer of dissolved substances, are found in music interchange. *Osmosis* and osmotic pressure can be observed in the tonal universum where they project themselves in just the same way as in the physical universe.

Values, fields of force and the yeast of musical

cultures, that is, the peculiar seminal particles, strive to penetrate from countries with a highly condensed musical culture into those of lesser musical tensity and culturally paler. By a more condensed musical culture I mean one possessing a higher creative attainment, or a more intensified general level of musical mass culture, or an exceptional and elemental freshness and impetus of racial expression, such as in the Eastern folk-song, Russian or Spanish music or American jazz.

In all these cases the main flow of tonal wealth is propelled by a sheer difference in emotional tension, in cultural level or simply in vitality. This corresponds precisely to the *difference of potentials* in physics.

If we take the two gigantic music processes, one inter-European and the other universal, each as an isolated experiment, we can easily observe and follow the current and the destiny of the osmotic waves.

Beginning with the second quarter of the nineteenth century, one of these great waves flows from the European West toward the East, in the direction of the least resistant Russian musical midst. Carrying the influence of Schumann, Meyerbeer,

Berlioz and Liszt, it crosses its impetus with the cult of Russian folk-art, set up by Glinka and the "Mighty Handful." This cross-fertilization is responsible for the appearance of the new Russian school with its creative summits, as Moussorgski's *Boris* and Rimski-Korsakov's *Cocq d'or*.

After having gathered a new flavor from the Russian folk-art, the osmotic wave turns back in Western direction. Unable to curb the robust, individual and aggressive new German current, that of Wagner, it presses upon that branch of racial art which, in the music of Saint-Saëns for instance, shows every sign of senility and non-resistance; it presses upon French music. The result of such blood transfusion is a new, boisterous bloom in the form of Debussy's and Ravel's tone-conceptions.

Now, our osmotic Western current, spiced and complicated by Wagner, Debussy and Ravel idioms, reverts again to the German and Russian East to ignite the creation of Scriabin, Schoenberg, Stravinsky, etc.

A similar process, but of universal dimensions, is found in the world music history of the second half of the nineteenth and in the already passed part of the twentieth century. The early waves of a classico-German type vibrate from the continental countries toward England and America. They strangle the dimmed voices of Anglo-Celtic song culture and give birth to the Victorian type of religious and secular composition, a slave-like echo first of the classical Mendelsohnian cliché and later of the Wagnerian.

Later and mightier streams carrying westward not only the yeast of the West-European tonal life, but also assimilated East-European intonations, melodic embryos and tone-colors, fructify the music of Anglo-Saxon countries, particularly that of the United States, in an even more significant way. On one side they originate currents which reflect new tonal influences, mainly French and Russian, as in the works of Bax, Bliss, Goossens, Holst and Vaughan Williams of England, and of Griffes, Carpenter and Howard Hanson, Hammond, Sessions and Taylor, Randall Thompson and Whithorne of America.

On the other side, these streams with their definitely racial igniters strike racial tonal flare-ups; such are observed in the younger American music. All her dormant racial rhythms and intonations, Anglo-Celtic, Negroid and Hebraic, have been awakened and have created a cutting whirl that has sent the oscillations back to Europe in the form of bacchanal popular songs and jazz. It is their turn now to fructify the old European æsthetics.

All these processes bearing distintegration and transmutation of harmony, melody and rhythm, again correspond to the laws of transformation of energy and radio-activity. Sudden disintegration of an atom generates a tempestuous, explosion-like outpour of energy, radio-activity. In the same way disintegration of melody, rhythm and harmony, evoked by the pressure of a foreign culture, produces a tempestuous whirling of musical thought, a tonal revolution.

One notices here a real transformation of energy. The tonal tension of the Russian national music has exploded the very foundation of the French musical syntax through Debussy and Ravel, and the American jazz with its rhythmic stringency has transfigured the traditional German polyphony, through Hindemith and Krenek. Exactly in this way the change of the direction of tension in atomic energy transforms electro-magnetic force into a radio-active one.

89

It is remarkable, however, that after all these concussions, contra-revolts and cataclysms our tonal language still clings to a fundamental gravitational formula of some sort, be it the *series* of Schoenberg, the *tropuses* of Hauer or the *supradiatonic* scaffoldings of Yasser.

It is only too evident that gravitation of this or another sort is imperative to organized tonal thought. In this lies one of the most interesting lessons to be derived from reading the spirals of the universal tonal osmosis.

Each of these osmotic waves sweeps along its own system of intonation or tonal inflexion, and of sound-color. Naturally, tone-color accumulation complicates the universal process of sheer numeric enrichment by the accruing of polytonics.

Harmonic cross-fertilization in itself brings in mighty coloristic forces which lie dormant in racial tonal taste. Call to mind the grandiose harmonic reaction brought about by some contacts. Picture, for instance, the mid-European tonal cultures, the German, for example, with its centuries-old predilection for the harmonic relationship of the fourth and fifth, think of their full cadences, wedded to the Slavonic harmonic taste, inclined to the harmonic relationship of the second and particularly, of the third.

However, I have now described but the superficial, physical play of the tonal universe. Let us abandon this comparatively minor process, that of the accumulation of musical wealth of a numeric and geographical order, and let us turn to the metamorphosis of tonal language as prompted by changes in the very directives of culture.

Then only shall we come close to the greater process of the tonal cosmos and be enabled to find our spiritual and historic position.

OUR HISTORICAL POSITION

The musical language reflects the type of culture which is its progenitor, with the same mathematical precision as does any happening in science or religion.[38] The musical speech of each period is the tonal image of its spirituality. This language is a triune stream of intonations, that is, of spiritual-tonal inflexions. Their character and chemical

[38] In the following exposition I use the term "religion" in a most inclusive sense, embracing the theological, gnosticological and sociological aspect.

combination crystallize the type of the tonal utterance with greater fidelity than does its technical or æsthetic structure.

In the river-bed of that triune stream named musical speech, one discerns the following strata:

first, the racial or national inflexion,—subsoil of the harmony and rhythm typifying a given culture;

second, the historical tonal traits inherent in the corresponding epoch's temporary tonal apparatus, —source of the form and technic of a given period;

third, the individual intonation with its fidel mirror,—melody.

These tone-inflexions, their release and transmutation in the course of the change of historical cycles, give birth to organic types of musical spirituality. History shows that of all these inflexions, the religious intonation and the racial one, as deeply elemental as the former and often its ally, are the most stable. They periodically renew their sway over musical speech. The very power of racial art whose influence also is an ever returning one, is functionally linked with the ever-green subsoil of religious tone-inflexion.

Many years after I had first formulated these

views [39] I have come across Spengler's book of genius *Der Untergang des Abendlands,* in which I read the following lines with deep emotion:

"The incorporeal world of early contrapuntal music was and remained that of the first Gothic and even when, much later, polyphonic music rose to such heights as those of *Matthew Passion,* the *Eroica* and *Parcifal,* it became of inward necessity *cathedral-like.*"

A renewal of the sovereignty of the religious tone-inflections over the musical language, appears in a direct form of religious folk-music or in an individualized form of tonal cult. This religious accent rings in the medieval cult of theocracy, tonaly translated into the hymns of Saint Gregory, as mightily as it does in the cults of social equality and of humanity. It lives in Beethoven's *Ninth Symphony* or in Mahler's *symphony of a thousand.* It lives aggressively in the worship of the proletarian messianic hero incarnated in Alexander Krein's *Lenin* and in the fanatical projection of the ego-worship of Strauss' *Heldenleben* or of Schoenberg's *Piérrot Lunaire.*

An intuitive sense of music's link with the sub-

[39] Articles published by the Moscow magazine *Music.*

93

merged powers of the universe, has compelled some of the great thinkers to allot to music a very singular place among the arts, and they legalize that place theoretically. I have in mind Leibnitz and especially Schopenhauer, who speaks revealingly of music in the third book of the first volume of *Die Welt als Wille und Vorstellung.*

* *

*

Each cycle and type of musical culture has its primordial, chaotic era, an era with tendency and impetus subordinated to racial-religious forces.

Each type of culture has also its ripe, organic epoch distinguished by the blossoming of personal intonation and personal creation. Musical art's final and eternal undersoil is the religious cult, no matter what form or direction music may take. As an outlet of our immanent thirst to draw near to the latent powers of Being who play with us, religious worship bears joy from a communion with the eternal and unknown source of order in the Universe.

Religious musical art is notably coexistent with the chaotic era of musical history. The primordial form of musical thought, the cyclic form in itself, just as the whole tonal-historical curve, is an embodiment of the religious tone-emotion. For the law of cycle, the elemental iron law of musical form, is wrought by our insatiable yearning to revert eternally to cosmic life-sense. We yearn to renew our joy in contemplation of Eternal Order in a repeated acknowledgment, for a single affirmation would not quench this thirst.

The torrent of creed-intonations carves for itself, in the course of history, a double channel. It flows together and together it returns, with the visible forms of epic and popular faith, for example, as in Rimski-Korsakov's *Kitesz*, in Wagner's *Parcifal*, in Malipiero's *Saint Francis of Assisi*, in Ernest Bloch's *Schelomo*, in Szymanovski's *Stabat Mater*. That stream also flows along with the fruit of a centuries-old refining process, individualized religion with all its conflux of personal emotion and æsthetic and sociological dogma. The flow of creed-accent is sensed in the blend of the artistic and the cosmic consciousness as looms in musical creations like *Prometheus* of Scriabin, *La Mer* of Debussy, *Friede an Erde* of Schoenberg or *After Shelley* by Gniéssin.

Thus we see that the inexorable law of the ever-

95

lasting cyclic return of religious tone-inflexions, but of a rejuvenated form, reveals its power in new music, too.

* *

*

The following is the historic scheme of the process that causes the downfall of the collective and imposed religious cult, clears the way to personal tone perception and personal creed, be it religion or a social consciousness, and thus throws open the gate to the organic era of musical culture.

The undiluted folk-religion of antiquity with its simple and unadulterated spiritual music, such as the hymns of Saint Ambrosius and of Pope Gregory the Great, is succeeded by an interminable era of utter union of the collective church cult with the state or nation.[40] The early medieval *Civitas Dei* of Saint Augustine designated an ideal scheme of such a church-state or nation-priesthood which had existed already in Judea and in Babylonia.

Even the musical art born about the close of the

[40] In his *Origin and Evolution of Religion*, Dr. E. Washburn Hopkins shows how the law of hospitality and that of asylum have formed a basis for the ancient temple-palace, which is still in existence among some of the primitive tribes.

Middle Ages, that of Josquin de Prè and Nicholas Gombert, of Orlando di Lasso and Heinrich Shütz, of Prætorius and Palestrina, is a tonal mold of that mixed loyalty, to the church and to the state. Even a Bach cantata and a Handel oratorio re-echoes that state-ecclesiastical intonation.

Disintegration of that bilateral loyalty and its downfall lent impetus to the kindling of the personal creed and to the refining and individualization of religious and civic tone-inflexion. Then later came a full secularization of musical utterance and pure individualism in it.

The new organic era of Western musical culture is thus being formed. Its three periods are the classical, the romantic and the cosmos-inspired.

CLASSICISM AND ROMANTICISM

The first great spiritual revolution in the European West, and the end of the church domination of the state (the Reformation and the Thirty Years' War), freed the individual from a strait-jacket of emotional regulations imposed by official religion and by its musical demand. Classicism

97

that lives on cultivation of physical tone-material, is the result of that freedom.

The style of the late Renaissance, in sculpture or in music, is the utterance of personality liberated from the æsthetic despotism of the church. But this freedom has been so far of an outward, a corporeal order. This new æsthetic sensation might be termed physical individualism.

The pure and true classical music, *i.e.* the music of the eighteenth century is the incarnation of the creative play of a personality unbound and giving itself to the joy of sound, *an ûnd für sich.* This is why that music seems to us apersonal and impassive. Incidentally, such a deceptive impression of the music of the eighteenth century is a sheer error of historic perspective. This impression is solemnly installed as a basis for the neo-classicist teaching of our day; music is manufactured by a pious following of the receipt.

Roger Sessions, one of the foremost American composers, describes the formula masterfully and to its great advantage: "music which derives its power from forms beautiful and significant by virtue of inherent musical weight rather than intensity of utterance; a music whose impersonality and self-sufficiency preclude the exotic; which takes impulse from realities of a passionate logic; which in the authentic freshness and simplicity of its moods, is the reverse of the ironic, and in its very aloofness from the concrete preoccupations of life, strives rather to contribute form, design, a vision of order and harmony." [41]

The second great revolution in the cultural life of Western Europe liberates the individual from state despotism. This germinates new personal and civic emotions, and corresponding tonal æsthetics. A new musical individualism, spiritual this time, is conceived. We arrive at the source of romantic music.

Since then both cultural types, classicism and romanticism, live side by side in Western art. We find such a distinctly romantic masterpiece as Mozart's d-minor quartet in the very midst of classical bloom. Again, a purely classical thought-form like Mendelssohn's scherzo from the Scottish Symphony appears when both Chopin and Wagner are already active forces of a stringently romantic epoch.

The newly born individualism or romanticism

[41] Roger Sessions: "Ernest Bloch," *Modern Music,* 1927.

transfers the creative center of musical art to the purely egocentric or civic emotions of the composer. Roland Manuel, one of the finest intellects in contemporary French music, has crisply defined the relationship of the romantic and the classical stands: "Before a musical fact an artist has the choice of two attitudes: that of the speaker who interprets himself and that of the actor who narrates." [42]

The purely æsthetic, tonal medium of classical music yields its place to the element of volition in romantic music, to the element of struggle of individual life with its spiritual and civic environment. The cultivation of the personal stamina of a creator is the essence of romantic music. Beethoven's Fifth Symphony is one of the most telling specimens of romantic art.

It is instructive to see how exactly this definition of classic and romantic art, arrived at by a patient scanning of the historical highways, coincides with the fastidious *aperçus* of modern æsthetics:

"It seems to me that to distinguish between the classical and the romantic artist one must consider

[42] "Devant le fait musical l'artiste a le choix entre deux attitudes: celle du *rheteur qui se* raconte, ou celle de *l'acteur* qui *raconte.*"

their attitudes toward actual existence, life. The art of the former is a closed world; that of the latter, has broad openings into reality. The classical artist treats reality as crude matter which he molds according to certain specific formal principles strictly pertaining to his art. . . . Thus, detached from the real, and forming an outside sphere, ruled by an artificial order, classical work does not enter life; its action remains exclusively æsthetic. . . . In this rests mainly the striking opposition of the two tendencies, the classical and the romantic one. For the artist of the romantic type pretends to influence reality, and he succeeds." [48]

This remarkable argument of Boris de Schloezer hides, however, an error of logic, a sort of a reversed *petitio principii*, for M. de Schloezer manifestly deducts the essence of a proceeding from its consequence and from its function. Romanticism is the cultivation of personal pathos including the civic emotion. *Therefore*, romantic art claims an influence on reality. This pretention is quite legitimate but it is not at all of an æsthetic nor still of a basic order, even though forwarded by romantic art.

[48] Boris de Schloezer in *Igor Stravinsky.*

101

But classicism, being the cultivation of physical tone-material, carries, of course, neither humanitarian nor civic issues. In this respect M. de Schloezer is perfectly right in his admirable remark that classical art is a closed world, "*un monde clos.*"

THE COSMOS-AWARE ERA

The two currents, the classic and the romantic have one trait in common. Being cultures of a purely tonal emotion, whether of an objective or subjective order, neither has admitted cosmic awareness into the circle of its creative stimuli.

It fell to the cosmos-aware musical art of the second half of the nineteenth and that of the beginning of the twentieth century, to unbind the forces of self-cognizance and cosmic consciousness, and to create a new musical structure: one built on higher individual religious intonation and religio-philosophic emotion. These emotions and intonations of humanity newly incarnated in music, acquire definite shape beginning with Beethoven's Ninth Symphony. Still, there are germs of such inflexion to be found earlier in

Mozart's *Requiem,* in the *Crucifixus* from Bach's *B-minor Mass,* and even in a more distant past, the ancient hymns to Mitra and Delphian Apollo. Wagner's *Parcifal,* Scriabin's *Prometheus* and the nature-poems of Debussy are the latest phenomena of the cosmos-aware tonal era.

In his fine book *"Les idées de Claude Debussy"* Léon Vallas quotes those remarkable words of Debussy concerning the force of cosmic insight hidden in music:

"In spite of their claim to be the sworn translators of nature, painters and sculptors can reveal to us the radiance of the Universe but in a loose and fragmentary way. They grasp and offer only one of its aspects, only one of its moments. Musicians alone are privileged to capture all the aroma of day and night, of earth and sky, to recreate their atmosphere and to transmute into rhythm their immense palpitation."

But when I consider Debussy's orchestral poems as examples of cosmos-inspired art, I see in them more than tone-painting. I trace there a reflection of main cosmic features perceived not alone through an instinctive reach in the artist, but grasped by his full mental hold.

Self-cognizance and cosmic insight brought to a highly conscious state, have ingrained themselves into the very flesh of musical art, formerly a culture narrowed to an artistic and egocentric scope. Both the form and the orchestra of the new epoch shrink from the proceedings and the tone-perception of earlier art.

The cosmos-conscious era instills in music traits correlative with the cognizance of the unity of the Universe and of the continuity of cosmic process. The monothematic structure of Liszt's poems, the endless melody of Wagner, the pantheistic traits of Rimski-Korsakov's and Debussy's tone-pictures, the spiritual unity of Scriabin's later creations, all these are rooted in emotions new to the composer, emotions of cosmic insight. The essential parts of Beethoven's *Ninth Symphony*, Liszt's *Faust*, especially its first movement, Wagner's *Parcifal*, Scriabin's *Poem of Ecstasy*, Debussy's *Nocturnes* and *La Mer*, all are specimens of cosmos-aware art.

Spengler's remarkable classification of space-symbols corresponds to image-ideals of various cultures. His "Magian Soul" parallels my definition of the cosmos-inspired era even in a greater degree than his "Apollinian Soul" approaches the traditional ideas of the classical element.

"Prime symbols—for the *Apollinian* (soul of the classical culture) is the sensuously present individual body as the ideal type of the extended, for the *Faustian* soul—pure and limitless space (Romanesque style of the tenth century, its beginning). . . .

". . . . The single world-volume, being conceived as cavern or as space demands the single god of Magian or Western Christianity. . . ." [44]

The religious intonation in its new metamorphose is incarnate in cosmos-conscious music in just the same way as it is embodied in the "Magian culture." The soul of our present tonal era also strives to embrace, to round everything into an entity, both in poetry and in music. What William James says with such marvelous instinct about Walt Whitman, is but a description of a Magian artist.

"The only sentiments Walt Whitman allowed himself to express were of the expansive order . . . a passionate and mystic entological emotion

---

[44] Oswald Spengler: *The Decline of the West*, Volume I.

suffuses his words." [45] Whitman is the poet of a cosmos-cognizant era just as Scriabin and Debussy are its musicians.

I would say here that the orchestra itself, seemingly a mere technical and individual contrivance of the composer, is actually a mouthpiece of the new type of culture. The disturbances in the new orchestral language—and they strike deeper than technical structure,—reflect with amazing fidelity all the shades of the epoch's mind. The organ-like orchestra of *Parcifal* is a faithful transmission of a new tense in a definite racial-religious mentality. I speak of the individualized and refined inflexion of mystical Germanism. The orchestra of Mahler's *symphony of a thousand* is that of exulting labor throngs, a mouthpiece of hilarious republicanism.

The orchestral ensemble of *Piérrot Lunaire* typifying but an inflexion of mutinous, even anarchical ego-centrism, and Stravinsky's orchestral tongue, in *Rénard* for instance, a servile and accessible parlance of industrial cast, are but other, different phases of our spirituality.

* *
*

[45] William James: *The Variety of Religious Experience.*

The organic types of musical cultures, those æsthetic entities which possess a face of accomplished expression and of poised and absolute content, have value independent of the historic moment. They are, therefore, true monuments of the spiritual existence of humanity. These are dispersed throughout the ages. Having acquired an absolute life, one outside of time, the organic specimen of musical culture escapes comparative valuation. A definition of its place in the so-called "progress" in musical history is senseless.

Of such organic instances of the classical era, as the clavichord d-minor sonata of Scarlatti or Handel's famous aria from *Xerxes,* of such perfect romantic forms as Mozart's D-minor quartet or Chopin's c-sharp-minor prelude, could one say that they have outlived their virility? Indeed not, they are beyond time now, quite as they were at their moment of birth. But *Tannhaüser* of Wagner, or Liszt's *Saint Elizabeth* bore a fatal seal of senility on the day of their creation. Even Stravinsky's *Sacre* already breathes symptoms of deadening. This is cruelly premature as the very era of *Sacre* has not yet ended.

In incompleteness, in the inorganic traits of a

107

creative type, caused by the non-consummation of the art-epoch's consciousness, lie the germs of its historical extinction.

The classical and romantic eras have given us in the course of their golden age complete, organic musical creations. Being rotating cycles of culture, both eras will probably have their recrudescence, in one form or another, but their rôle is definite and accomplished.

The latest return of the cosmos-aware musical age beginning as early as with Mozart's *Requiem*, has not yet offered a perfect, eternal casting for the new tonal mind. Of the events in cosmos-conscious music that followed *Requiem*, even the works of great majesty, all are stamped by the non-completion of their creative type. They all are organisms deprived of a single impulse, of a unified mentality. Beethoven's *Ninth Symphony*, also an instance of the early universe-cognizant thought of the nineteenth century, is an evident spiritual cripple. Its head and legs are of the religio-cosmic tonal cast; the torso belongs in part to the classical (the scherzo) and in part to lamentatious and rickety, prematurely enfeebled romantic type (the andante).

108

The *Ninth Symphony* is succeeded by Liszt's *Faust*-symphony and Wagner's *Faust*-overture, both of which suffer from romantic elocution. Then comes Liszt's *Les Preludes* whose cosmism reaches only in single drops the pure, real vision of universal entity. Generally it does not rise above drawing-room tone-painting and philosophy. Wagner's *Parcifal*, one of the most consistent creations of the cosmos-conscious era, is corroded by the theatre, and its musical pulse is deadened by a Berlioz echo, an outmoded pictorial tendency.

All these works were symptoms of a maturing cosmic awareness in music. A new great musical epoch and a new organic type of tonal mind had been ripening. But the process was cut short.

The premature death of a great artist, the greatest creative force of post-Wagnerian times— I speak of Scriabin—and an historic and cultural cataclysm that has turned modern taste toward industrial directives, are responsible for that break-off.

No matter what measure of might and vitality we assign to Scriabin's music, we cannot deny that *Prometheus,* even if not an organic work, has constituted the beginning of a culmination in a new tonal age. Already the main theme of Scriabin's *Third Symphony*, that admirably tense and forceful statement, not inferior to any Beethoven theme, is a clear cut, dynamic arabesque belonging to a cosmos-inspired art. Scriabin called it "theme of self-assertion" or the "*I am-motive.*" Indeed it is a distinct crystallization of self-cognizance and self-assertion. But the characteristic Scriabin passion for a display of technical gears, and the weight of European academism as well as spiritual immaturity, make the whole symphony but a vague image of a perfect cosmos-aware piece of art.

Coming after the clear, peremptory form and parlance of the *Poem of Ecstasy*, the not quite sure and not quite formed tonal language of *Prometheus*, and its not quite articulate syntax, point to what *Prometheus* tended to be and might have become.

A specimen of art interrupted in its flow to full fruition, *Prometheus* was the symptom of a completion about to come to a great period in music. Erroneously taken by some for neoromantic, that period might well have accelerated hope for a synthesis of East and West in music, for Scriabin's art is of a perfect Eurasian type.

From the beginning of the World War and after the death of Debussy and Scriabin, music flounders in a torment, in the unsolved crisis of the cosmos-aware age. That age did not take full cognizance of its own march, did not complete itself, nor did it incorporate itself into an organic type of some new tonal mentality. The pain of not having given birth to what had been ready to come to light, is the predicament that now tortures the subconscious tonal mind of our day. It remains for us to realize the situation.

Dissatisfaction, upheaval, a flinging of self from one style to another, sickly recidives and flares of neoclassicism, neoromanticism and neoimpressionism, expressionistic struggles and others of Schoenberg, Miascowski, Honegger, Bax, Malipiero, Hindemith, Ernest Bloch and Szymanovski, even the cold and calculated contortions of Stravinsky, are all phases of the crisis.

Such an abrupt clipping of a great culture, ready to shape itself and to grow to full bloom, has antecedents in history as instructive as itself.

111

The Mozarabic style in Spain which united in so delicate a harmony the Gothic and Moorish art emotions, was about to come to its full fruition in a glowing era of architecture and music, when the invasion of Roman craft distorted and clogged its effort.

The same thing occurred in the French Gothic, as can be seen in the very old ornamental designs to be found in the Chartres Cathedral or in the decorative profile of the medieval French chants of Guillaume de Machaut.

The pressure of the Italian art flood diverted the natural flow of medieval French craft into artificial Latin channels and cut short the formation of an original and potent culture.

Returning to a consideration of the cosmic period, one finds that impressionism really is but a non-crystallized and as yet, a self-unseen outgrowth of a cosmos-inspired current.

This is why impressionism has never faded with finality; some germ of it is eternal. This is why we sense in Debussy a close kinship with Scriabin, in spite of the absence of official cosmological profession of faith in Debussy's music. Debussy is perhaps the first in whose creation the petal of

112

cosmic awareness becomes pure music with such a divine ease.

All the elements of pain, struggle and achievement in the music of our day, as well as those in Scriabin and Debussy, point to the looming traits of the future creator.

The coming composer is destined to transmute into pure tonal gold elements of self- and cosmos-cognizance. This task will fall to the artist who will be born to combine a blind elemental force of creation with the highest mental adroitness. To the artist who will be capable of a sharp individual creative attitude and of an immersion in the eternal springs of race and creed, subsource of ever-living religious tone-inflexions.

* *

*

The vibrations of our tonal day flow toward a united goal, which splitting it for clarity, I would term:

a) *euphonia rediviva;*
b) *ecclessia rediviva.*

The coming oneness which is to embrace the resurrection of euphony and the resurrection of cult in tone-art, will suppress the duality in the

113

creative type found in the present. Our art has not been granted full fruition, and its death struggle is prophetically incarnate in bilaterals of creative attitude. Hierophant versus master, priest versus technician and tradesman, temple versus gild-hall, Debussy versus Ravel, Scriabin versus Stravinsky, Schoenberg versus Hindemith.

The cosmos-inspired art eventually drawing to completion will evolve, together with the resurrection of euphony and cult, a creative type of its own. It will cause the inflated art-priesthood, as well as professional and technical cerebralism, to disappear. And indeed, the more vulgar images of our present creative duality, the tonal pyrotechnician and the *Schulmeister*—will perish first.

A many-sided, encyclopedic creator, synthesis of priest and master, drawing his creative impulse from the megacosm and the microcosm, the Universe and the Ego, is the one to restore to music the fullness of content which is its universal nature.

PART II

RACE AND REVOLUTION

RACE AND REVOLUTION

THE ever changing tonal world of today has at least one stable islet. Music rooted in the race is perhaps the only one that has successfully resisted the great historical and social-industrial catacylsm of these decades.

But the aggressive and dogmatic pre-war attitude, the attitude of an aloof political mission, is greatly transformed. Even the cruder zoological nationalism of yore has undergone substantial changes. Whatever the war peers and the industrial barons may think, in the course of these doleful decades we have measured the waste of cultural separatism. We have acknowledged the blessing of racial interchange and cross-fertilization.

The art credo of Georges Migot reflects the new and humanized racial stand most interestingly in *Cahiers de la Douce France:* "I believe in internationalism in art when confined to the comprehension of works of art. As to creation, I believe

117

in an ethno-geographical influence which does not mean nationalism of the frontier."

* *
*

Race is a controlling force in art. But this maxim is open to misconstruction. A persistent prejudice today holds that race is the stronghold of reaction. This view is arbitrary; a simple examination of the progress of modern music will disclose it.

The three races whose individual characteristics have been least affected by their European environment are the Vélikorossy or Great Russians (the people of Glinka and Moussorgski, not of Tchaikovsky and Borodin), the Hungarians and the Jews. And it is just from these three races that the musical revolution of the twentieth century has received its greatest impetus, through the contributions of Scriabin, Schoenberg, Stravinsky, Bartok, Milhaud and Prokofieff. Their race, not their nationality, fanned the insurrectional ardor of these composers. Generated in their blood, it was not nurtured in the well-trimmed and levelled lawns of civilized art, in the cultured thought of

118

their countries. It overstepped and broke through their national palings.

From the very beginning of their careers, Stravinsky, Prokofieff and Bartok, whose racial impulse is vigorous and clearly obvious, show the unmistakable signs of struggle against their heritage, against bequeathed cultural habits. The power of this inner racial impulse determines the outcome of the conflict and, as their gifts reach maturity, we see it triumph over the civilization that nursed their creative self. In the *Sacre,* in Prokofieff's *Scythian Suite,* and in Bartok's *Piano Concerto,* we witness the victory. Here the sources, destructive to inherited cultural practice, revealing new formative powers, can be seen almost in the act of springing from the soil of Vélikoross and Magyar folkdances. *Ceci a tué cela,* to use Hugo's solemn dictum.

Even more significant, if less openly violent, is the conflict between culture and creative impetus in Schoenberg, Scriabin and Milhaud. Educated according to the strictest regulations of civilized art, they broke away more gradually but even more definitely; Scriabin from the comfortable Liszt nursery, Schoenberg from the stagnant and exhausted *tristanesque* and Milhaud from the post-Frankist coteries. With the dawn of creative maturity, their racial voice rises high and clear above the prompting habits and pressure of national culture.

Thus in Scriabin racial vitality suddenly, illogically but peremptorily, spurred him to the creation of those extraordinary whirligigs of music, the ecstatic voodoo dance-codas of his last sonatas and of *Prometheus*. These pages of the true, the essential Scriabin, reveal a deep kinship with the *radeniya* of certain Russian sects, those religious services that develop into orgies of dervish dances. Nothing could be more radically opposed to the whole cultural aspect, to the square, smooth, formal conceptions of Chopin and Liszt, Scriabin's spiritual fathers.

Nor can we fail to recognize in Schoenberg the nature of that fire which, kindling in his period of revolt, led him to destroy the established, complacent European tonal structures topped, with such seeming finality, by Wagner. It is the high-strung restlessness, the unassuaged mental thirst of Schoenberg's race that forever frets at local boundaries, forever strives for a supernational and exalted speech to break down cultural bars opposing its own spiritual domination.

As for Milhaud, with a definitely academic tendency of mind and the special musical inbreeding of his country, nothing but the power of his alien race could have veered his course from the safe fairway of the Schola Cantorum meadows.

The difference between the two groups is clear. The revolution of Stravinsky and Bartok is race-conscious; while involuntarily and with pain and struggle, Scriabin and Schoenberg are driven by the inner force of race against their inheritance.

With the question of race in mind, let us for the moment try to isolate and define those elements of music which carry the germs of reform. For melodic, harmonic and rhythmic means, let us use the term, *vocabulary;* for the laws governing the changes through which they pass, the collective expression, *etymology;* and for the formal relationships of the tonal units, *syntax.* In all the revolutionary derangements of vocabulary, etymology and syntax in music, the force of race is seen to be peculiarly and persistently potent.

The perennial re-invigoration which race gives to the vocabulary and etymology of music, is attested by one of the newest occurrences of our own time. The convulsion generated by jazz in the rhythmic conceptions of today has too often been misrepresented through false historical perspective. These new rhythms are neither an isolated phenomenon nor solely a result of contemporary militant internationalism.

The synthetic rhythm of a Gershwin passage is no more advanced or international than is the $1\frac{1}{4}$ structure in the chorus from Rimski-Korsakov's *Sadko*. Neither of these rhythmic formations is a citizen of the world at large; both are native born. They belong in the same historic continuity and what is more important, spring from the tree of racial art.

Not only the vocabulary and its manning in racial music, but also the syntax is more pertinent to the boldness and flexibility of contemporary revolutionary art than is the canonized pattern of the Occident.

In the Irish folk-song, *The Next Market Day*, for example, the structural formula (a) + (b+ b+a), has a freshness, a grace, a bold fling of emphasis that make into dry platitude our revered classical song formulas. The extraordinary structural daring in the savage songs of the Transcaucasian Houri tribe far outdistances today's masters of heterophonal speech. This ancient music is a natural synthesis of both polytonal and polyrhythmic clusters.

In such tonal creation lie the germs of new and powerful stimuli. They contain the potential force to modify the syntax of all inner relations, to change the chemistry of the elements of music. They would be able to bring about more than a reform of musical dress, more than a chromatization and a dynamizing of our old music.

American art gives us an almost perfect illustration of the fundamentals in the relation of race to revolution. Why is the music of America reactionary? Certainly not because the racial soil is too rich. In fact the racial factor is just what is needed to revolutionize the adopted musical syntax.

Wherever racial elements have appeared on the American scene they have created definitely disturbing currents. Even such hybrid native music as the assimilated American negro jazz rhythms and the Celtic-American melodies have impressed themselves on the music of the world, though they

123

have entered through the back door, the music hall.

Such influence has been, of course, only superficial, because the racial background proved neither stringent nor homogeneous enough to sustain a profound modification, a lasting growth. Perhaps America is still to give its own revolutionary voice to music. The original manifestations in its other arts, the daring spatial logic of the Grand Central Terminal in New York, the torrential sweep of Walt Whitman's verse, are not these an indigenous and authentic racial evocation? Are they not the expression of a driving power emanating, if not concretely from the soil of America, then from the spiritual flux above it?

THE DOWNFALL OF STRAUSS

THE glittering inventions of Stravinsky, the grand master of tonal fireworks, and Schoenberg's aloof and violent soliloquies have swiftly eclipsed the glory that was Richard Strauss.

In their hurried adoration of new idols, people have forgotten that it was really Strauss who was responsible for the return of "dynamism" in music. And, as a matter of fact, it was his use of polytonal effects, or possibly a single master-stroke of this kind, the famous A-flat major plus a-minor passage of the concluding scene in *Salomé*, which so profoundly affected the harmonic vision of the young moderns and germinated the new technic. We seem to forget how the down-pour of disturbing rhythmic movements of the *allegro* in *Tod und Verklaerung*, the impetus of the opening pages and of the coda of *Don Juan*, and the sheer drive of *Till Eulenspiegel*, has all but overwhelmed the patriarchate of Wagner, Debussy and Rimski-Korsakov.

Yet time, the fair judge, as the Italian proverb has it, discards false claims. The downfall of Richard Strauss could not have been stressed in a stronger manner than by the official eloquence which flooded his last jubilee. Nor is the end of his musical reign as Europe's Iron Chancellor merely a by-point to the entry of new masters of sensation. For, if today we have accustomed ourselves to their rhythm, color and accents, if we have grown bored, and now face the twilight of these fresher gods, our yearning is toward anything rather than *Heldenleben*. We may finally accept complete annihilation of tonal logic, or a return to Monteverdi, Mozart, or the old Netherlanders, but we will never again set up altars to the hollow colossus of Strauss.

His crash was inevitable. He held a place too exalted for the measure and quality of his spiritual power. The historical niche of heir to Liszt and Wagner was assigned to him imprudently. We often mistake impetus and violence for genius; we have granted the honors that Strauss claimed. He was, however, not the heir of these two great men of German art, but their victim, and by his pretensions he wrought damage both to himself and to their cause.

What is most characteristic and genuine in the work of Strauss is not the romantic impulse but the spirit of the middle-class mid-European drawing-room. It is that peculiar blend of domesticated elegance and self-respecting vulgarity that finds its perfect expression in *Der Rosenkavalier*.

Till Eulenspiegel, the subtlest of his works, aroused a hope that he was destined to incarnate in music the gaiety and charm of the German Renaissance and its *Büergerschaft*. Here he seemed to discover a happy fusion of gentle whim and new classic clarity of design, the promise of a novel tonal imagery.

Paraphrasing Ernest Newman's admirable description of the composer "who was once a genius," I prefer to think of Strauss as a man of genius when he wrote *Till Eulenspiegel*. Alas, his glowing thought was quickly exhausted; the romantic pasticcio too soon re-enveloped him.

Victim of "historical succession," he was destined to vulgarize the spirit of Liszt and Wagner. In comparison with Liszt's main theme in the *Faust*-symphony even the better musical ideas of

127

Strauss, such as the opening of *Zarathustra*, seem the creation of a military band master playing philosopher.

Ruthlessly he laid hands on the loftiest visions of mankind, and he accommodated them to his own enterprise. Into the pure spiritual air of the Greek tragedies, the Scriptures, Nietzsche, he infused that compound of oily and violent expressiveness which haunts us when we now invoke the images of Elektra, Jokhanaan or Zarathustra.

Salomé, bad enough *chez* Oscar Wilde, in the hands of Strauss becomes an encyclopedia of fulsome and noisy platitudes. Music offers us few other works in which tastelessness, lack of imagination, and unspeakable "orientalism" unite so blatantly as in the *Dance of the Seven Veils*. *Salomé* has become the horn of abundance for exoticisms such as those of Krenek's *Leben des Orest* which H. H. Stuckenschmidt, the well known German writer, calls very excellently "an abortive attempt to sell us a Hellas with jazz accompaniment."

It is impossible to refrain from setting this auctioneering of sacred objects against the aristocratic disgust of Schoenberg: "Even radical propa-

gandists in the world of music do not now try to
howl their thought; true artists never do. Even
the listener begins to understand; things need not
be shouted into his ears."

Strauss was among the first to inject into contemporary musical thought the elements of com-
mercialized sex appeal and deliberate sensation,
which, quickly adopted by the younger men, seem
almost typical of our time. It is amusing to observe some of the youngest and noisiest of our day's
composers repudiating Strauss. To be sure, there
is an intimacy in our young music which is at the
opposite pole from Strauss' grandiloquence. But
he was the first to give musical shelter to that mixture, snobbery and a worship of the mob, *le dernier
cri* and a catering to the man-in-the-street, which
is so joyously assimilated by the cleverest of our
young authors.

Strauss has stamped out the continuity of life
in romantic music and made it, for the time being,
the laughing stock of every petty officer of modernity. Schoenberg and Szymanovski, Arnold
Bax and Malipiero, the aristocratic representatives
of neo-romanticism, all strive to restore the line.

To clarify the debilities of Strauss' claims I will

ompare him with a younger herald of the new German art who, in my opinion, voices his race more directly. I speak of Paul Hindemith.

He possesses racial robustness, specific and high technical intellect similar to all the grand and to the merely outstanding German creators, Kant or Weber, Lenbach or Helmholz or Reger, whereas Strauss' utterance is of a markedly reflected nature. It is weakened by the distilling apparatus of culture. In Hindemith's more spontaneous works, such as *Die Junge Magd,* the choral songs to medieval texts, in the delectable *Landsknecht's Trinklied,* for example, his race speaks with victorious directness.

* *

*

The street, the dance-hall and Luna Park, authors of today's "folk-lore," have flooded us with a new stream of vulgarity. But Strauss' influence carried a graver menace: the domination of the middle-class musical mind and a stifling of the voice of a great race with echoes of hollow burgher-romanticism.

MAHLER AND BUSONI

BUSONI'S remarkable, in many respects, extraordinary opera *Doctor Faustus* yielded surprise. It revealed to us that Busoni's creative power was much more potent than we had thought, and that it was at best when applied to the theatre.

The legend of Busoni's cerebral instrumentalism proved to be unwarranted. There is in *Faustus* a mellowness and a warmth which is granted only to creators with a feeling for the human voice. Also, it is curious to find in *Faustus* so scant an influence of Wagner; what one discovers rather, are tints of Berlioz and of Meyerbeer. Peremptory, stark must have been Busoni's personality to have withstood the triumphant Wagnerian pressure of his day, for the range of Busoni's assimilative artistry was colossal.

Busoni was in truth a gigantic sponge forever absorbing. His eclecticism as well as his miraculous musical flexibility and his responsiveness to new tonal concepts, is reminiscent of Mahler's.

However, the genius of each as performer and assimilator, distorted and crushed his creative gift. In spite of strong racial difference and an even wider divergence in taste and vision, there is a great similarity in their musical natures. As a composer they both were constructors rather than creators. They had the power to assimilate the melodic and harmonic wealth of the past, and yet they joined eagerly in frantic pursuit of new tonal acquisition. Both had the ability to melt down and mold all the gathered musical ore; both were able to construct now light and graceful, then vast and powerful frames. But neither could animate those scaffoldings with a voice distinctly its own. Some of the sphinxlike structures seem inherently inarticulate, in spite of a driving loquaciousness and multicolored Babel tongue.

Strange as it may seem, Mahler, so discriminative in performance, reeks with a peculiar kind of platitude as a creator. He is not free from even a nude and plebeian sentimentality *à la* Tchaikovsky. The ardent exponent of Mahler's works, Dr. Paul Stefan, still places them as transitional, as tonal thought full of retreats and eclipses.

Their parodies and burlesque anticipations are

132

strangely reminiscent of Berlioz. But true and valuable as Mahler's rôle was in being a forerunner of the new tonal concepts, his false position as prophet and demiurge trumpeting through immense formal structures but aggravated their queer hollowness. In his best creation there is a touching love for the field, folk-song, the child. An engaging, a delicate glimmer of humanness is felt in the best pages of *Totenkinderlieder* or in *Das Lied von der Erde*. These precious emotions, unique and gentle in their power, were stifled in Mahler's grand constructions. Dr. Stefan is quite right when he speaks of Mahler's "magic and fascinating force." But it is that of a builder, of a master stone-mason, not of a creator.

When one considers how similar is Busoni's nature to that of Mahler's, both men of genius, with assimilative and compiling capacities in triumph over creative force, one marvels the more at the great musical vision of Busoni, at the extraordinary discriminative grasp which is sensed in *Faustus*. In this work his inbred eclecticism is much less manifest than in any other—the *Piano Concerto* or *Clarinet Concertino*, for example. He has contrived to give his opera a unity, a style and a flexibility of musical action that might serve as a challenge to any creator. His fastidious speech and pure, exalted musicianship usher Busoni into the sublime circle of Liszt, Scriabin, Debussy and Schoenberg. Busoni is one of the few embodiments of that elevated artistry surviving into our own busy time.

As an operatic conception *Doctor Faustus* is a relief from the stodgy and artificial continuity of the Wagnerian drama. The return to the fantastic and picturesque, to whim and episode, to the elegant adventure in art sought by Berlioz and Delacroix, is more relevant to our time and to the new opera than the tedious consequentialism of Wagner.

Another feeling that remains after hearing *Faustus*, is one of profound admiration for a race that still gives us masters who are, much more than Titus was, the "consolation of humanity." In their aloof and noble artistry, in their disregard for fads worshipped by the modern jungle, Busoni and Toscanini, Malipiero and Pizzetti are true masters of new Italian Renaissance. They are heirs to Monteverdi and Mantegna, Sebastiano del Piombe and Vivaldi. And it is thrilling to watch these flames of Ausonian spirit and to find that their divergent art tendencies are allied to a typically racial, sublime dramatic sensibility. Each answers to Guido Gatti's description of Pizzetti: *"Noi lo vediamo a poco a poco tendere tutte le sue facoltà al raggiungimento dell'ideale drammatico."* [1] This dramatic elevation permeates pages of Busoni's *Faustus*, of Malipiero's *Torneo Notturno* and of the fine *Trenodia per Ippolito morto* from Pizzetti's *Phoedra*. Their tragic and serene majesty are of Hellenic parentage.

Particularly does Busoni's element of sheer tonal play, especially his *junge Klassizität*, propel a true Hellenic breeze. The distinguished German writer, Paul Bekker, elucidates this trait of Busoni with rare sagacity when he says:

"Diese junge Klassizität lehnt sich ebenfals an die polyphone Kunst an, als ihre besondere Aufgabe bezeichnet Busoni den definitiven Abschied vom Thematischen und das Wiedergreifen der Melodie." [2]

---

[1] "We see him straining little by little all his powers for a recapture of the dramatic ideal." Guido M. Gatti: *Musicisti moderni d'Italia e di fuori.*

[2] "At any rate this new classicism leans on polyphonic art, as it particularly marks Busoni for a definite parting from the thematic idiom and for a recapture of melody."

Dr. Paul Bekker, *Organische und Mechanische Musick*, Deutsche Verlag, Berlin, 1928.

Fateful and irrepressible, the recapture of melody seems becoming to this racial artistry, especially when one realizes that the riverbed of melody is underlaid with dramatic conflict.

AN AUSTRO-GERMAN TRIAD

Schoenberg, Bartok, Berg

IN spite of a wide difference in creative stature, in human stringency and native direction, Schoenberg and Bartok have affinities, notably in their clearly defined racial strain and art ethics.

The latter, a minor point of their affinity, discloses the necessity and vitality of their revolutionary pace. In their candor they truly tower over the new academician, the doctor of modernity, insolent and well-fed on musical insurrection.

But the most engaging quality in Schoenberg's and Bartok's utterance is the triumphant stream of their racial *psyche*. The nervous, laconic angularity of their language, the language of a new age, and even their respective *grotesque*, is tainted by race-streaks of almost biological intensity.[1]

[1] Speaking of Bela Bartok's creation, Alexander Jemnitz points very justly to the source of instinctive and laconic firmness of Bartok's speech: "Blut wird zu Gedanken und Gedanken werden zu Blut. Die tief organischen Zusammenhänge zwischen Leib und Geist werden vom Volk zwar unbewuszt, aber mit instinktvoller Sicherheit erfühlt. Deshalb ist es wortkarg." (*Anbruch*, May, 1931.)

One recognizes without fail the neurotic, bitter overstress of a Semite in Schoenberg, and the bizarre touch of infantilism, of barbaric playfulness in Bartok. From Israel, The People of the Book, streams the virility of Schoenberg just as does his aristocratic, inextinguishable worship of cultural heritage, to reject which he has called on all his emotional poignancy and his technical power. Behind Schoenberg's tortuous, wry design of darkly-bitter color that conveys so peculiarly the stinging mixture of wisdom and suffering, one can perceive the heir to an old, a unique race. At the same time one recognizes a master who has explored the past domains of art before he rejected them.

Bartok's creative self embodies his own racial peasant-laden *psyche* and an art newly rebarbarized by the reappearance on our tonal arena of an old Mongol race.

The very peculiar spontaneity of Bartok's deep gray melos, the biting freedom of his rhythms (second string quartet, *scherzo-finale* of his second violin sonata), the sylvan freshness of his form, herald the cultural resurrection of a race whose remote ancestors fought and then amalgamated with Attila's Huns in ancient Pannonia.

But certainly, the grotesque of Bartok is but imaginary, as is every art-peculiarity of a distant and polar race, whether Japanese, Kaffir or Indian. Bartok's is a vernal and fertile, a racial singularity opposed to our flat, sterile and city-born, modern tonal *bizarrerie*. Into this degenerate mire of cinematographic impressionism, even Schoenberg's speech lapses now and then.

I have pointed expressly to the second quartet and second violin sonata of Bartok as exhaling that vernal racial freshness; I could well add his delicious orchestral *Dance Suite*. The pressure of Stravinsky's dynamism and "objectivity," and the horizontal twelve-tone web and calculus of the Schoenberg school have made, in Bartok's later works, ruinous inroads in his monolithic mentality. In spite of these "European," "modern and impersonal" digressions of Bartok's art, it has resurrected for our tonal dwelling and within it, the linear or graphic delicacy of the old Mongol art. Overwhelmed and overfed in the last half century by the oily orientalism of the Near East, Russia and Spain, we have come to think of the Orient as a color gusher. We have lost sight of the subtle

graphic orientalism and the coloristic restraint of
the old Mongol and Persian art. We have forgotten to what source we should trace the old linear
phenomena of European art, to whom we are in-
debted for the fresco craft and for the decorative
pattern of fifteenth century Tuscany into which
old Persian miniatures found their way.[2]

We fail to remember the font of the later *chinoi-
series* of Rococo art, the potteries of Saxony and
Rouen, etc.

Bartok is thought to be among the first to con-
front our new tonal perception with a graphic or
linear orientalism of exceptional freshness. But
I would say here that Michel Glinka, the father of
the new Russian music, absurdly considered by
many an amateur,[3] but in fact an admirable master,
a creative force on a par with Mozart and Schubert, had displayed, almost a century before Bartok, a keen sense of linear orientalism in music.
The Arab Dance, Finn's ballad and other gems
from Glinka's *Ruslan and Ludmila* are marvels of

[2] *Influence orientales dans la peinture toscane* by J. Soulier reveals extraordinary facts.

[3] It is comforting to see that an excellent connoisseur of Russian
music and a fine writer such as M. D. Calvocoressi, takes the true
measure of Glinka's genius in his book "Glinka," (*Laurens*, Paris).

graphic Eastern art. Glinka's restraint was extinguished later by the coloristic orgy of the "Mighty Handful."

Bartok has shown his keen perception of linear orientalism not only directly through his creation, but also through the ethnological work in which he collaborated with Kodaly. Their extraordinary collection of Hungarian folk-songs and folk-dances, a veritable gift to the century, has purged Hungarian music of the muddy admixture of Gipsy and Rumanian melos, whose introduction into Hungarian art is a blot on Liszt's sagacity.

In liberating Hungarian music from tawdry Near East color, and in accentuating the Mongoloid foundation with its graphic clarity and precision, Bartok, however, has not in the least grown to be a *cultivator* of folk-songs in composition.

Leigh Henry says lucidly of Bela Bartok, that though he employs certain scale and form elements proper to Hungarian music, "such a procedure no more renders his music archæological or conventionally *national*, than does the employment of the ballad form by Rossetti, of the sestina by Swinburne, of certain verbal reiterations by Maeter-

141

linck, or certain images by Van Lerbergue and Claudel, render the work of these writers mere imitations of the troubadours and the Renaissance."

*   *

*

To Bartok's monolithic self I have opposed the complex and tortured racial psyche of Schoenberg, his cruel, neurotic overstressing of a rebellious art-creed, so typical of the new Hebrew generation and yet so startlingly allied in him to the typical Hebrew deference for inherited wisdom.

The well-known American writer, Pitts Sanborn, has stated subtly that the instrumental web of *Piérrot Lunaire,* Schoenberg's pivotal work, reminds him of El Greco. Indeed, one feels in *Piérrot Lunaire* the same mixture of wisdom and cruelty, of suffering and beatitude that is written on the old, blue-ashen hands of El Greco's portrait of Luigi Cornaro, in the London National Gallery. Still, by no means would I assert that the power of *Piérrot Lunaire* is only a neurotic force.

One is disturbed, indeed, by the outbursts of an hysterical creator, but one is also conquered by the descriptive grip of Schoenberg's *toucher,* by his polyphonic vision, by a mastery that might be

142

expected to follow *Die Verklärte Nacht* and
Pélléas. The poem in *Piérrot* entitled *Die Nacht*,
is music of genius. Its stupendous effect is almost
incomprehensible in the face of the modesty of
means employed. Using four shades only, the
lower register of the piano, the whispering singing-
speaking voice, the bass clarinet and the mourn-
ful, lamenting cello, he has created a poignant
night desperately black, cruel, and a sinister, a lone
corner where human suffering is condensed to tor-
ture and suffocation.

Semi-colors and semi-shades are so tenderly
blended with purely spiritual elements that at the
end of *Columbine* one can not define what actually
in one's own being is listening to the music, the
ear or the soul. . . . Great and ingenious is his
art in selecting instruments and his blending of
registers! One is sometimes unable to grasp which
of the instruments is entering the ensemble, the
viola, the low register of the flute or the voice of
the clarinet's *chalumeau.*

One must, however, recall the art of Gustav
Mahler as the source of this new descriptive and orchestral mastery. Could we forget the magic
finale of *Lied von der Erde* where the low tones

of the contralto, the flute and a contrabass' pedal form one of the most divine tone-garlands ever heard?

Schoenberg's use of the voice, of the gamut of its inflexions is just as extraordinary. In the poem *Parodies* the singing is as poignant as the tears of some tortured Bacchante.

*   *
*

The stir of Alban Berg's opera *Wozzeck*, so manifestly a sequel to *Piérrot Lunaire*, forces upon us the juxtaposition of Schoenberg and Berg, two remarkable personalities basically different, yet living in a close æsthetic kinship and communion.

Berg, just as uncompromising in his art-tendencies as Schoenberg, is at the same time more human, or, shall I say, less superhuman than the latter. Less sharp and angular than Schoenberg's, Alban Berg's speech is much more to the German taste than Schoenberg's neurotic virulence of accent and strongly Semitic exaltation.

There is a marvel of humanness and poignancy in all the lyrical parts of *Wozzeck*, but this is strongest in Marie's arioso found in the third scene: *"Maedel, was fangst du jetzt an? Hast klein Kind*

144

und kein Mann." Vapor-like and gray, chaotic emotionally, deliberately strained, melodically diffuse, but whimsical and attractive, Berg's tonal thought is yet ironclad in its formal logic and construction. Here is one of the actual victories of the Schoenberg school of æsthetics.

Not only the steel-clad form, but the irresistible and true *Sprechstimme,* the tone-building, in fact each strong feature of *Wozzeck,* comes from Schoenberg. But each cell of the opera—it has a cell-like structure—is laid in with supreme intelligence and talent.

Some compare *Wozzeck* with Debussy's *Pélléas.* An affinity in their deep impressionistic breath does exist. But *Wozzeck's* neo-impressionism is that of art degenerate and rebarbarized; there is something of the poster and of the motion picture about it. The whole is kept a unity by the sheer fundamental force of the work which Olin Downes, that very active American writer on music, defines so well as "its dramatic integrity and relentless frankness of expression." Perhaps, also, by its acute, visual theatrical clarity and self-sufficiency.

However, we find in Berg neither the expressive might, nor the elevation, nor that grim aristocracy of speech that are Schoenberg's. There is more whim than invention, and more invention than creation in Berg's music. And it breathes a subtle and charming domesticity, that forms the substratum of all typical Austrian music, from Haydn to Berg. That domesticity, however, we find neither in Beethoven, nor in Schoenberg.

AMERICANS OF SINGLE AND DUAL
ALLEGIANCE

THE following is what Americans themselves say of American music of today:

"Since 1914 musicians of every country on earth have flowed in upon us in an unending stream. . . . Under the vast mass and variety of influences that now swept in upon us our modest powers of assimilation were hopelessly deluged and gutted. We became vast stomachs to swallow at one gulp the music of the universe, while our legs, just timidly sprouting, gave up the unequal struggle and withered away. In short, American music from 1914 to 1928 is the Music of Indigestion." [1]

"One is impressed by the great quantity of music written by Americans, particularly in recent years.

[1] Daniel Gregory Mason: *The Dilemma of American Music.* Macmillan.

In opposition to this is the very excellent information gathered in "American Composers" by Claire R. Reis and published by the American Section of the International Society for Contemporary Music. The freshness of the younger Americans' conceptions and the diapason of their striving is quite reassuring.

One is impressed also by the obvious advances that have been made in the acquisition of technical facility. But one is depressed by the paucity of any real contribution of that larger world of music which is not greatly concerned with nationality. . . .

"The hope of American music was the great outdoors. . . . Our trend to the cities seems to have all but stifled the outdoor urge. It is the night club, not the great vault of the open sky, that enlivens so many conceptions of what our music should be. It is the city composer who babbles most of capturing the spirit of the machine age. . . . What is true of America is, in varying degree, true of the European countries. But there is this all-important difference. Their music had opportunity to blossom before the blight of the machine conception came." [2]

"Compositions of a marked individuality have recently begun appearing in America at the hands of Americans; and individuality, we know, is the sign and condition of the strong natural impulse. . . . Like so much American life, American music

[2] Oscar Thompson: Review of the valuable book *Our American Music* by John Tasker Howard. Crowell.

148

is still in bonds. But a certain warm integrity of style and independence in the release of form is current." [3]

* *
*

Of these statements that of Oscar Thompson seems to be the most just and lucid; still they all somehow miss the root of American music's dilemma. They all depart, willfully or unwittingly, from the elusive image of an American race or an American culture or, at least, from a unified American creative psychology. The finely worded lamentations of Dr. Mason greatly and unjustly underestimate the resistance and creative strength of the younger American forces. Laments could be shed quite as well for former periods. Prior to the "indigestion of 1914-1928" American music suffered from other and un-American diseases, namely, from a lymphatic Victorianism and from a decolored, regenerated Wagnerism that has not yet abandoned us. In as much as America is not a land of racial uniformity,[4] in as much as neither one single race, nor even one mixed but definite

[3] Paul Rosenfeld: *An Hour with American Music.* Lippincott.
[4] I do not lose sight of the controversies over race; I preserve the right to use the popular definition of race as a working hypothesis.

racial compound can claim supremacy, the definition of American music must arise in the national
moment rather than the racial one.

We need not be tortured by an imaginary
dilemma. American music exists as that of allegiance. I mean by this: as music born of, or at
least, born *with* the creator's unshakable feeling
that America is his native soil, physically or
spiritually, ancestrally or individually, collectively
or personally.

However, the racial ingredients of the American
nation, whatever their positive force may be, have
indubitable power to split, to cleave this allegiance
and to vary its meaning in very subtle ways. The
spiritual allegiance, held by those creators who
come of a stock firmly rooted in American soil,
may be no more ardent, than the fealty of those
of a mixed or exotic extraction, racially remote
from the older American stock. But the former
is certainly more monolithic, more productive of
a music closer to the historical conception of Americanism.

For the sake of reasoning and for clarity of
perspective, let us eliminate the vast group of
American composers of a decidedly eclectic and

cosmopolitan hue, however important they may be. We will then be confronted with two limited but typical groups. I shall define one group as Americans of single loyalty and the other as those of dual allegiance. In speaking of allegiance I now mean racial, not national fealty.

To the first division belongs an Anglo-Celtic group of American composers, particularly the New Englanders.[5] As their race has formed the kernel of the American nation since its birth, there is no incongruity in their racial and national psychology. Such allegiance as theirs is eminently single.

There is both health and profile in each of the composers of this group, whether they are salient, virile or merely attractive. In the positive yet flexible artistry of John Alden Carpenter, in the strangely crude intuition of Charles Ives or in the stark and stubborn single-mindedness of Roger Sessions and Carl Ruggles, in the delicate and alert sensibility of Charles Griffes and Richard Ham-

---

[5] With pleasure I saw that such a subtle observer as André Coeuroy adopted unreservedly in his book *Panorama de la musique contemporaine* (Paris, 1928), my division of the Americans into groups —Cosmopolitan, Anglo-Celtic and Neo-Hebraic, exactly as I have used it in my articles and lectures abroad for the last ten years.

mond, in the lively pictorial gift of Douglas Moore, Deems Taylor and of Emerson Whithorne, in the racial exuberance of Roy Harris and Randall Thompson, or in the hard Western color of Arthur Shepherd, in and behind each of these creative silhouettes looms the stem of an Anglo-Celtic race.

A neo-Hebraic group of younger American composers I call Americans of a dual allegiance. They are loosely related to the traditional, national and historic psychology. But in some respects they are a sharp example of my main, elucidated statement that American music is that of allegiance, not of race. Because of the variations in its racial compound, welded with a broad diapason of transatlantic psychology, æsthetics and emotion, the group of Hebrew-American composers is truly a test-case. Therefore, a more detailed survey will be desirable.

* *

*

Of all the representatives of the Hebrew-American group, Aaron Copland possesses the strongest Jewish traits, mental and creative, and Frederick Jacobi bears the least pronounced Hebrew profile, in spite of his devoted interest in Hebrew culture

and fine contributions to Hebrew music.[6] Jacobi
has a warmer attachment to his race than the
others; however, this does not yet intensify the
racial color of his music to a marked degree. On
the other hand, Jacobi's originating from an older
American stock than other Hebrew-Americans
and his profound emotional Americanism do not
prevent a distinctly cosmopolitan strain in his creative mentality.

In his little book on American music [7] written
in a state of ecstasy peculiarly his own, Paul Rosenfeld has greeted with an exalted solo on the drum
each failure of American music and each fraud of
Ersatz-American music. But he speaks thus about
Copland, one of the best grounded and most deter-
mined of the younger Americans:

"His gift is decidedly proficient but small, as
yet so immature that it makes the impression not
so much of something human, as of something
colt-like: all legs, head, and frisking hide; canter-
ing past on long uncertain stilts, the body oddly
small in proportion to the motorpower, the head

---

[6] The choral *Sabbath Evening Service*, for example, published by
the Bloch Publishing Company, New York, one of Jacobi's most
inspired works.

[7] *An Hour with American Music.*

huge and as wooden and devilish as that of a rocking horse."

In this overburdened description the statement regarding immaturity is quite unfair. It would be more correct to reproach Copland's music with being precocious and over-ripe, designing and *altklug*. In these traits, the well-known mental ghetto-type is recognizable. One could accuse Copland of being too clever, too deliberate and too cerebral an observer and exploiter of modern European ways. His neurotic drive and stringent intellectualism are typically Jewish, but of the worse sort. It is curious that he was inspired by the play *Dibbuk* of the Jewish ghetto-genre to write a trio on Hebrew themes. He is a *Dibbuk* himself, a possessed and spiritually emaciated receptacle of an odd soul. However, one senses in Copland's music a second, so to speak, Hebrew soul such as flows in the gentle, nobly warm and wistful melos of the slow movements in his *Music for the Theater*.[8] This second Hebrew nature is one of the

[8] Marc Blitzstein, one of our most active younger composers, a musician of acute intelligence and brilliance, also points to this quality in an indirect way when he says: "In Copland's work the propulsion of the ego outweighs the natural gift, although the gift comes out strongly in the more quiet music."

sources of the peculiar outline and attractiveness of part of Copland's creative kernel. I say, "one of the sources," for in Copland's intellect one unveils also an incisive strain of American mentality. In its definiteness it can counter any composer of the above listed Anglo-Celtic group. When Mr. Rosenfeld says: "Copland's work is symbolic of the new world on every green page of it . . . it places us immensely alertly in the stream of metallic, modern American things" . . . one cannot deny that Copland's *Jazz Concerto*, perhaps, warrants these words.

* *

*

The other outstanding Hebrew-American composers, Ernest Bloch, Louis Gruenberg and Leo Ornstein, are also stamped by that strength drawn from a dual spiritual allegiance. They come of a race that had much to say and belong to a nation that had much to do. In their case, too, we see that to be part of the young land of America spiritually may on occasion prove of greater advantage than to be its child by direct inheritance. For the "old American" the insularity of his culture sometimes sheds æsthetic limitation, even technical provincialism. But this same restriction purges the "new American" of his inherited Continental long-windedness and a tradition, that is often more of a slavery to dead music than a creative conviction.

Of these composers Leo Ornstein seems to have lost the most through his adoption. His music says with eloquence that he has been rudely torn from his true spiritual fatherland, Russia. A fatal nostalgia, present even in his later works, reveals itself in a strange succession of influences. In the allegro of the *Fourth Sonata* Rachmaninoff is felt, in its scherzando, Borodin, and in its andante, the later Scriabin.

His music has given us the fine main theme of the piano concerto, the subtle pages of the violin sonata, and yet the emptiness of the scherzando in the fourth piano sonata as well as the trite orientalism in one for the cello. Yet in spite of a labored radicalism, a forced tempestuousness, this last-named work reveals a kinship with Scriabin and Szymanovski who, whatever else is said of them, are the later-day aristocrats.

Ornstein's strong creative nature has been corroded by a native American disease, auto-didacticism, and by a typical virtuoso failing, facility and omnivorous absorption—which is also, to an unfortunate extent, a characteristic of Gruenberg. The self-taught man is apparent beneath an over-abundance of episodic material in Ornstein's larger forms such as the cello sonata, in the provincial radicalism of his harmonic methods, as in the *Poems of 1917*, and in the inadequate orchestration of his piano concerto. Facility and eclecticism, together with a typical Jewish loquaciousness, keen and pleasing, however, give his musical ideas a curious, all-embracing range.

In a sense, Louis Gruenberg is the most American of the group; I am tempted to say, he is a New Yorker by vocation. He is as definitely American in spirit and expression as any composer today, yet he exhibits in his creative personality certain strong Jewish traits. In him the typical racial loquacity has a Heine-like strain. It is spirited and untamed. His music is a sort of multi-colored, whimsical *rondo a capriccio*. In fact, this label is more suited to Gruenberg's whirlpools than to Beethoven's Biedermeyer, *The Lost Penny*.

There is little that is European in Gruenberg's music, except a definiteness of musical culture and a high level of technical achievement, by far the highest in the American field. No one can forget the brilliant orchestral writing of Gruenberg's *Jazz Suite,* its dazzling verve and color. In some of his work, in his second violin sonata and the *Jazzberries,* for instance, vitality is lowered by a certain Continental and sophisticated morbidity: one might call it Busoni-ism.[9] But the magnificent aggression and range of American life, at least of American mental and industrial life, an ecstasy that belongs to builders of the future, fairly sweeps through his *Creation.* In it as in his other compositions, are to be found confusing byways, pictorial, humoristic and minor designs, evidence of an over-abundant *remplissage.* His tonal dress is at times too sumptuous, too magnificent.

One other American trait of Gruenberg's is that gay and attractive showmanship. With this is amalgamated a profound feeling for culture, more warm and pulsating than Bloch's ascetic, passionate intellectualism.

---

[9] A. Walter Kramer, one of the leading American musicians and writers, is even more definitely negative, when he says about Gruenberg's jazz works: "They are artificial; they lack pulse. One feels certain that they are essays propounding a jazz theory, rather than emotionally felt utterances."

Bloch is, of course, less American than either of the others. The revered W. J. Henderson said delightfully and justly: "Even Ernest Bloch's *America* sat down by the waters of Babylon." Bloch is a creator of a single scheme, a single color. The tenacity of color in Bloch's tonal raiment has often been mistaken for formal unity. But, as a matter of fact, it is the tenseness of his human kernel and of his mental impetus coupled with a rare mastery of form that account for the monolithic construction of his larger works.

Many foolish things have been written about Bloch and his prophetic vision. Leigh Henry, the British writer-composer, has very brilliantly said, "Bloch is of the line of Job, not of Jacob." There is indeed more of Judaism than Hebraism in Bloch; the spirit of the ghetto frustrates that of the Promised Land. He studiously wails over his own and the world's misfortunes, he exhibits his wounds, even in such priestly music as *Schelomo*.

But a different Bloch appears when the profounder Israel possesses his spirit, the spirit of a conquering race which has bequeathed Law to the world. Then we are given the fine major coda of *Schelomo* and the glorious opening of *Israel*.

Less original and vital than his gift for construction, which is the greatest in his equipment, is his thematic invention. This is obvious even in the piano quintet,—like *Israel* and the violin sonata, his best work. It is startling to discover in the main theme of the quintet, with its trite succession of fourths, a dangerous kinship with the leit-motive from D'Albert's *Tiefland* (the clarinet yodel), not to mention the obvious quasi-Hebraic localism of *Schelomo's* first subject and the Franckism of his *Sea Pictures*.

In *America* the thematic platitude and general facility, to say nothing of the final chorale, cross the threshold of vulgarity, painful to find in a composer of Bloch's stature.

However, Bloch has more than one claim on grandeur. A true son of his own age, a master of the present-day technique, he burns no sacrifice to "today." He does not care for path-breaking of the well-known sort; for this he is neither destined, nor artificially trained. His æsthetic and human aloofness isolate him from the man-in-the-street and from the new *mondain*, the law-givers of our ephemeral time.

160

I have said that the Hebrew-American group provides a test-case combining as it does, the complexity of racial shades with subtle variations of typical transatlantic psychology. The lesson we may draw, is illuminating. It would seem that race of extraordinary definiteness of *psyche*, race mentally polar to a nation aggressively Western, would preclude even a shade of sterling Americanism in a composer of recent adoption. In even a son or a grandson of an outlander.

However, in spite of its definite and compelling Hebraism, the whole group of a double allegiance breathes all the moods and runs of creative Americanism. It turns on an American mental axis.

Many are the arrows pointing to an unmistakable American gravitation. The hilarity and tension of the "shrieking wilderness of steel" is sensed in some of Copland's music. The passionate self-adaptation of Frederick Jacobi to the Red Melos of America and of Louis Gruenberg to its Black Melos, are also significant.[10] The personality of this

[10] Describing the valuable activities of Dr. Howard Hanson in Rochester, the well-known composer, Bernard Rogers, speaks of the best Negro compositions performed under Dr. Hanson, as contaminated by some outside influences. (*Modern Music*, volume VIII, p. 4). It is interesting to learn that phenomena of co-national order include also the travel of influence from the white to the black lines.

devotion is a happening of co-national order, rather than a purely æsthetic adherence. Even Ernest Bloch's religious love for and tonal reconstruction of those great spiritual quantums of American history, Lincoln and Walt Whitman, is another symptom of a mentality gravitating to American life-symbols.

All this is music born of, or at least, born *with* an unshakable feeling that America is native soil. This music is American not because of its racial or national loyalty, but because of its emotional and cultural allegiance, the only effective unifier of American music, so far.

* *
*

In his *Future of America,* H. G. Wells quotes with relish what Henry James says with superb arrogance to the Americans:

"It's all very well for you to look as if, since you've had no past, you're going in, as the next best thing, for a magnificent future. *What are you going to make your future of,* for all your airs, we want to know?"

Indeed, the premiss is superficial and wrong: those who have airs, have a past. But the question and its stress are tangent to everything American, music as well.

Had American music been that of one uncleft race or nation, the American dilemma in music and its solution would have been prearranged by its past. But American music is that of an empire, of a commonwealth of races, and its allegiance is that of cultural loyalty. American music is mother to any composer who feels the land, or even its spiritual medium alone, to be his native soil. The future of American music lies clearly in a tonal culture grown from this emotion.

Possibly, music of a single racial fealty might expect longer life. When of a powerful cast, mixed spiritual allegiance arms its music with a mightier range and a sharper profile.

AMERICA, CELTIC AND LATIN

THE length and the curve of musical growth depends of course, on the nature of a nation's musical mind. The French mind is rather instrumental, decorative and urbane; the Russian —vocal, rhythmic and rural; the Italian—capable of taking the instrumental as well as the vocal line when allowed a long span of culture, as the art of Scarlatti, Corelli and Vivaldi shows.

What kind of musical mind have the people of the American North? This query may open the true perspective of American tonal culture, may also lead to an answer as to what is wrong with the American composer of today.

But let us think first of what is right with him and his inherent tonal mind.

Firstly, the American is "a natural." There is an alertness and eagerness of melodic gusto in his music, the same native agility and efficiency as in his language. Then he has an excellent tradition of melos back of him and musically worthy genetic antecedents, Anglo-Celtic, Saxon, Jewish, Italian. He is, in his strongest and most typical representatives, personal rather than original, as Hermann Scherchen, that brilliant musician and famous conductor, sagaciously observed.[1] And such may be a rather healthy basis for the initial growth of a culture.

What is amiss with American music? Being primarily of a vocal vein and, more than anything else, Anglo Celtic, the pressure of German instrumental culture has forced into American creation habits and grooves that run counter to the native American musical mind. The yoke of technical Mid-Europe of the eighteenth century, to say nothing of the three B's, still works havoc with our contemporaries. The "absolute music" cult and the worship of the Hindemith type of craft with a highly distilled Germanic instrumentalism and structural obsessions, are by-points of this servitude.

And yet, when the versatile Deems Taylor, one of the leading Americans himself, says "We Americans are not a race; America is a club, not a

[1] Hermann Scherchen: *American Composers*, Musical America, December 1938.

motherland," [2] he looks into the wrong corner inhabited by Loeffler, the half-German, and Chadwick and MacDowell whom Taylor himself calls "two German composers." I would rather look to the real salt of this land, true aesthetically as well as physiologically,—Harris, Ives, Sessions, Ruggles, Whithorne. I would take a close look at this Celtic American pleiad and its youngest stars, Robert MacBride, Ruth Crawford, Elliott Carter, Gardner Read, when speaking of America as a tonal motherland.

This hurried glance does not give us, however, a full or even correct account of the deeper agonies in the American music struggle of the present. Its shortcomings, its strange incompleteness, easy surrender to cross-Atlantic dogmas, have a deeper source, than long historical spells of imitation or slavery to a technical order alien to the native musical mind.

That incompleteness of type and artistry is present in each of the five creators who together form the American musical landscape: Roy Harris, its finest, most natural and original creative gift;

[2] Deems Taylor: *Of Men and Music* (Simon and Schuster, New York, 1937).

Charles Ives, its sharpest instinct for newness rising from the soil; Howard Hanson, bearer of various basic life-traits here, our practical energy and efficiency; Louis Gruenberg, conveyer of the highest of our artistry and technical finesse; Roger Sessions, its sturdiest palladin of culture as opposed to the sterile froth of "international" art which American youth is taking in so piously.

Those adjoining the Hanson line in American music reflect the practical alertness, combative energy and populist leanings of the type. Of them, Deems Taylor is of the American cosmopolitan mind; Arthur Shepherd, Harl MacDonald, Herbert Elwell and Leo Sowerby, all fine musicians and composers, reflect in a subtle way the spirit of their native places. As does Harold Morris whose body is in New York and soul in sun-baked Texas, and Mark Wessel whose wanderings have not effaced either his discreet personal accent or the ardent note of the Westerner. In his technical elegance and worldliness Emerson Whithorne stands somewhat to one side, yet an alert, practical aggressiveness ties him to this typical American set.

Speaking of Louis Gruenberg I have in mind also the contiguous group which could be described as cosmopolitan—eclectic—Hebraic, and is driven by worship of minutiae in technique. In Bernard Rogers' *American Frescoes*, a beautiful piece of tone-painting and orchestration, as well as in some pages from Isadore Freed's *Sacred Service*, such as the luminous chorale "This is the Tree of Life," the spirit lifts itself beyond the short reach of an aesthete's strivings. As to Copland, in spite of their faint Americanism and rather bloodless charm, the best pages in *Billy the Kid* lead us to a significant clew. In a small way, the cowboy songs and the delicate, attractive Ravelesque watercolors of the opening of *Billy*, are a response to the bankruptcy of city music. The whole is a naive and timid crystallization of an awareness which Ives states boldly.

*   *

*

The will for a return to the racial song of the American people, to its musical "grassroots," is with us again. Communion with one's people or race is, indeed, an indispensable preliminary to the creating of an integrated type of musical expression. In America, music has not had the opportunity for a complete cycle of growth from the Anglo-Celtic seed of its folksong. Unfolding methodically and doing it now, as Charles Seeger suggests, may be inspiring to some, may even result in lasting works, but as a cure-all it is *une chose manquée*. The old folksong's germinal strength is gone; the New England hymn-tune, the Southern ballade, the Mississippi shanty, these are no more the ruling folksong of the American people. Something else, a tonal bend which is still to be defined, has taken the place of the traditional melodic spirit of the old folksong.

Neither grassroots, nor melody for the new masses, nor the *gebrauch*stune, jazz, swing and other mass-dance utilities, are points in the real issue of American music of today. They are only avenues of evasion of the real issue, evasion of which the new American composer is not yet aware.

The end to which American music flows, anxiously and fitfully, is the formation of a rounded creative mind reflecting the fullness of American life and responding also to the breadth of the universal. Stylization or musical adornment of a single angle of our American spirit—native melos,

169

mass song, aggressive social ideas, will not do. This land will eventually find and follow a well-rounded, integrated creative ego. Original and personal, yet responsive to the spiritual, this ego will be fitted to shed its light and a human warmth over field and mine, over the street and the "ivory tower," in an obsession of the oneness of the creator's task. *E pluribus unum!*

With this in mind we can more easily gage the breadth and the limitations of the leading spirits of our day.

*   *

*

In no cast of American creator does the struggle for and against a universalism in direction show more clearly in the tonal mind than in the New England type, with its clear-cut denominators, racial and historical. Of them Roger Sessions may be called an apostle of the universalist creed, Charles Ives—a defender of the narrowing of our creative stand to the national power lines.

Sessions is a leader of high distinction, an intellect of exalted power, a master of cultured craft that is in itself a valuable force in setting our art-levels.

He is a neo-classicist of the Hindemith and Prokofieff kind. Not a stylizer, not a clever manipulator of tired pasticcio, but a man aroused by a vision of the orderly frames of the classical world, swayed by their lucid reason.

However, Sessions' reset classicism is possessed of his own, very individual emotion; and so is the tonal material he uses.

There is a sharp personal tang to his cryptic melos, a peculiar weight and color to his tonal plaster. Swarthy and of powerful mold, these drastic steles of tonal plaster used by Sessions to lay his spacious forms remind one of the Egyptian bas-reliefs.

This also is the impression—an extraordinary one—from the physical appearance of the composer himself. Most unexpectedly, a very deep and remote ancestry lurks in the emotional make-up of an American artist, and an Anglo-Celtic, too—in his parlance, physical type, in his ways.

In the opening *Giusto* of his *First Symphony,* an obstinate force with glints of emotion clearly racial yet personal and centripetal, streams through the cyclopean lines of its structure. And, one must add, this force is coupled with a stark innate rigidity that allows for only well defined, limited and predictable swings of creation.

But equally typical of this drastically Anglo-Celtic nature, in the following Largo of Sessions' symphony, his very personal melos is delicately crusted by a chilled heartiness and humanness. One is moved by the same quality in the opening measures of the song from the *Black Maskers,* one of the most beautiful lines ever created by American art. One is bewitched by its dark glow and caress.

Of Sessions' latest works, the *Concerto* for violin and orchestra exhibits in its *Largo tranquillo* a melodic thread of steel-like resilience. This music is marked by a spiritual climate in some way related to the sharp freshness and hidden aggression of the very air of New England.

But again, the opening bars of the *Romanza,* in the *Concerto,* has that alluring melange of sombre glow and humanness that strikes one in such related acts of art as Edgar Poe's *Ulalume* and Sessions' song from the *Black Maskers.*

The principal weakness of Sessions' larger forms is a too copious unfolding of all the derivatives,

sequels, side-thoughts drawn from his main thematic idea.

This draconian completeness, a fully exhausted
development, does not appeal to my own creative
taste. But one watches with respect such frenzied
tenacity of aim.

*   *

*

If Charles Ives is a good test of what the American tonal mind is—and I believe it to be so—the
creative vein of this country is predominantly vocal, chromic, rhythmic and decorative. Yet Ives is
reassuring as to the presence of the instrumental-
polyphonic phase in the tonal gift of his race, a
race holding the promise of a still more inclusive
type of culture. The music of Sessions, Harris
and, of our younger composers, that of Elliott
Carter and Robert MacBride, is an added proof.

It is in the songs that the Celtic American nature
of Ives and all his stark personal traits transpire so
definitely. To his songs Ives' peculiar homely
technique linked to no tradition or science is as
proper as that fresh breeze of an uncommon yet
deeply racial nature. He is indeed original, but in

173

fits; in willful whim more than in basic pattern. And here is where he differs from Roy Harris whose originality is inmost, contacts the deepest lines of creation.

What Henry Cowell says of Ives admiringly, might be re-echoed in condemnation:

"No element of music, no matter how unpopular, is left uninvited—all possible elements are included. . . . It is a music most universal in its use of different materials and shades of feeling, of any music which I have ever heard." [8]

Ives can be as obvious and homespun and imitative as any other man, and he is crudely and wildly spontaneous. Restraint and elimination, the two points of a master's control, are something he is entirely innocent of. Yet there is, at times, an artistic instinct of quality, even genius, in some of his melodic thought.

Ives' song *Evening* is irresistible in its exalted simplicity and peculiar emotional accent; *Down East*—uncommon and very typical of Ives in its blend. A serene Anglo-Celtic pattern is deliberately scrambled by savage thrusts of jagged meter.

[8] Henry Cowell: *American Composers on American Music* (Stanford University Press, 1933).

A melange of ballade with cross-rhythm rising to a rhythmic debauch. Yet it is true that even in *Down East* Ives reveals his predilection for the type of "tunes which are the experience of every American who has gone to church, been at a ball game, or heard a band concert." [4]

Still other facets show themselves frankly in the song *Charlie Rutlage,* vital and of crisp humor, and in *Two Little Flowers,* too comfortably naïve and polka dot.

This profusion of facets, aspects, materials, emotions driven by a strong nature and an expansive crude talent, fairly riots in the *Concord* sonata.

The opening movement "Emerson" is Lisztian but with a gleam of American exuberance giving it distinction. "Hawthorne" is tonal lacework without pattern. The lovable short poetic episode "The Alcotts," the best in the sonata, has the same fragrant simplicity as his song *Resolution.* "Thoreau," the *finale,* is again full of Lisztian inflation. But in all fairness, one must admit the "imaginative and spiritual vastness" claimed for it

---

[4] Quoted from the excellent study of Ives' work by the young New York composer Goddard Lieberson (Musical America, February 1939).

by Lawrence Gilman, spiritually a New Englander himself.

In both, the soul and body of his music, Randall Thompson, too, belongs to the New England coast, and Quincy Porter is a native son in many respects, in his New England solidity of texture, for instance.

In Randall Thompson's *Second Symphony* there is a typical vivacity of theme and gait. His technical assurance and gift for pruning symphonic verbiage reward us for the somewhat conventional thematic and formal profile of his work. The rhythmic oases in the *Scherzo* are refreshing; neither is the more ceremonial *finale* lacking in air, a delicate jazz-breeze driving it. In Thompson's choral *Odes of Horace,* the finesse and elegance of writing respond to the parnassian crispness of the poet. Of these choruses, *Montium Custos,* with its spare euphony, is of winning propriety and loveliness.

Quincy Porter's moods seem to be wholly instrumental, and in his chamber music, the subtle skill in marshalling the tangled voices dims their emotional message. There is, however, a greater warmth in the *Ukranian Suite* and in some slow segments of his string ensembles.

As to Douglas Moore, if nothing else does, his opera *The Devil and Daniel Webster* sets him firmly in the spiritual air of New England. And in its quaintness, idiom, mannerisms of musical parlance, this opera is one of the few staunchly American works. At any rate, it is traditionalist to the core. It is also one of the best in operatic technique and theatrical unity. That spirited music in the scene of the neighbors' marching on Jabez Stone who has sold his soul to the Devil, and the delicate moving song of Mary, his wife, when left alone with Jabez, is something that clings in one's memory.

There is still another, a contiguous group whom one is tempted to name "academic New Englanders." After a mental gliding by the trim line of the opuses by Walter Piston, one observer at least prefers the music of the adopted son, Werner Josten, with its delicate subsoil of religious emotion (*Concerto Sacro*), minute yet fervent tonal elaboration, and interesting psychological mixture of traditional Germanic and modern spirit.

In a certain way Frederick Jacobi, a native

American, still only faintly an "adopted" son of New England, is of the same type. But he essays to break through the glacis of academic rigidity. Then he gives us his best. In spite of their eclectic spirit, his piano concerto and second quartet, skillful and spirited, are among the best in the copious rosters of American instrumental music.

Speaking technically, it would be easy to say this much for Piston's music. Of it, the *Prelude and Fugue* take first place. But its elegance is academic; its grotesque dross and juiceless, not even entertaining.

And it is fitting to count in this group, not through regional but academic points, the agile and polished Bernard Wagenaar.

* *

*

There is one composer in American music, whose gifts and achievement place him in a unique class. His story is fantastic. Before our own eyes Roy Harris began as an uncouth, almost ignorant musician, as foolishly conceited as the usual ignoramus, yet keen and exuberant.

Before our own eyes he has developed into a

composer of high attainements, has become a musical thinker of distinction, a master of a broad and
powerful technique, creator of works the appeal
of which is practically universal and entitles their
progenitor to a place in the peers' gallery.

Yet even in Harris' earliest or occasional works,
such as the early piano sonata or the choral *Song
for Occupations* full of turns that are gauche, un-
derdone and homespun, there is much that is alluring and of high order. Taints of crudity and
technical limitation never could hide a creative nature of the first water, ever articulate, virile, the
racial note tense, the diction clear and winning.

Pointing to the traits which Harris has in common with Carl Sandburg, another typical offspring
of American soil and genius, the well-known
writer on music David Ewen says aptly:

"His melodies are obviously the speech of a
Western temperament in its angular line. Its vitality is an expression of American health and
youth."[5]

One readily subscribes to this. There is a Westerner's expansiveness and the warmth of a stark

[5] David Ewen: *Twentieth Century Composers* (Crowell).

179

Anglo-Celtic nature in the verbose yet loveable "Chorale" from Harris' *Concerto for Six Instruments,* still another early work. The *Finale* is confused and overstated; but the opening *Prelude* striking in its rhythmic vitality, melodic play, in its exuberant precision of speech.

The Harris of this *Prelude* never fails us. In his best symphonies, whenever his higher spirit prompts him to forget technical scullduggery, his armour rises to the power of his great gifts. Thus in his *Second Symphony,* as soon as we leave behind the set of obdurate technical whims of the allegro, we are left to inhale the exquisite melodic air of the slow movement, to delight in its intoxicating freshness of pattern, in its subtle weaving.

Harris' *Third Symphony* is the best, its thematic flesh of a basic nature yet alert and maleable, the melodic invention magnificent, the form of fresh vision and masterfully controlled. All the traits of a splendid talent born to build vast, powerful forms, are there. Thinking of this imperious work one dislikes even to recall certain rough episodes and naked patches in the orchestration. That opening long theme sung by the strings, a melodic thought of rare beauty, refuses to yield place to any other impression.

Harris' greatest work, however is his piano quintet. The *Passacaglia* of this composition is, in my opinion, a work of genius and the best piece of American music that has been written during the three hundred years of its history.

It is interesting to compare this quintet with another piece outwardly, perhaps, even more brilliant, from the pen of another American composer of the first water, with Louis Gruenberg's *Second Quartet* for strings. In this work, also, the opening movement is the best. Admirable in the drive and color of its emotion as well as in the transparent might of its structure and the finesse of episode, this music is dramatic and chromic, while Harris' is of inner concentration, of a steady enveloping grip that suggest Beethoven.

The sweep of outline in Harris' quintet is a marvel of form vision: *Passacaglia-Cadenza-Fugue.*

True, the last two sections do not fill their superb concept as well as the first does. With all its ingeniousness of planning, the second movement stoops to a sort of an experiment in sonority, the ever-lurking temptation of a man of our day. Only in the exalted piano cadenza the depth of the *Passacaglia* theme is mirrored again as if in a noble lake.

In the *Fugue* the deepest resources of polyphonic craft are applied with the skill of an artist of very high caliber. Many points of contrapuntal finesse can be seen here. But the *Fugue* also reverts, once more, to Harris' obdurate worship of labored technique in minutiae. And the glorious spirit of his opening movement that should have shaped the whole, wilts.

It does not matter, however. The *Passacaglia* is a world in itself, and its achievement is a summit of American artistry.

The splendid main theme, one of the best born on this soil or on any other, is a manly, broad, seminal thought; it holds a deep breath of emotion and personal might. In that wonderful spaciousness of Harris' theme one is tempted to sense the vastness and abandon and the epic stillness of the Colorado Desert. The unique modal structure of the theme is polytonal horizontally, that is, in the long run, and tonal vertically, that is, seen as harmonic cuts. This theme has a strong sense of cadencial centre within a polytonal web. The whole is something that only a master mind can achieve.

And how marvelous, and of what personal otherness is his play of rhythm in this superb *Passacaglia*. Not figured out and not calculated but conceived through the sheer vision of a creator *pur sang*, a vision of mutations lying dormant in his main motive. How enchanting is the whim of the *molto cantabile* where a still newer mutation of the theme appears as an exquisite piano arabesque set against the theme left intact! And how delicate the *mot juste* of his harmony, how true the sense of modulational order!

Indeed, here one stands before a vast artistic nature, a creative and technical vision reaching out for a perfect craft. That broad, rounded creative psyche which is to combine a native flair for racial melos, a technical imagination of a high order, and a greed for technical perfection inherent in this transatlantic race, with a response to universal life, this wide and complete creative mind for which American music yearns unaware of its own anxiety, is in sight, at last.

* *

*

As to the lively phalanx of the younger Americans, it is not possible to disregard their heel of Achilles seen at a glance. Their fault is not so much that of being half-baked, as that of following half-baked standards. They are still unaware of the difference between a master's negation of tradition and that of an apprentice. Their lusty radicalism is still that of ignorance.

There is, however, among them a coterie of which one can have little of interest to say, the school of American *chi-chi* (pronounced *shi-shi*), our own homegrown smarties. It is comical when this circle of odd oldish youths, a timid glance on its leading musical dandy, swears that its music has purged itself of all literary aspect. Why, these men are the very flesh of the latest and most spurrious literary chapels uniting Paris and Kansas, the Gertrude Stein revelation, for example.

This group is so light of consequence that there is scarcely anything to relate except that they exist. But their leader is interesting. I speak of the father of our own American *chi-chi,* an Ameri-

184

can version of Eric Satie, the unbending, ferocious Virgil Thomson. He reminds one of Satie not a little, in his wit and perverse humor—his is more fierce, however, and also more weighty. Like Satie he is marked by a smallness of creative gift and an even smaller turn of invention. The basis of Virgil Thomson's music is the most obvious American-Victorian church chorale. His method of perversion is that of a Red Mass without murder. The rites and mysteries are blackened out and made mildly sacrilegious *à la parisien,* and whether mock (*Capitals, Capitals* and the *Four Saints*) or serious (*Stabat Mater*), they sound the same. Roseate and faintly sour outpourings of the soul of an organist gone wrong. It is a pity that the swift intelligence of Thomson is put to such poor use.

Now to the younger set that counts.

The *Prelude to a Tragedy* by Robert MacBride shows creative vigor and a craftsman's gift of high promise.

In Elliott Carter we have achievement of heartening scale. This young artist has a mind of his own and the kind of technique that augurs a real ripening in the young American craftsman.

Carter's choral *Heart not so heavy as mine* (to Emily Dickinson's verse) is a piece of rare loveliness, a neatly crystalized bit of Anglo-Celtic melos in a new mutation, and also, one of the best examples of polyphonic writing known here. In Carter's ballet *Pocahontas* the same subtle vigour, directness and a remarkable technical gift transpire in spite of an overstrained "dynamism" which inevitably tempts young people of our day. The music of the scene in which Captain John Smith is saved by the Indian princess Pocahontas, is exquisitely finished.

In naturalness of talent, sureness of craft and an inbred artistic solidity Evelyn Berckman belongs to the same type as Carter. Only the color and the dramatic strain are different. A rarely and variously gifted nature, Evelyn Berckman has produced works of uncommon and fine quality, such as the orchestral suite *On Board the Morning Star,* the pieces for voice and string quartet and the song-cycle *Dr. Johnson's Tour in the Hebrides.* She is one of the best and one of the least noticed talents in this country.

As to Paul Nordoff, his *Concerto for Two Pianos* exhibits a temperament bright and prolix, apt

186

to shower undigested, vast material. In both his lyrical and technical "modernisms" one is at times annoyed by the facility. But a certain winning verve, energy and fundamental youth, one to remain, which one likes in Nordoff's music, cannot but sway the hearer to sympathy.

And he has that kind of attractiveness also, William Schuman. His *Prologue for Chorus and Orchestra* show, however, a greater concentration of craft, a lesser exuberance and a restrained dramatic tone arising from Schuman's civic temper.

Of David Diamond's works, *Ashen Pages,* songs of a subtle and somber line, still remain the best. His orchestral *Psalm* as his numerous other opuses are tentative, in scheme and accomplishment. His personality and technique are still nebulous, and it remains to be seen whether his shrewd intelligence and mental subtlety may not cheat his creative ego out of something essential.

Some of our youngest are still only names. Charles Naginski's ballet *The Minotaur* reveals a talent of much vigor and a gripping imagination. The *Incantation* based on a Chippewa chant for viola, piano and organ and the two-piano *Suite* by Miriam Gideon are marked by attractive emotive traits, high musical intelligence and delicacy of tonal thought. Something engagingly uncommon dwells in this music.

*   *

*

In the novel tonal world, so strange to us and, at times, so untranslatable, that of the Latin America, let us seek out the deeper currents.

This immense habitat still lives under the musical sign of folklorism, the initial stage of any original culture. The basis of the true Latin American music is Indian music, and its chief ingredients, Ibero-Spanish and Portuguese. There are, indeed, formidable reserves of native folk-chant. Such leading composers as Humberto Allende of Chile, the gifted author of *Tonadas,* Honorio Siccardi, the presiding composer of Argentine, Silvestre Revueltas of Mexico, the two outstanding Cubans, Alejandro Caturla, composer of the frenzied *Cuban Dances* and Pedro San Juan, author of the loveable *Sones de Castilla* and of the Afro-Cuban pieces, Gillermo Uribe-Holquin, premier composer of Colombia, Carlos Pedrel of Urguay and Segundo Louis Moreno of Ecuador, all of them cultivate the native folksong as a basis for their compositions.

Two outstanding Latin American musicians, Dr. Francisco Curt Lange of Montevideo, Professor of the National University of Uruguay, and Burle Marx, the well-known Brazilian composer-conductor, have initiated important movements for Pan-American musicology and a study of the folk-chant, and the musical interchange between the two Americas as well.[6]

But, indeed, the creative life in Latin America moves between far wider limits than the tilling of the native chant.

Burle Marx, a gifted and remarkable colorist of fine technical prowess as his orchestral *Fantastic Episode* shows, is himself an isolated phenomenon and an issue of the German tradition.

In Argentine, the picture is even more vivid. Honorio Siccardi and the talented and vivacious Jacopo Ficher lean toward traditional and classical lines. Of the two gifted brothers, both leaders in the "Grupo Renovacion" (Society for Modern Music) José Maria Castro is a stern neo-classicist.

[6] I owe part of my information to that admirable and indefatigable observer, Nicolas Slonimsky (articles in Christian Science Monitor and Musical America). He has traveled and conducted in Latin America.

Juan José Castro is the author of a delightful *Children's Suite* for piano and the luminous, graceful and transparent music of the *Sinfonia Biblica* for chorus and orchestra. Pictures of fine blood and color, these leaves of the life of Jesus hold something quite uncommon in the music's line and tonal light, something of a counterpart of the lumen of Fra Beato Angelico as it were.

Among the Argentinians we find also a sharp radical current. Its leader is that staunch and dynamic palladin of the twelvetone system, Juan Carlos Paz whose works were acclaimed at the international festivals in Paris and Bruxelles.

* *

*

In the best works of the two foremost composers of Latin America, Carlos Chavez of Mexico and Villa Lobos of Brazil, it is easy to observe how the first stage of national integration, the folklorist stage, fades before a deeper intake of their soil and inheritance. And it is easier even than in our own case, to follow the wonderful play of dual allegiance in this music of such rugged force, an allegiance reflecting the somber fertility of the

190

Indian wedded to the ardent gait of a Southern Latin race.

Carlos Chavez is a creative nature monolithic yet rich in variety and sensibility, and a composer with whom the material is not the overruling element. In his *String Quartet,* emotionally compact and of clear diction, glints of a mind unknown to us, oddly distant, glimming through a background almost classical in its crystalline quality, are unmarred by a somewhat ordinary material. One finds the same striking trait in Chavez' attractive *Sonatina* for violin and piano where something forceful and rounded coming from the unsplit racial spring, offsets the lack of distinction in the flesh of the music.

But his most impressive, and also most delicate work, *Tierra Mojada* (Wet Earth) for chorus, oboe and English horn, is extraordinary. It is an encyclopedia of the emotions of a remote, inscrutable race, utterance of a soul lone and sullen. There is nothing like this piece in its cold whimsy, in its stark seclusion.

One finds more splits in Villa Lobos. In *Song of Our Land,* in parts of a delectable rhythm and choric abandon, it is a pity to see the emotion drift

191

into smallish, facile lyricism. And it startles one to listen, in the Aria from *Bachiana N 5*, to a cluster of poignant unusual voices deployed over a quasi-Bachian whoof. The juxtaposition itself is magnificent, however, as is the very original form and substance of the second movement.

It is, however, in such a piece as *Chorus N 8*— orchestra and two pianos—where the gift of Villa Lobos streams in an unabated substance and splendor. With an odd reflection of barbaric glimmer *à la* Stravinski and pointilist spangles *à la* Webern, this music is Latin American to the depth. Here is a tense stillness and rhythm of the jungle. And when the music rushes into a savagely moody play of pointilist accent and showers astonishing sheets of tone colors (piano plus muted brass plus unheard of percussion), one visions the gigantic shadows of the virgin forest, and one inhales the epic magnificence of the waters of the Rio Negro.

How significant that in both Chavez and Villa Lobos the native speaks in stronger voice than the Latin! The traits ardent and debonnaire, those of the Spaniard, sink into *Tierra Mojada*, into the silent night and fertility of the Indian soul.

SIBELIUS, A MIND TWO-DIMENSIONAL

EUROPE has a new crowned head. She has insisted upon having one ever since Liszt and Wagner prompted the habit. And when the exuberant, moody brutality of Strauss had spent itself, Stravinsky's steady drive came to a standstill, and Schoenberg had wheeled into the sidelines of atonal calculus, a vacuum was created. A new god had to be enthroned, and Sibelius was brought forth and crowned with good titles and with false, with sensible appraisal of his art, and with impassioned sophistry.

The odd thing about it is that Sibelius' work has been well known, even in Western Europe, for at least a quarter of a century,[1] long before our musical stock exchange began to speed quotations up in high fever. He was weighed and measured with much critical calm long ago; for decades he has been assigned to a very honorable, but definite

---

[1] He has been well known in the United States, Russia and, of course, in the Scandinavian countries since the turn of the century.

shelf. There is nothing mysterious, or incomprehensible or unexpected in his music.

How much of an actual discovery has occurred to single him out for this strange hysteria of worship? The aloof, rural, venerable Sibelius, a creator of greatness, to be sure, but of a limited intellectual world, of an even more limited craft?

How fitting is the investing of his work with a universality, how sensible the looking for ideological electrons which are simply not there? How much of this craving to see a new leader in Sibelius should be credited to the breath of the green earth in his work, to symptoms of a return to the native old ways of music, to the yearning for the song and the canticle?

I am not prompted by a shallow aim to burn the Temple of Ephesus. Neither do I relish the necessity to pour cold water on the valiant but runaway championship of Sibelius by such writers as Rosa Newmarch and Cecil Gray. Whatever I may say here, is predicated on high esteem for the revered artist with his deep emotional nobility, for his beautiful land which I know well and love, and for his race, so civilized and distinguished.

* *

*

The salient trait of a creator of high order, composer of lasting forms, is the gift for basic patterns, that is, *thematic* inventiveness as opposed to creation of melodic episode. This primacy of creative invention a genius of the first water couples with the primacy of craft, handling of tonal light and shade, developing, building. A composer of the highest stature is one capable of syntactic originality, of a potent and subtle otherness, whether in laying out his monumental building plans or in molding his microform, the cells and bricks of his tonal material.

By sheer syntactic originality a creator of power manages to grow large and lasting forms from seedlings that may have little melodic distinction in themselves. It means that in such plantlets the faultless instinct of their user foresaw primal patterns capable of gigantic growth.

Of such is the difference between the inner working of a first rate genius, a mind of many dimensions, and a mind two-dimensional, the one who visions a beautiful tree but cannot conceive a great forest.

Compare the allegros of Beethoven's Fifth and Mozart's G-minor symphony, their main themes all but inarticulate in the former and almost obvious in the latter. Take their development sections and set them against the opening movements of, say, Grieg's piano concerto or Rachmaninov's Second Concerto.

The basic melodies of the latter pieces are of heavenly beauty; they fairly stifle us with fragrance and emotion. Yet they are not pregnant musical theses; no lasting structure has nor could come out of them. This music is a medley of beautiful melodic bits strung together without inner necessity, by the whim of an improviser. On the contrary, the developments in the Fifth or the G-minor of Mozart, or, for that matter, in Tchaikovski's *Pathétique,* are the summit of relatedness, naturalness of growth, superb logic of modulational flow, superb art in wielding tonal shade and light in a climactic order.

* *

*

Now, the case of Sibelius is precisely that of Grieg and Rachmaninov, even if the nature of

Sibelius' material and particularly, the tone of it, is different, even if the size of his spiritual self is larger.

The canonization of Sibelius began on the basis of a discovery of the "song-symphony" as the original trait of his major works.

This term is a *contradictio in adjecto;* it is wooden iron. The song as melodic episode is a static form. The symphony as an intricate but *definite* structural unit embracing manifold patterns dynamically driven, is by its very nature inimical to the spirit of song.[2]

The idea of symphony has nothing to do with dimensions or size; is concerned with only the structural spirit and the intricacy of building. The spirit of symphony with its sonata and its building scheme, form within form, is dynamic. The spirit of the song is static, its form built of cells lying next to each other.

Symphonic works that must be described as "song-symphonies," those made up of "songs" or melodic episodes in loose, catalogal sequence, are

[2] It is possible, of course, to call a work a "song symphony" substituting "song" for "chorale." This author did so once but suppressed the name finding it confusing.

really rhapsodies. Sometimes original rhapsodies, tactful as to length and proper ingredients, and therefore vital; sometimes dull and marshy as an overdrawn rhapsody can be.

Let us take a symphony which Sibelius devotees consider a revelation in new form building, the Second. Cecil Gray tries to show that here a great symphonic work has been created by the reversal of the usual structural proceeding. Instead of splitting a theme and playing on the variation of the bits, Sibelius presents his splinters first, and then, in the development section, shows the mother theme all straightened out and bandaged up.[3]

This could have been a great new achievement had the motives paraded first in the Second Symphony been basic patterns, as pregnant with parenthood, as full of inherent development as is the main theme of the Eroica or that of the *Finale* in Brahms' Third Symphony, a perfect symphonic structure. But Sibelius' building bricks are not that; they are mainly episodes, motives without a future. This is why his Second Symphony is, in spite of its structural intention, another product

[3] Cecil Gray: *Sibelius. The Symphonies* (Oxford University Press).

of a typical two-dimensional mind, a genius of episode and improvisation, a "heaver of rocks, not a shaper."

The spirit driving this music is magnificent in many respects, but without sufficient artistry of a high order to fill the vast form. The size of the work is too large for the nature of the thematic units, the binding material badly chosen. There are in this symphony none of the traits of the new symphonic thought, it is claimed it has, such as a sense of organism rather than of dramatic discourse, a drastic relatedness of all material in a vision of unity or laconic objectiveness of thought.

There are of course, wonderful things in the symphony: the superb climax at the end of the first movement or the enchanting opening of the second, a typical bit of Norse melos that contributes blood to the symphonic body.

Again, these are but episodes ever ready to spend themselves in insipid improvisation. The swift change in the opening music of the second movement illustrates this only too well. And how distressing it is to hear the smallish, shallow, *petit bourgeois* closing segment of the symphony, and to see the instrumental ineptness, that naked brass for instance, that blows at us from everywhere.

Of the *Fourth Symphony* Gray himself says that its formal structure is "elusive and baffling." A fine compliment to a symphony, the most set form of all!

Nor is this symphony, perhaps Sibelius' best, an issue of pregnant mother-themes. The two initial subjects of the work are episodes at their frankest. Fine episodes, they do not sound as preludes to anything and engender nothing but a light literal repetition of one of them at the end of the allegro. And after the desert of the second part we find still another full-blooded but rather obvious kind of episode in the finale subject.

With their darkly shifting melos reminding us of the *Swan of Tuonela* the motives of the opening movement, in the *Fourth Symphony*, are again but bits of a lyric melopee lacking resilience, lacking those direly needed thematic hooks and angles that give a Bach fugue, a Beethoven or Brahms symphony their unforgettable face. The face of all Sibelius symphonies is the same.

And how poverty-stricken is that everlasting homophony of the Fourth! And how unbearable

the square doubling in his orchestration which can
not boast of one individual *tutti!*

But it is essential to note that there is a certain
compactness and brevity that saves the form itself
and gives it a semblance of efficiency, just as the incomparable racial color and emotion gives it a
semblance of unity.

We must not be deceived by the fact that the
symphonies of Sibelius are full of unusual, fanci-
ful, even potent harmonies. Like Grieg and Rachmaninov, he has only color vision, no real harmonic
imagination as indispensable to a three-dimensional
creator, as is the gift for pregnant theme-patterns.
There is no harmonic movement in Sibelius' webb,
none of that wonderful modulational order and
climactic flow of harmony of which Mozart, Wagner and Mussorgski are the unsurpassed masters.
Sibelius has learned nothing from that astonishing
slowly sinking harmonic sequence at the end of the
Confutatis in Mozart's *Requiem,* or in the description of the Impostor's dream in *Boris,* or in the
sword scene in the first act of *Die Walküre.* There
Wagner's harmonic genius creates a superb play of
shade and light by switching from the basic C-major ray to a side glow of E and A major, thus

kindling an extraordinary feeling of harmonic movement and suspense.

This kind of gift for handling of tone-light is indispensable to a creator of large forms. In Sibelius' case, we unfortunately find a blind spot on his musical intellect. Intuition of genius, uncommon sense of color there is. But the third dimension, the one which binds the outpourings of the former and molds forms eternal, that is, the dimension of artistry, is absent. His technical imagination, harmonic vision, architechtonic sense fall far behind the power of sheer individuality.

In leaving the symphonies if one harks back to the dark grief of *Tuonela* and the *Lemminkainen* cycle, one finds there everything which denotes Sibelius' fate as a composer—that of an improvisational genius. Bardic, rhapsodic, anti-thematic, anti-symphonic, Sibelius' music is for all its severe speech misty and, at times, baffling in tonal turns and tongue-tied. But in its noble bleakness it poises on a splendid racial melos. Everything in this music is enhanced by race and habit, and the light of the *aurora borealis* shines over all of this lone art.

Sibelius of the *Tuonela Swan,* and of the *Lem-*

minkainen sagas is the true Sibelius. He is a racial and regional genius, and all attempt to magnify his spiritual reach, to universalize his thought by naming him an enricher of music with novel forms, the "song-symphonies," are a lawyer's sophistry whitewashing improvisation.

Like Grieg's best music, Sibelius' rhapsodies are an issue of an old and fine but limited culture, of a rare folklore moving and sublime, but a limited one. And while this parentage lends its music the green stillness and wisdom of the earth, and something of a grandeur of things immortal, it does not insure its offspring continuity in the flow of great art. This music has all the closeness of a regional culture, and its craft is of short breath.

* *
*

Sibelius is a natural flame, of the same kind in some respects as Schubert and Mussorgski, but with this variance. From Sibelius like from Grieg, nothing emanates that may infuse itself in the new art. Sibelius' song has something of the same immediate potency as that of Schubert and Mussorgski but surely not the same germinal power.

203

Out of one *Lied* of Schubert's, *Des Krieger's Ahnung,* the whole first act of *Walküre* and much of other Wagner arose. And one single passage of Mussorgski's song-cycle *Sunless* is the evident progenitor of Debussy's *Nocturnes.* What has emanated or is likely to come from a Sibelius pattern?

We ask ourselves: "Who then is the great composer of today?" And the word of Saint-Beuve as to who was the greatest writer of France, comes to mind.

"Hugo, *malheureusement.*"

Sibelius is, indeed, the greatest composer of the day but *malheureusement,* he is one to glorify and canonize, not to follow. He is a genius without sequel, one from whom craft has learned little and will inherit nothing.

SAXON VERSUS GAUL

ONCE more, I am afraid, one must hark back to the well-known facts of France's and England's respective physical position and history to understand their musical currents. These geographical and cultural conditions still hold their sway after centuries crammed with change and catastrophy.

The difference in kernel, flavor, direction of the two musical cultures is greatly conditioned by this main fact. The tight quadrilateral of France favored bearing a race welded into oneness early in history, a creative life self-centered and integrated. The narrow island of England forever overswept with ethnic and cultural waves from eastern and southern lands across the seas, was given by nature itself to diffusion, a spreading out of creative life, and in the latest period of English musical history, to an emotional expansiveness arising from a peculiar and exhuberant imperial awareness.

Such is the reason why the French tonal mind

is restrained, concise, centipetal, and the English— expansive, catholic and centrifugal.

And another important source of variance in these cultures. The French tonal mind, rather instrumental and monolinear, is countered by the English, vocal and by nature, if not always through action, polyphonic.

* *
*

The diversity and catholicity of the British tonal mind can be seen with great clarity in the four present leaders of English music, in Vaughan Williams, the fervent populist, Arnold Bax, the Celtic voice in English music, Arthur Bliss, one of the keenest speeders of its pace, and Eugene Goossens, its keenest internationalist.

In the work of the most prominent of the younger composers one finds a veritable jumble of tendencies. In Constant Lambert's lively *Rio Grande* for chorus, piano and orchestra and his graceful ballet *Pomona* there passes a rainbow of colors and melodic turns, some frankly and directly British, some exotic *à l'espagnol,* others of current devil-me-care modernity, or of delicate impressionistic slant *à la gaulois.*

As to the gifted Walton, his *Façade* is full of russo-parisian spangles and *Belshazzar's Feast* reeks with Oriental melopee of not always the freshest strain.

Arthur Bliss is, in spite of all his modern gait and continental externals, more essentially British and Saxon, than his above described juniors. I would like to repeat the admirable characterization by two brilliant English musicians.

Of Bliss' *Madam Noy* Goossens said that it is "neither too objectively fussy nor subjectively vague." [1] And Leigh Henry added that this music "does not amplify the incidents but synthetises the images; is not illustrative but decorative."

The typical emotional pointilism of Bliss and the motion that results in a peculiar exhilaration, are ever present in his work, whether the early *Rout,* vigorous and of delicious verve, or in his latest *Concerto* for piano, with its amiable, discreetly romantic *Adagietto* and mischievously spirited *Finale.*

Goossens himself has kept to his personal lines just as sturdily, in craft as well as in creative trend. In Goossens' recent work, the opera *Don Juan de*

[1] Eugene Goossens in an article on Bliss in the Chesterian, 1921.

Mañara which enjoyed a glorious reception at its première in London, we find the well-known Goossens idiom. This music is virile, multi-colored, full-blooded. The harmonic vocabulary of *Don Juan* is catholic. A frank polytonal scaffolding (the opening choral exclamations) is as natural to him as a clear flowing modal melopee. Such is the attractive serenade of Don Juan before the boudoir of his half-brother's mistress whom he, of course, seduces. Being Don Juan—Mañara or Tenorio, makes no difference—what else could he do?

* *

*

Edwin Evans, the authoritative champion of the new British music, who thinks as many other competent musicians that Arnold Bax' *E flat Symphony* is his best, defines this composer's craft very concisely:

"His texture was at first over-elaborate. . . . Its warp and woof have not changed as much as might be expected after a quarter of a century of active composition, but the pattern now stands out with a clarity that was lacking in some of the earlier works." [2]

[2] Edwin Evans: *Arnold Bax* (Modern Music, Volume V).

The music of Bax owes its strong impression of unity not only to the sturdiness of its pith, but notably to the sustained Anglo-Celtic lyric force. The latter screens the presence of any alien corn in Bax' music, the French and Russian pigments, the Brahmsian lines of his larger structures. This ruling Celtic voice is heard in the best and the true Bax, in his early orchestral poem, the delectable *Garden of Fand,* in the undisturbed message of his *First Symphony,* perhaps his most vigorous and close-grained, and in the dreamy leaves of the *epilogue* in the *Third Symphony,* music of great loveliness.

There is a still deeper communion with his people's creative life in Vaughan Williams. All his music and his best, from the fresh youthful *Norfolk Rhapsodies* and the superb *Fantasia on a theme by Tallis* to the symphonies, all of it grew from the seed of racial and traditional song. How true is the excellent remark of Gerald Abraham that "no composer has yet succeeded in 'digesting' Celtic folk music as Vaughan Williams has digested English folk-song." [3]

In the *London Symphony,* one of his best

[3] Gerald Abraham: *A hundred years of Music.* (Duckworth).

rounded works, one of complete expression, there does not seem to be any visible trace of folksong. Yet it breathes the same warm "folkiness" as Parry's *Jerusalem*. In the limpid and exalted introductory motive of the *London Symphony* and in its luminous mutation closing the work, one senses the renewed play of the racial tonal mind that has lain dormant far beneath the English musical life since Fornsete and Dunstable, the Tudor madrigalists and the great era of the modal church chorale. And there is a telling kinship with Mussorgsky, another exalted singer of his people's soul. In *Alla Marchia* and the *Epilogue* concluding the symphony one is stirred by the same sacramental glow and sublime humanness.

Vaughan Williams is the heroic figure of today's English music. More than anyone else, he has helped to reverse the process of diffusion and "continentalisation" which came near dissipating the great musical wealth left by the English Renaissance. Williams helped England to regain her own tonal mind.

* *

*

Hundreds of years of cloistered, close-knit spiritual life and, probably also, the deeply imbedded traits of Gallo-Roman civilization, gave French music its strong stamp of integration. On the surface, it may seem that the remote and diverse racial springs have added to the French tonal mind no more than nuances. But the latter are so telling that again we stand before a powerful showing of blood stronger than civilization.

The well-known outer shell of French music has every trait of the Gallo-Roman mental type, brevity, a certain cool, collected stubbornness of logic, clear line of form, controlled evenness of diction. Yet the puissant passion of Florent Schmitt, the cerebral Ibero-Semitic finesse of Ravel, the dark glimmer of something intricately exotic in Debussy's *Nocturnes* as well as the swarthy Oriental coloring in his physical type, come from the same source as the Gallo-Mongol, or perhaps, Gallo-Finnish face and subtlety of Roussel, and the Black Madonna of Chartres. These racial "nuances" go as far back as the epoch of the Moorish invasion, the battles of Charles the Hammer, the raids of the Norse and Finnish corsairs, and perhaps much earlier, the visits of Egyptian and Phoenician traders.

211

* *
*

The most intricate nature among the masters of French music, intricate and almost indefinable, yet racially tangible, is of course Debussy.

Catlike, solitary, artistic, amorous—so runs the felicitous account of him by Oscar Thompson. "Feline, not feminine, is the adjective most used to suggest his walk, his manner . . . the voluptuousness that covered his whole relation to life and art. He was a hedonist, a sybarite, a sensualist." [4] A priest of Phoenician Ashtoreth! Does not this portrayal call up one? And one thinks too of the airiness of his creative touch, his horror of crude color and of over-stressed epithet, all these subtle qualities of a part Celtic nature which Lawrence Gilman captured in his delicate *apperçu*. "In his search for all loveliness that is fugitive and interior and evanescent. . . Debussy is often more Gaelic than Gallic." [5] Still he is, more than anything else, Claude Debussy, *musicien francais*.

Even more French, if restraint is the criterion,

[4] Oscar Thompson: *Debussy, Man and Artist* (Dodd-Mead).
[5] Lawrence Gilman: _Toscanini and Great Music_ (Farrar and Rinehart).

is Albert Roussel whom two eminent French critics portray with a precision much easier here than in the case of Debussy. "He venerates the clearness and discretion of our race." [6] says Jean Aubrey. In his outstanding lectures at the Sorbonne [7] Robert Bernard, a young musician of great subtlety and remarkable science, and a gifted composer himself, points to Roussel's being the banner-bearer of resistance to the post-Debussy current. Roussel's was a nature deaf to anything extra-musical as an incentive to creation. Yet his anti-romantic and anti-impressionistic rigidity do not exclude a sensibility of a very subtle order. One wonders where the serenity of Albert Roussel really comes from. Like that extraordinary mandarin face of his, it makes us dream of the soberly delicate lines of the early Chinese painting and the taciturn soul of the Mongol.

Another Asia lurks in the commanding, burning parlance of Florent Schmitt, the greatest living composer of France and the highly revered keeper of its best traditions of technique and culture. He

[6] G. Jean Aubrey: *French Music of To Day*, translation by Edwin Evans (Paul, Trench and Co.) London.

[7] They are embodied in the book of Robert Bernard *Les Tendances de la Musique Francaise Moderne* (Durand, Paris).

looks like an Assyrian king, and his blood carries as much energy, tempest and eloquent fury. But the Gaul in him and the heir to Roman culture as well, temper his richly imaginative creation with that incomparable precision of thought and refinement of craft, that is the patrimony of French civilization. This superb spirit shows in such early masterworks as the starkly lyrical *Quintet* and the choral *Laudate*. The latter is enchanting not only in the naturalness of its full-blooded melos and power of diction, but also in the polyphonic transparency native to a master of the highest mark. But it is, indeed, in Florent Schmitt's Psalm *XLVII* for chorus and orchestra, one of the greatest monuments of French art, that all the forces of this mighty imagination, all his gifts and technical powers whirl in their unrestrained splendor.

* *
*

Of the conflicting racial currents and religious tangles harking back to the Renaissance and the Huguenot Wars, conflicts after four hundred years not yet exhausted, the most surprising musical ramifications show in the neo-Catholic musical group as countered by a neo-Protestant current. A strange spectacle this, in the sea of modern music!

Georges Migot, an independent and very unusual musician, is a cultivator of the Protestant musical tradition. A descendant of the famous Huguenot minister Jean Migot who was burned at the stake during the Religious Wars, he is a fiery exponent of very remarkable ideas. He believes that by root and essence French art is Gothic, not Latin; that the dynastic and religious interchange of the French Renaissance under the Valois kings made the Italian-Catholic influence rampant and diverted French culture, and so French music, into a Latin channel contrary to its nature.

The æsthetic range of Migot's music is as broad as his ideology. His *Trio* and the *Zodiac* suite for piano are pieces of rare freshness and of delicate water-color quality, a little too wordy for their *genre*, perhaps. The *Sermon on the Mount*, an oratorio ingeniously planned as a cortege of all creeds toward the Mount of Revelation, seems over-concentrated, of almost excessive violence. Vast forms like this are rarely even, in either interest or quality, but on the whole, it is of striking power and contrapuntal skill.

The group of *Jeune France* is dominated by the neo-Catholic creed of their highly gifted young leaders, Olivier Messaien and Daniel Lesure.

In *Action de Graces* of Messaien, striking and somehow of our day—in spite of its archaic bent and strange Gregorian-Hindu flavor, is the pathos of its chanting line. And just as notable is the grace of Messaien's polyphonic ornament. The tonal basis of his work has very original points. Enamored of the ancient Catholic canticle he does not follow, however, the medieval modality. He has one of his own. His modes are non-transposable: he calls them *"modes de transposition limitée"* as are non-tempered scales. He has also a trick of using the accruing metres (*"unités de valeur ajoutée)"*, of accelerating them as it were, not for contrapuntal purposes, *à la* Bach, but for intra-melodic development.

His remarkable song cycle *Poèmes pour Mi*, a set of luminous and delicate litanies, is a clear issue of the ancient Catholic melos. When Messaien sings them he looks like an intent, almost possessed monk, like a twelfth-century chorister, a member of the great Ekkehard chorus from medieval Mainz, or a presbyter celebrating the Nativity before a Hohenstaufen emperor, on the shores of Lake Constanz.

Messaien himself is as interesting as his music. The same blend of churchly softness with iron character sounds in his tonal texture, lurks in those intent gray eyes, somewhat softened by a halo of light chestnut hair.

Daniel Lesure, the most elegant spirit and the subtlest craft of *La Jeune France,* is enchantingly spontaneous, far from any scholastic or academic revival of a form that in our own day should be an incentive rather than a mold. In Lesure's *Passacaille* the opening ostinato theme of a Dorian turn and the beautiful diatonic texture of the piece, its quasi-classical, radiant sensitiveness and fancy, are of a rare technical finesse, so individual and yet so French.

André Jolivet is the tonal anarchist among them. Yet even he is swayed by the neo-Catholic tendency of his group; he also, wishes to render to music its original antique character, give back its incantatory expression of a creed animating a large human mass.

Of these "youngsters" it is no longer possible to jest as did Eric Blom, one of the leading British writers on music, aiming, no doubt, at the *Six* and the still younger *Ecole d'Arceuil*. Mr. Blom's finely pointed dart reaches as well to their much advertised father, the "velvet gentleman of Arceuil" Eric Satie, who is supposed to have given Debussy his ideas of art and points for tonal innovation. One suspects that Debussy would have appeared in any case, and carried on exactly as he did—without a prompter.

"The youngest," says Mr. Blom, "delight in the spicy *capitolo* whose artistic material is of set purpose so meager that brevity is its greatest excellence." [8]

* *

*

There is a far more important point in the rise of these new creators of France than their return to solidity of craft and pith. I speak of the centripetal movement of these young musical forces.

Messaien hails from Avignon, the city of the Popes, and he has grown to be a leader of the young Parisians.

Jean Françaix, who, in spite of the light weight

[8] Eric Blom: *The Limitations of Music* (Macmillan).

of his work, has the clarity and the exuberance of that undying Gallic race, comes from Anjou.

Henri Tomasi, author of a ballet and a colorful orchestral poem *Bocero,* premiered in Paris, conductor and organiser, is a Corsican, and in his *"oeil clair, dent dur,"* there is the stamina of a southern mountaineer.

Of the "older" and now famous men, Milhaud hails from Provence, and Honegger from the Swiss Borderland.

This movement of musical forces, from the country's periphery to the center, is, perhaps, one of the most fruitful in the musical life of France. For two centuries the music of Paris has been the music of France. In all its creative implications this state of things is as harmful as is the fact that over a long period the music of New York has been the music of the States.

The tremendous hold of Paris on French music (as that of New York on the creative music of our country) has been both valuable as well as harmful. Valuable in the setting of a high technical level and sharpening of the composer's craft, harmful in segregating the young creative forces

219

into stifling pockets of highly specialized cults and chapels.

The earth, the wide fields of the far hinterland of France are coming into their musical own.

PART III

NEW RUSSIANS AND THEIR ALMA MATER

NEW RUSSIANS AND THEIR ALMA MATER

THE reform of the Western World's tonal language, in progress during the last three decades and accelerated by the post-war upheaval, is rooted in the *Alma Mater* of the New Russians, headed by Scriabin and Stravinsky. By *Alma Mater* I do not mean the whole "Mighty Handful," Moussorgski, Borodin, Rimski-Korsakov and other creators of the Russian national school, though their pregnant influence on Debussy and Ravel, reflected later in Schoenberg, Stravinsky and even in Strauss, deeply disturbed the Wagner-infested European art. However, the teacher of Stravinsky, Miascovski and Prokofiev, the leader of the Petrograd school and its greatest technician, Rimski-Korsakov, was the source of much of Stravinsky's backbone, in artistry and novelty.

In this rôle of a precursor of a mighty phalanx of young creators leading the revolt, Rimski-Korsakov was lonely. The other great light in Russian musical learning, Serge Tanéyev, held a spiritual position directly opposed to that of Rimski-Korsakov.

Serge Tanéyev, leader of the Moscow conservative school, teacher of that triad of great Russians —Rachmaninov, Scriabin and Siloti, was an unexcelled master and the mightiest contrapuntist since Bach. Tanéyev's glorious *Treatise on Counterpoint* means to musical science as much as Newton's *Principia* to cosmology. It is most unfortunate that this extraordinary master and theoretician of genius left no impress on new Russian music except a mere technical influence on the art of Rachmaninov and Scriabin and an evocation of the magnificent missionary work of Alexandre Siloti.

In spite of having been Scriabin's teacher, Tanéyev, the "old believer," could neither be, nor be thought of as the source of "newness" or "revolutionism" in Russian music. The newness he strove for, was admirable and prophetic, but of quite a different hue.

Leonid Sabanéyev, another outstanding disciple of Tanéyev, says very admirably:

"Our [Russian] Gothic viewpoint, our European and partly our *Slavic* conception, unbalanced, putting the supremacy of spirit and chaos over that of the body and cosmos, this type of thinking could never be attuned to Tanéyev's Appolinism and Hellenism." [1]   Sabanéyev adds that in his letters to Tchaikovsky, his teacher, Tanéyev noted that Russian music should follow a different road than that of Western Europe: "Only after having created its own epoch of strict counterpoint and ensuing polyphonic style, will Russian music get under way to a normal profile of development."

However important and revealing this stand of Tanéyev is, it is evident that to Rimski-Korsakov alone falls the honor of being the true fountainhead and *Alma Mater* of the tonal newness that has played so great a part in the tonal reform of the last three decades.   At Rimski-Korsakov's side stands Anatole Liadov, his pupil, first lieutenant and his successor in the class of composition.   A fine master was Liadov himself, and in his severe school Gniéssin, Prokofiev and Miascovski received their first and essential training.

[1] Leonide Sabanéyev: *Sergei Tanéyev*, Tair publications, Paris, 1930.

Rimski-Korsakov and Liadov were fascinating human figures, the very mouthpiece of old Russia and its fanatic artistry. To help in restoring their true portraits is a joyous debt of devotion.

RIMSKI-KORSAKOV AND LIADOV

A CREATIVE artist, who has been active on the larger and more open roads of art, accessible, well seen by the mass, is liable to be thought of in terms of one definite stamp. Humanity, or less pompously, the human mass as a whole, is very apt to judge a creator known to them by his accessible platitude, by his popular pattern rather than by the exquisite exception and *aperçu* born in a singular second of whim and genius. We know and proudly count up the "sweet" Madonnas of Rafael. But we faintly recollect his work of such individual allurement as the portrait of Juanna d'Aragon, wife of Prince Ascanio Colonna, persecuted by the awesome Caraffa, Pope Paul IV. . . . Rubens means to us hardly more than bacchanales of huge, bestial women and satyrs. Where is the observer who poses in rapture before that exquisite "Diana of the Hunt" in the Dresden Gallery? How much is the trait of shy delicacy in Rubens perceived by Every-man?

For that matter, are we fully conscious of the fact that Beethoven, creator of those honestly European quartets op. 18, creator of that rigid example of classical pedantry, the adagio from the *Fourth Symphony*, is also the composer of *The Ruins of Athens*, of the extraordinary Chorus of Dervishes? Do we realize how much of a strange medium, almost bizarre, to us racially inconceivable, was hidden in that gigantic soul? Do we stop to think that it is entirely possible that Beethoven could have been greedily immersed in conceptions of an *altogether different* sort than those of his habitual pattern?

Rimski-Korsakov's image sifting through popular memory, suffers from the petrified, one-sided general perception which Bacon termed *eidola fori*, prejudices born in public places. The real Rimski-Korsakov is locked and stifled in a chest of platitudes of common acceptance. His silhouette is shrouded in the thickness of myths, myths of dryness, professionally cut pedantry, artistic cruelty typical of a *Schulmeister*. The notorious campaign dealing with Rimski-Korsakov's "mutilating" of

Boris, contributed not a little to these myths. In 1908-1909, the period of that campaign's early phase, Diaghileff, the *Monsieur Sans-Gêne* of European art, was much behind the coulisses; later one could not help perceiving the scent of publishing interests.

* *

*

From the day when, waiting for my entrance examinations, I first saw the fantastic form of Rimski-Korsakov descending the grand staircase of the St. Petersburgh Conservatory—in August, 1906—until my last meeting with the master in May, 1908, a few weeks before his death, I knew but one image of him: a giant of northern sagas with the wide eye of a benevolent sorcerer, a tenderly passionate and delicate artist-aristocrat, religiously in love with the freshest, airiest walk in art.

The world at large has created a popular image of Rimski-Korsakov in conformity with the naked orientalism of *Schéhérazade* and *Chant Hindou,* an image conformed to all the accursed flummery we hear of the relationship between Moussorgski and Rimski-Korsakov. But can the world at large have a true idea of Rimski-Korsakov without knowing his tenderest, his most radiant, his subtlest creative dreams? I speak of the *Fairy Tale* and *Mlada,* of *Kastchei* and *Kitesz.*

For that matter did the world at large, who had had an inkling of the real Rimski-Korsakov in *Cocq d'or,* sense all the import and historical consequence of this work? Do we realize that both Stravinsky and Prokofiev are *hardly possible* without this source and forerunner of both, their grotesque and their technique? Have we truly measured the many art-sides, all the enchanting and significant tonal avenues hidden in this work, quasi known to the world? We have all heard the *Snow-Maiden,* but who has turned scarcely more than a deaf ear to one of the most divine pages of music, the scene where the Snow-Maiden, at the dawn of a glowing summer day, calls her mother, the Spring, from the waters of a forest lake? Who has judged Rimski-Korsakov by these tenderly poignant evocations, by these magic tonal garlands; who has probed the human and artistic depth hidden in these pages of genius?

The one who does not know the soft glow and the evil-bearing fires of *Mlada,* her gentle threads of archaized melos, her demoniac choruses, such as the awesome devils' *Kolo*, copied with dangerous exactness by Stravinsky in *Kastchei's* dance from the *Fire-bird*; the one who does not suspect the singular pictorial and tonal wealth of *Kastchei*, with its velvety-sinister, hissing undertone; the one who has not been stirred by the night scene and choral prayer to the Madonna of Kitesz, has no right to join the parrots' choir shouting down Rimski-Korsakov, as the schoolmaster to the Russian national group.

Inspiring was that master's pure and enamored musicianship, his devoted, ever-tested artistry.

*   *

*

The western world does not know Anatole Liadov, the teacher of several famous composers of our day. He was not only an important link between Rimski-Korsakov and the new Russians; he was also a very extraordinary representative of the now dying type of Russian craftsmanship and art morals.   He was, as I have said, the veritable image of old Russia.   Both his activity and indolence blend in a most picturesque page of musical history.

In November of 1913, St. Petersburgh cele-

231

brated a jubilee of Liadov's creative work. Of course, Liadov would not go near any such festivity. He was impossible to be found anywhere. I remember how later he grimly joked about the title of "councilor of state" and the order bestowed on him on that occasion.

We, his former and his immediate pupils, felt at the time a pang of devotion and gratitude for all we had learned from that fascinating man and master. I took it upon myself to write the following letter to the press:

"A jubilee is now being celebrated to honor the glorious master whom Rimski-Korsakov did not mention otherwise than 'the most gifted, the wisest.'

"Of his disciples, either those who are welcomed in Liadov's austere school, or those who are in disgrace and have gone, not one would deny a deep gratitude, deny respect and love for one of the most fascinating of Russian artists. Not one could fail to see in himself turns and traits for which he must feel a debt to Liadov's noble school.

"In our day there scarcely lives a master, other than Anatole Liadov, who has a right to the title of *arbiter elegantiarum*, the supreme arbiter in artistry. In his hatred of everything obvious, casual, plebeian, of everything smacking of the market-square, he is verily Petronius of our day, day of predilection for painted rubbish.

"Another trait that commands a singular respect, is his gift of effacing himself, of retreating from the swampy public music-bazaars where each must beat the drum of his own glory. This gift a young musician who would serve lofty creative dreams, must envy and emulate. Then glory to our master who shuns the loathsome market-place."

This letter was published in the Moscow magazine *Music*. In his reminiscences Victor Walter, concert-master of the Imperial Opera House, says that Liadov was greatly touched by the letter. Four years before he would not permit me further studies under him (after the fugue) as he violently disliked my independence or temper, my desire to work the technique in my own way, and my other "revolutionary" whims. However, I was greatly devoted to Liadov and wanted him to know this before he passed on, in 1914.

Liadov's life was that of a phantom. He was almost never seen at concerts. Very seldom and then imperceptibly would he slip into his class of composition at the St. Petersburgh Conservatory. And very, very sparsely this still, lazily swaying existence sent out its creative message. An artist scarcely exists whose embodied creation is so mercilessly small a coefficient of great hidden gifts. The immense interval separating his early *Music Box* from the orchestral *Apocalypsis* and the later piano works, this interval calls on those potentialities all too slightly.

His unusual, taciturn nature and even his extraordinary indolence had a singular spiritual tinge, and they shed a peculiar fascination.

He hated teaching, the very effort of it, and our director, the gentle-hearted Glazounoff, had to resort to all manner of petitions and diplomacy to get Liadov to come to his class of composition.

Liadov would appear finally. With a grimace of disgust, dropping each word with an effort, he would design the exercise or theoretical formula on the blackboard. Then with a singular, languid elegance and a face reflecting genuine suffering, he would play on the piano his pupils' written exercises, lighting with inimitable ease and grace on each bit of harmonic mud.

234

In recalling now those adorable scenes I am tempted to evoke the image of Frau von Breuning driving young Beethoven from the house to visit his pupils. Young Beethoven's stubborn distaste was notably that of a young donkey.

Then indeed, we did not take Liadov's negligence easily. And we did not think of gay comparisons, we who gathered from all corners of Russia, who threw overboard our university studies, our occupations and our positions, with the sole aim of study under Liadov.

His hatred for teaching can by no means be disposed of by saying that he had no capacity as an instructor. On the contrary, he possessed all the gifts of a remarkable one: a powerful and lucid theoretical mind equipped with clearly devised principles and plans for teaching, a neat and concise elegance of explaining formulas, a wise compactness of exposition. In its forging of a conscious technique and artistic judgment Liadov's instruction was of enormous value; his casual remarks were priceless.

Only aloofness of unusual order, a complete locking in of self and his hatred of conversational necessity, can explain that strange resistance to imparting his knowledge to others. That dislike often lit his witticisms with an amusing ferocity. To a clumsy pupil in counterpoint, in whose primitive two-part exercise in "six notes against one" the multinoted voice had become a garland of neighboring notes, stalking helplessly by the *cantus firmus*, Liadov would say: "Your contrapoint looks like a convict; attached to a chain and unable to take a free step."

An unskillful exercise where the soprano climbed aft to additional staves, and the bass trespassed the lowest lines, Liadov named "a love affair of the flute-piccolo and the contra-bass." A tearful experiment in composition smacking of provincial *Stilleben* he dubbed "Aunt Kitty's sonata," etc.

Humor, both subtle and ferocious, added irresistible personal charm to a nature of exquisite intelligence and artistry, a nature capable, even in its last years, of a singular spiritual growth, gravitating to the subtlest occurrences in new poetry and painting.

Even as a teacher was Liadov marked by rare mental freshness and openness. In spite of professional despotism, in the form of his demand of complete surrender to his teaching methods, there was not a tinge of *Schulmeister*-ship in the quality of his musical taste. That *freedom in slavery* enchanted us: a rigidity strictly limited to school requirements, combined with a grant of liberty to the individual musical viewpoint of the pupils, even when opposed to the excellent art perspective of the teacher. This leeway rendered invaluable the rare talks granted to us by Liadov.

In his own creative life all was fantastic and invisible. His shyness was proverbial. Liadov's timid form hiding behind some column at the première of his works, was unique and unforgetable. Of course, he *never* appeared in acknowledgment of plaudits. The preparation and rehearsing of a new work of Liadov's was always a fantastic affair. Sometimes up to the very last rehearsal one could neither extract the new score and parts from his mysterious hiding-place, nor find the man himself and force him to some explanation of his work. But invariably, at the friendly and copious supper following the public performance thrown together at the last moment, Liadov would place himself at the piano and most willingly and amiably play his work to the conductor, tell him in all detail the meaning of the piece just performed, and how it should have been presented.

I would like to quote here from lines of mine written as a memorial, shortly after Liadov's death: "In our time of musicians—business men, travelers and organizers, deeply concerned in both the performance and the success of their work, how extraordinary and fascinating looms that remote, almost legendary figure of Liadov!

"A famous Russian historian juxtaposes Louis the Ninth (the Saint), the man of the Middle Ages with outmoded ideals, the God-fearing romanticist, to Louis' successors, destroyers, organizers, 'whose hearts echo the wistful voices of the past no more.'

"This is the time of the business man in art. Since our day wants or needs him, there is no use to bewail the fact. But how touching they are, the phantom-figures, those Liadovs, artists of the past!"

*   *

*

I have said that Rimski-Korsakov's and Liadov's school had a tremendous bearing on the new Russian music. Because of them many phases also of the new Western music are clarified, the many features, for example, that we find in Debussy, Ravel, Stravinsky and others. A closer examination of these two masters' teaching principles will illumine many a dark point.

In his essay on Stravinsky Ernest Ansermet remarks: "The teaching of composition in Russia, as far as I can gather from that received by Stravinsky from Rimski-Korsakov, is much more in the spirit of the corporate apprenticeship of the Middle Ages, than is our own teaching, generally of an academic nature." [1]

But it is not quite correct to define the school of Rimski-Korsakov, that is of Liadov also, as essentially a practical one.

I would not wish to appear ungrateful to the cherished shadows of my beloved teachers, to whom I owe much as a composer; but I owe more even to the code of *magis amica veritas*.

It is quite necessary to define as closely as pos-

___

[1] "L'enseignement qu'on donne de la musique en Russie, autant que j'en puis juger par celui que Stravinski a reçu de Rimski-Korsakov, est beaucoup plus dans l'esprit de l'apprentissage corporatif du Moyen Age que l'enseignement academique qui est généralement le notre." *La Revue Musicale*, July, 1921.

sible the true *value of the teaching principles* of Rimski-Korsakov and of his art. But let us immediately note that this has nothing to do with the estimate of the *artistic value* of Rimski-Korsakov's work. His adversaries and would-be detractors are wrong when they confuse the two points. The teaching of Rimski and Liadov was practical in its episodic and exterior part, rather than in its essential lines. Their instruction was indeed based on certain theoretic *principia*, quite inferior and harmful, I regret to say.

These principles were evidently rudiments of those masters' own primitive training in their youth. Having become routined *Gebrauchsformulas*, they were never altered in spite of new artistic experience acquired.

Thus their training in counterpoint was based on the antiquated system of the mid-European levelled major-minor. It was, in essence, the false or substitute counterpoint, that of harmonic passing notes, so well known to many European schools. This sort of training narrows at the very outset the harmonic and polyphonic horizon of the pupil, hides from him the richness of new and inexhaustible polyphonic combinations, all the fresh

240

dissonant chords discoverable in the old modes.

It is even strange that a creator of a strong racial nature, such as Rimski-Korsakov, would lead his academic following in a direction quite opposite to his racial harmonic taste. It is *à propos* to quote the remarkable statement of the eminent British writer, Edwin Evans, pointing to those racial tonal predilections:

"In contemporary music there emerges even a technical aspect of racial division. That form of chromaticism which leads first to tonal ambiguity and finally to atonality, reveals itself more and more as being a tendency congenial to the Teutonic mind. Latins and Slavs alike, whilst availing themselves of extended resources, seem to cling obstinately to the diatonic and modal basis of their music as a means of definition and clarity."

But, of course, when attributing the shortcoming of the Petrograd group, as well as faults described further on, to the Russian school in general, the West makes the mistake of forgetting the Moscow school headed by Tanéyev. His instruction was based on conscious cultivation of modal polyphony, of form and development, which excluded an abuse of sequence and other primitive

241

formal proceedings ingrained through the Petrograd school in Russian music, and even carried into the West. Still, fictitious counterpoint and abuse of the sequence are minor sins of the Petrograd school. Constant use of thematic modification instead of the dissection of themes into segments usable in development, a lack of stress laid on the vital difference in the exploiting of themes or motive-bodies capable of evolution, as opposed to melodic episodes, these are the school's worst shortcomings.

I must add also, that the Petrograd school has perpetuated the "crime" of their forerunner, "The Mighty Handful," in applying without restraint all the set and trite proceedings of Western form building, development, figuration, to the Russian folk-themes, and even to purely Eastern folk-songs, so unamenable to forced "civilized" ornamentation.

Following in the footsteps of my revered masters, I passed through a long period spent in the cultivation of Eastern songs. After much creative experience I have come to the conclusion that the use of folk-songs in large forms will seem the least forced and the least alien to the whole in these three cases: (*a*) when used as fanfares; (*b*) as episodes or *codas*; (*c*) as material for figuration. But even then, the folk-theme must be skilfully modified that it may fit into a large form of universal nature.

* *

*

This analysis of ways typical of the Petrograd *Alma Mater* of the New Russian music, provides more than the just evolved technical and a, so to speak, minor lesson. Important vistas of historical, even of prophetic order, are opened when contemplating the Russian *Alma Mater* from our distant position.

It is evident that the great historic cycle which began with Bach, is at an end. That cycle was based distinctly on a Ptolemaic conception. Visibly, it narrowed down the confines of the tonal universe to a set and limited mid-European musical civilization. The Bach culture and the Bach cycle were essentially scholastic. Our final modern harmonic extracts, ultra-chromaticism and atonality, are in fact the last word of the Ptolemaic, mid-European culture initiated by Bach. We are dwelling now in its æsthetic and creative impasse.

In influencing the West through Stravinsky, Debussy and Ravel, the newer Russians and their *Alma Mater* have already contributed greatly to a Copernican revolution of attitude. They have deflated the universal pretense of mid-European music and have widened our tonal cosmos. The Orient's ever beneficial rôle has been to remind the European West of the damage brought about in universal art, when the conceit of a regional musical culture set up an imaginary universal focus of tone-art.

The real, great East of the mountains, villages and temples, not that of city-lanes and caravansaries, the true great Oriental music is still to be discovered and assimilated by us. Russian influence was only a beginning. We have forgotten that the modal and the melodic root of the entire tonal universe, derives from the ancient village and temple life of the East. In the Orient lies the hope of our liberation from the scholastic, levelled and narrowed tonal thought of mid-European cast. There lies dormant the germ of a reunion of the great musical streams of the Two Worlds.

SCRIABIN AND STRAVINSKY IN REVIEW

IN *Modern Russian Composers* Leonid Sabanéyev, one of Russia's leading critics, has given us a brilliant and subtle book. His gallery of portraits is extensive—it ranges from Alexander Scriabin to Alexander Krein, an outstanding figure in his country today. The strength of this portraiture rests on the excellent and thorough information of a musician who vivisects with a sure hand. Its weakness can also be traced to the fact that Sabanéyev is a musician, and as such, too keen, too interested, too active a protagonist in Russia's musical life.

He is, of course, a partisan, in fact an apostle, perhaps even—*horribile dictu*—the originator of the Scriabin doctrine. He is a defender of the Moscow "old believers" (Tanéyev, Rachmaninov) against the Petrograd group of aggressive modernists (Stravinsky, Miascovski, Prokofiev). In all fairness, however, one must concede that he tries hard to suppress his prejudices, and to give as impartial an appraisal as his fighting temperament permits. So obvious is this that in the chapters on Miascovski and Prokofiev one can almost feel the strain of self-repression.

The most important parts of Sabanéyev's book are naturally taken up with Scriabin and Stravinsky, the creators of the two channels along which the main streams of modern Russian music flows. The Scriabin chapter opens with the remark that in the world of music this composer played the rôle of "drawing-room demon," a man of maniacal self-adoration and pose, a re-incarnated Childe Harold, but with more intensified neurotic and philosophic traits.

However, Scriabin was infinitely more than a drawing-room Mefisto. He was sharply cognizant that he headed the culmination of a great creative era. Boris de Schloezer defines Scriabin's inner stand very closely when he says: "Scriabin possessed the characteristic traits of a revolutionary mentality. A sense of the non-continuity of the historic process; of gaps in the web of Being, of empty spaces that must be leapt over; an apocalyptic expectance of a new earth and a new heaven dominated his mind."

Nonetheless, with his picture Sabanéyev strikes at the real root of Scriabin's creative disabilities: the lack of elemental virility which diminishes Scriabin's human stature. Æsthetically Sabanéyev's image is a misrepresentation. All the themes of Scriabin's *Third Symphony,* called also the *Divine Poem,* particularly those of the introduction and first allegro, are titanesque; they are magnificent thoughts capable of limitless development. Scriabin failed to fulfill their broad range, not because of his philosophic and poetic *remplissage* but because of the inflexible quality of his technical imagination. In his otherwise fresh sonata forms with their extraordinary whirlpool codas, the development is never organic. It does not spring from the theme spontaneously, as the tree from the seed, in the fashion of the Beethoven and Tchaikovsky symphonies. His development is rather rigid clock-work whose little wheels whir along, side by side, with toneless persistence. In almost all the Beethoven and Tchaikovsky symphonies the development is more vital and inspired than the themes themselves, while in Scriabin's larger forms, just the reverse is true.

Sabanéyev's emphasis on Scriabin's harmonic

innovations is another valuable critical contribution, for these are far more stringent and so more vitally important to European tonal conceptions than the harmony of Debussy and even Schoenberg.

In his attitude toward Stravinsky, Sabanéyev is again more just about the man and what one might call his musical ethics than in the appraisal of his creative gift. He is right in his general outlook, but wrong about the individual works. I subscribe to Sabanéyev's assertion that "Stravinsky's fame rests chiefly on his virtuosity in making full use of musical conditions and taking full account of fashions and fads. . . he is a deliberate innovator, deliberately glittering, sharp, shrill voiced, flickering and blinding like electric signs" and that "like Berlioz, he combines genius in the field of color with definite lack of talent in a number of other musical elements, and, like Meyerbeer . . . sells his music for the potage of fame and recognition in his lifetime."

And yet after all, one cannot very well pronounce such torrential music as the *Sacre*, that marvel of invention, color, structural unity, one of Stravinsky's most spontaneous creations, to be merely "the production of a commercial genius."

Here I would take exception to the seemingly reasonable placing of Meyerbeer in the same moral rank with Stravinsky. The innuendo in Heine's "Paris letters" defiling Meyerbeer's pathetic concern for the success of his operas is always repugnant to me. I wonder, how a subtle soul like Heine could miss the touching, the maternal nature of Meyerbeer's worries. How very different is the moral position of a composer who sends presents to his first tenor or to his flute-player, so that they may take better care of their parts, from the ethical level of one who continually changes his creative stand to keep the new consumer interested.

On the whole, Sabanéyev's book is a negative one. Nevertheless, it is admirably vigorous and perspicacious. Perhaps, after all, it is only with negativeness coupled with such intelligence and musicianship, that the very core of human and creative ego can be probed. Surely indignation is a far stronger incitement to thought than the platitude of "constructive criticism."

GNIESSIN, PROKOFIEV AND MIASCOVSKI

EACH of this puissant group, who have passed jointly through the austere school of Liadov and Rimski-Korsakov, is endowed with concise and deep individuality. Prokofiev is an elemental force, a savage cascade compressed by a chain of unicolored rocks. Gniéssin unites in his spirit of a possessed Oriental priest, the sophistication of modernity with a finely archaic turn. Miascovski, of a tensely cultured lineage, is a musical sage, and though a nature full of personal torment, he listens benevolently to both the voice of today and the refrains of the past.

In this group Serge Prokofiev has the advantage of freshness. He is neither gnawed by the expressionist self-analysis of today, nor overburdened with accumulated science like Miascovski.

One could well apply to Prokofiev the wise judgment of Guido M. Gatti passed on Ernest Bloch: "The exceptionality of his speech either with regard to the harmony or to the rhythmic designs, does not strike us as *provoked* (we do not say *designed*) by an excess of refinement and intellectualism, as in many a page by contemporaries, but, as it were, by a primegenial instinct impatient of bonds and conventions. The music of many moderns seems to us beyond the school; that of Bloch, before it." [1]

Prokofiev is satisfied with the direct wisdom of his creative instinct. The latter is proudly manifest in his earlier works, in the youthful exuberance of the *Ugly Duckling*, and in the singular and savage eloquence of the *Scythian Suite*, perhaps Prokofiev's most lasting work.

In this early speech, foaming like an irritated torrent, laconic and free from bequeathed technical habits, is all that is real and attractive in Prokofiev. Leonid Sabanéyev characterizes these and parent traits with admirable precision: "After the solemnities of the immediate past his *naiveté*, freedom from psychological obsession, fresh humor and healthy rhythmic verve were startling. He almost seemed to give music a fresh grant of laughter. This liberty, humor and mocking irreverence lent him an air of rowdyism, of *gaminerie*, which

[1] "Ernest Bloch" by Guido M. Gatti, *Musical Quarterly*, 1921.

was accepted from the beginning as an expression of youthful vigor."

In the middle period of his overstreaming creative life two works, the adorable *Shout* (Buffon) and the cyclopean *Sept, ils sont sept* are distinct recidives of the early, the best Prokofiev. In the later works, such as the ballet *Le fils prodigue* and the *Divertimento*, one finds, however, in spite of Prokofiev's fidel and firm classicism, a somewhat stale and studied simplicity,[2] and a diatonism, less fresh and even less certain than the neoclassic parlance of his youth. To be sure, there is a greater cultural height, a new and delicate wisdom, a new transparency and tenderness in Prokofiev's later music. But do these fit into the singularly definite and elemental racial frame?

The *Classical Symphony* arriving years after the *Scythian Suite*, and the *Le fils prodigue* following after *Shout*, are sorry disgressions. I resent the regeneration of that superb creative cascade, of that supremely individual human compound. I regret the change from angularity and attractive

---

[2] The well known Paris writer-composer Raymond Pétit describes however these qualities as *"une réelle gravité . . . une fantaisie précise et mécanique."*

bumptiousness even, into a well groomed *habitué* of Paris, affected by Greek and other grimaces of the greater and lesser Stravinskys. One wishes Prokofiev's native overpouring freshness, his inborn rhythm, had never been severed, spiritually at least, from the rich race ,to which he owes his self.

* *

*

Gniéssin's creative youth was nurtured by *Tristan,* by Scriabin's poems, by Rimski's *Kastcheï.* One senses these pulsations in the beautiful early song *I Ever Picture the Sea* and in the delicate weaving of the symphonic fragment *After Shelley.* A short transitory spell, strangely uniting fits of neurotic complexity with labored stylistic preciosity, follows. It has given us the provoking *Hymn to the Pest* (from Pushkin's drama) and the cold and wistful *Snowflakes,* one of the most elevated and finest in Russian song literature.

The long period of the later Gniéssin, the period begun with his music to Euripides' *Phœnician Women* and with the poem for voice and orchestra *Wrubel,* crystallized the pantheistic pathos, the solemn Hebraic accent, the strange, singularly individual exaltation, which one had already sensed in his early songs. The dual spiritual parentage of Michael Gniéssin is now manifest: the visions and tonal tales of archaic Russia as embodied in Rimski's *Kastcheï*, and the cabalistic dreams of illustrious Lithuanian rabbis, professing a pantheistic creed akin to Giordano Bruno and the neoplatonian dogmas.

In Gniéssin's later songs like *Rachel's Tomb* or *Laron, laron, velaron* (On the Heights) there is a radiant and transparent solemnity and a feast-like, sacramental Hebraism, compared with which Ernest Bloch's Hebraic parlance sounds crude, provincial. This priestly luminousness raises Gniéssin's biblical fervor to an Hellenic elevation. Once again it seems that Russian Hebraism may be nearer to Hellenic order than any other European spiritual trend.

* *

*

Miascovski is a somber and fastidious spirit propelled by stark impulses, even storms of restlessness, a spirit avid to translate into music the delirium of Edgar Allan Poe, of Shelley and of Maeterlinck.

One of the most brilliant Russian musicians of

today, Igor Gliébov, portrays Miascovski's psychic color in a way that makes one shudder: "The main trait of Miascovski's music is its utter darkness: a gray, awesome autumnal darkness transmuted into a moonless night, a tenebrious blackness. The power and action of this music come from its dynamic idiom, which one could describe as a state of anxiety of various degrees and colorings: from timorous apprehension, to dread of the immobility of nature, of its terrifying silence and menace."

Miascovski's personal creative medium is a strange amalgam of lyric and Slavic traits, in kinship with Tchaikovsky and Rachmaninov, with purely European and radical technical predilections. He is a fervent adherent of Scriabin, Schoenberg and Debussy, and he wrote of them revealingly. He is an erudite musical thinker and a contrapuntist of excellence. It is remarkable how his creative self combines purely feminine features in its expression, features so typical of a Slavic mentality, with energy and virile economy in the formal casting. However, even his wistful contemplation reaches at times the pressure of a masculine poignancy and despair. In his noble songs *Uniformity* or *The Moon and the Mist* or in the symphonic poem *Alastor*, for example, one unveils the somewhat dormant virile powers of Miascovski, mainly in his formal invention and building.

His tonal thought is not free from a strange lyric facility which is often, as in Mahler's case, inflated to the point of facile emotionalism. The blemishes in Miascovski's early *Second Symphony* and those of the late *Reminiscences* op. 29 for piano (particularly the fourth piece) are of this nature. However, there is more of a spiritual concentration in Miascovski's smaller forms, such as his *Third Piano Sonata* or the songs I have mentioned.

In his *Eighth Symphony* he suddenly, but for a short time, turns to the populist tonal line of the Russian national school. One finds a succession of diatonic spells, oases of transparency, and brisk Moussorgski squalls in portions of that symphony. But Miascovski's inborn cosmopolitanism exerts its grip even here. Already the second theme of the first movement, a very noble line in itself, has a racial and even a spiritual vagueness. And when his *Ninth Symphony* begins its flow with a somberly meditative Lisztian motive and then deploys a tumultuous *Mefisto-walzer*-like figuration as the *allegro* theme, one feels that Miascovski of this music, not the one of the nationalist pastiche, is the real self.

Like Stravinsky, he is a leader of Russian cosmopolites. If nothing else, his Occidental dynamism and radical predilections make this certain.

THE LATEST RUSSIANS

THE younger creative lights of new Russia can be placed in three well defined groups. First, personalities of unusual gift and cast, the geniuses as it were. Then, the theoreticians and ideologists of the new Russian currents, those who contribute to revolution by both deed and word, sometimes more by the latter. The third, an overrun class, comprises the young Russians of uncommon gift and merit who without creating any particular disturbances in the new music of Russia still form its true yeast and dough. They are now building up its body with perhaps greater assurance and solidity than both the ecstatic and the learned ones.

In a country whose insularity and traditionalism are so deeply rooted that they stem and discolor even revolutionary tides, it is not so much the creative force that counts as the spiritual uncommonness, the human size and color.

* *

*

Among the names entirely unknown to the Great West, I deem it indispensable first to mention the twenty-two-year-old Alexeï Stantchinski, though he has now passed on. During the war he was found drowned in a lake near Moscow, after a passionate dispute with his innamorata, a beautiful peasant girl. This young boy, an extraordinary genius, could have hewn a new channel for Russian musical thought, a course on a par with those fashioned by Scriabin and Stravinsky.

Blessed with a much greater nervous force and impetus than Stravinsky, and with even more freshness and whim than Prokofiev, he was also infinitely more the true son of Russia.

The child of a mad peasant-musician, Stantchinski became a student at the Moscow Conservatory, a pupil of the great contrapuntist and theoretician, Sergei Tanéyev and of Professor Giliayev. Later he was singled out for his talent by the eminent critic, Leonid Sabanéyev, of Moscow.

Stantchinski left a great number of works, all for piano. In his second sonata both the themes and the exposition breathe a virginal freshness, a freedom coupled with enchanting, fastidious diatonic harmony. But into this exhilarating tonal atmosphere Stantchinski's fancy sends now and then rays of sharp-edged chromatic successions which are quite unusual.

In Julian Krein we approach another extraordinary figure. His age—he was born in 1913 in Moscow—his creative *stage* (an opera, a symphony, a piano concerto, two quartets, several sonatas and suites for various instruments, an endless list of piano works), and the fact that conductors such as Koussevitski, Monteux and Stokowski favored and have already presented his works, has brought this frail, melancholy boy within the circle of the world's attention.

Reared in the intense musical atmosphere of the Krein family, a well known dynasty of Moscow musicians, and thus having such extraordinary and natural teachers as his father, Gregory Krein and his uncle Alexander Krein, both composers and men of remarkable personality, young Julian became a competent and sure musician at an age when most boys begin to be less interested in their toy horses. At four Julian played the piano and was able to repeat with the precision of a phonograph a prelude of Chopin or Scriabin after his father had played it three or four times. He was composing at six; the Universal Edition in Vienna published his works written at the age of eight.

But even knowing this, one is struck by his technical freedom and precocity, by his extraordinarily competent use of voice and instruments, by the amazing sureness of his writing.

His creative idiom is, of course, still derivative; one would expect this from a mere boy. Nevertheless it assumes now and then individual coloring.

One cannot deny that Julian Krein's music has well known traits of *wunderkind* composers of the Korngold type, namely the dangerous facility, the technical genius prevailing over a conscious and critically controlled mastery. There is in Krein's music a prematurely old, *altklug* expression, a languid hothouse precocity, a certain monotony and sameness due very likely to the leveling atmosphere of three Kreins living together.

But in some of Julian Krein's songs, like the delectable *Hebrew Song*, in his sonnet *Mon Pays* with its naïve gravity, and in the toccata and finale of his suite for cello and piano, enchantingly

261

alert and whimsical, there are strains of an unusual personality *in statu nascenti.*

The very appearance of this morose and frail youth is convincing; there is a ray of genius in its somber repudiation of life, in its boyish austerity.

Another composer of unusual gift and individuality, like Stantchinski, omitted from all reference books and biographies, is Moses Milner of Leningrad, author of an opera, *The Flaming Heaven,* of many songs and choruses.

Born near Kiev, in southern Russia, Milner started his career as a pianist wonder-child and boy chorister in a synagogue choir conducted by an eminent Kiev musician, critic and conductor, Abram Dzimitrovski, now director of the Russian division of the Universal Edition in Vienna.

Milner grew to be the François Villon of Russian music, a fascinating vagabond in life and art. He moved along the immense highways in ever-changing capacities such as accompanist, opera conductor, choir leader in synagogues, arranger or musical adviser in dramatic theaters. Still, he snatched instruction here and there from prominent musicians or his own comrades.

Milner is a creative force of the first order, very much akin to Moussorgski. He resembles the latter in melodic and dramatic power, but also in technical debilities. He is possessed by the same moving and frenzied humility of an almost ascetic pitch, but also he is weakened by the conceit of an "autodidact," of a self-made man.

This strange, pathetic personage has created songs of lasting beauty, such as *El Hatzipor* (To a Bird), Bialik's poem, and *Tanz, tanz, Meidele, tanz* (Dance, dance, little girl).

These three figures, Stantchinski, Julian Krein and Milner, mirror some of Russia's submerged creative streams, untamed, immense and manifold to absurdity.

* *
*

Quite different characters represent New Russia's sizzling art doctrines, with their conscious shaping of the revolutionary path, which is still largely thought rather than actual music.

This second group is composed of theoreticians and ideologists; among them Nicolai Roslavietz and Joseph Schillinger are the most prominent.

Roslavietz is perhaps the keenest and most original mind among the modern Russian radicals.

It is curious that this sophisticated musician and thinker should be a peasant *pur sang*, his parents being former serfs and he himself a shepherd boy up to the age of twelve. A happy turn of destiny then sent Roslavietz to a provincial music school. Later he became a student in violin and composition classes at the Moscow Conservatory and won its *grand prix* for a cantata based on Byron's *Heaven and Earth*. Already while at the conservatory he was disliked for radicalism.

He rid himself of the conservatory prescriptions very quickly. As early as in 1913 he formulated his own æsthetic and creative principles and applied them to his first violin sonata and his first songs.

Roslavietz's thought took at once the direction of replacing the obsolete classic tonality by the idea of "tonal unity." Thus he links up all his six- and eight-voiced "synthetic chords" which cover the immense variety of harmonies inherited by us and those created today.

This system has some kinship with both the Scriabin and the Schoenberg harmonic innovations, although Roslavietz's ideas were conceived independently and have important individual points.

From his harmonic foundation he evolved several years ago a peculiar system of voice leading and a new polyphony which led to his "tonal organization."

Whatever the direct and creative value of Roslavietz's music is, one must admit its implacable logic and also its remarkable kinship with the fighting principles of our time, its objectivity and its destruction of music's emotional lining.

However, Roslavietz criticizes today's music in a very stringent way. He describes it as a state of "impressionistic-expressionistic anarchy." He dubs it an impasse where "rickety neoclassicism" draws nourishment from "two mothers, the yesterday" and the "today," and seeks their synthesis.

Failing this, we throw ourselves into "barbarism" and whirl along the fateful circle—"from Debussy to the Negro."

Roslavietz sees the future not in "radicalizing" the past or in co-ordinating the new with the past. The future lies in the formation of a new tonal logic which will organize our tonal riches.

Leaving Roslavietz's doctrines aside, one finds in his music individuality and independent invention. His harmony is quite unusual. If there is in the pathos of his music a relatedness to Scriabin, and if there is in the neat logic of his harmonic scaffoldings a suggestion of Schoenberg (the third string quartet and the two piano poems of Roslavietz), neither is imitation or epigonism. Roslavietz's music is full of a very peculiar and attractive intelligence of its own.

In Joseph Schillinger we have a mind of different cast and temperament. Its character is very typical of the Petrograd school, which is less radical and doctrinaire, more practical, more interested in actual art making than the Moscow school.

Joseph Schillinger, born in 1895 in Kharkov, Ukraine, a graduate of the Petrograd Conservatory, author of a symphonic rhapsody, *Octiabre*, of a violin sonata, many songs and piano pieces, quickly attained the leading position of professor of composition in the State Musical Institute in Petrograd. He lectured at the Institute of Art History and was also one of the chief officers of the State Commission of Modern Music.

The constructive principles which Schillinger

has evolved and applied to his composition, notably to his aggressively "proletarian" sonata-rhapsody for piano, are of much interest.

They are somewhat related to the Stravinsky idea of the new sonata, whose development is dialectic—*i. e.*, based on purely tonal and dynamic difference between the themes or motives.

This is opposed to Beethoven's dramatic method, where the conflict generating the development arises from the emotional differences between the main motives.

However, Schillinger puts not only a more catholic meaning into his "dialectic unfolding of the thematic material," but embraces also the dramatic method. He also clearly defines the nature and relationship of all thematic elements. This material he lists as organic and mechanic. The organic element is based on folk-melos and dance rhythms; the mechanic element, on rhythms of machines. These are linked by man who is dominated by the organic stratum, on one hand, and on the other, is himself ruling the mechanic one. The struggle of these media creates the development in Schillinger's form and defines its character.

Despite the rationalism of these art tendencies,

267

Schillinger's works are by no means deprived of elemental stress and abandon. In his songs, *Orientalia,* written under the influence of the primitive airs of Transcaucasia, one finds an attractive melodic and emotional turn. This remarkable fusion of a sober and highly cultured meditation with an understream of Oriental sensibility is the outstanding trait of Schillinger.

* *

*

Russia's insularity, even more underlined now by political and spiritual isolation, plus typical Slavic racial inertia, is likely to keep Russia's new music in old channels for a long time yet. So far, her social cataclysm has not been able to produce a marked repercussion in her music.

As I have said, Russia's musical revolution is still in doctrines more than in action. The new music, when of any value, is, through and through, individualistic, *à la Russe.* The attempts to make musical creation conform to the Communist creed are so far flabby and unsuccessful artistically. They are usually undertaken by mediocrities whose only chance lies in commercializing revolution in music.

There is still a strong academic strain in new Russian music. It struggles to rid itself of the "Korsakovstchina," "Glazounovstchina," "Tanéyevstchina," of that crushing system of art morals, prescriptions and creative routine inherited from the great teachers, (Rimski-Korsakov, Glazounov and Tanéyev). Their regime still petrifies the young Russian thought not a little.

The very type and form of musical expression inherited from the old academies is slowly giving way, alas, to no fresher thing than impressionistic tendencies or the metamorphosis of Scriabin's mysticism.

Another important factor in the picture of new Russian music is the struggle for Scriabin's supremacy; it is still going on. This contention is not so much in opposition to Stravinsky's influence, almost negligible in Russia itself, as to the western European waves, to Schoenberg, Hindemith, the younger Frenchmen, etc.

But perhaps the greatest difficulty that the young builders have to overcome, is the real curse of modern Russian music, its spiritual and technical provincialism, an outcome of obstinate isolation and academism. One may reply that in our

era of the domination of capitals with their snobbery, provincialism of spirit might prove to be a
blessing. However, *technical* provincialism is indisputably a blemish, a sore and pitiful burden.

*   *

*

Having in mind the handicaps of the younger
Russians one marvels at the buoyant stream of
their creative activity, at the variety and color of
their talents. Among the most attractive and
gifted younger composers of today, Russia's daily
workers, so to speak, who form our third and most
active group, I would list Alexandre Mossolov,
Dimitri Shostakovitch, Vassili Shirinski, Vissarion
Shebalin, Alexandre Veprik and Liév Polovinkin.
Almost all of them are pupils and some are
ardent disciples of Miascovski, whose austere
school, great musicianship and great personality
fairly dominate the modern movement.

Alexandre Mossolov, a Ukrainian who studied
and lived almost all of his life in Moscow, has revealed an energetic and individual talent in his
string quartet, which had an exceptional success
at the Frankfurt Festival of Modern Music in 1927.
An excellent pianist, he appeared in concerts very

often. His list of works is striking in its abundance and variety and what is more important, in its inventiveness. Beside five piano sonatas we find a sonata for voice without words and piano. Mossolov's string quartet is supplemented by four cadenzas and a coda played *ad libitum*, a delightful spark of improvisation within a rigid form. A symphonic episode for orchestra, *The Steel Mill* (at last something linked with Communist industry!), tone pictures for piano, *Nights in Turkestan*; interesting chamber orchestra combinations, an opera, *The Hero*, all point to a mind never contented with ordinary subjects.

It is true that even in Mossolov's best works, like the second piano sonata, we find again that typical Russian weakness, the thinking in sequences, and also a harmonic radicalism of somewhat naïve and facile nature. But we see also a green boldness and personal vigor which are enticing. The Parisian professors of polytonality would profit by a glance at the first page of Mossolov's second sonata, by seeing how music built on very unsophisticated polytonal segments can be made vibrant and compelling.

The very young Shostakovitch, who was born,

studied and lived all his life in Leningrad, is the author of five symphonies, of many piano works and of a comic opera, *The Nose* (after Gogol), staged in Moscow and Leningrad.

The most promising qualities of Shostakovitch are a youthful verve, a temperament that in his age is allowed to pass for individuality. There is an unpleasant facility, almost a technical braggadocio in his string octet, Op. 11. But this is evidently a passing fault, since there is less evidence of it in his admirable *Second Symphony*, a gleeful and virile work.

Vassili Shirinski, a Cossack from North Caucasia, born in a family of musicians, is also an excellent violinist and member of well-known Russian quartets who have concertized with great success in Russia and Germany. This accounts for his thought being given mainly to string ensembles. He is a strong technician, far above the ordinary. His harmony, involved, highly seasoned and cerebral, does not leave, however, the chromatic paths. Precocity and neurotic pretence mar his songs, *The Lily*, for instance. His violin sonata is labored along the Scriabinesque pattern. With all this, Shirinski is a man of excellent culture, a good writer on music, a propagandist of Hindemith. He has written valuable articles on the new forms in modern chamber music.

Vissarion Shebalin was born in Omsk, central Siberia, in 1902, lived and studied music and agriculture there up to 1923; then he migrated to Moscow and became at once Miascovski's pupil and most fanatical follower. In his two symphonies, string quartets and numerous songs we find a talent of undeniable vigor; its development is rapid and uncommon.

In Shebalin's second string quartet everything is of rather an ordinary nature; a very adequate and neat technique of the Miascovski type, a quasi-elegant melodic line, somewhat melancholy and gray, à la Tchaikovsky, symmetric, well ironed forms. But in his later songs from the cycle *Podorojnik,* the harmony grows so fresh of nature and so personal, his ornamentation acquires such an exquisite tonal aroma that we notice no more the emotional grayness. Shebalin belongs already and indisputably in the really "new" Russian art; his music truly looks forward and is of a fresh current.

Alexandre Véprik, of Moscow, after study with

Max Reger and Janacek, passed also through the magnificent Miascovski school and was under its strong influence. Véprik's is a talent of exceptional strength and character. In two piano sonatas, suites for viola and piano, and songs, Véprik reveals a driving vitality and a racial color of unusual nature. His excellent *Dance*, Op. 13, for piano is full to overflowing of elemental temperament and harmonic imagination, vital and vibrant.

In Liév Polovinkin's ballet *The Little Negro and the Ape*, and in his incidental music to a comedy, *Sirocco*, is seen something of the Poulenc quality, a microscopic and cloying musical thought and a quasi-classical, labored simplicity. Some of Polovinkin's piano pieces and songs are of the same sort.

But in the delightful *Berceuse* for piano, there lurks something finer and more deeply rooted, a very intimate lyricism resembling the later Prokofiev. The other pieces from the same opus are impregnated with youth and force. And when one reads the delectable, lively songs of Polovinkin, one realizes that he is typical of Russia resurrected. He symbolizes the understream of its folk-melos newly mounting to the art thought of modern Russian youth, a phenomenon so strongly represented in Prokofiev.

I wish to mention also a highly interesting gift, almost entirely unknown, and coupled with a personality of charm and promise. I speak of a very young woman, a Leningrad composer-pianist, Viéra Vinogradova, who, in an imposing list of works including a piano concerto, a *Ballade* for piano and chamber orchestra, a string quartet, a suite for violin and piano and numerous smaller works, has shown not only an outstanding creative ability, but also an excellent technical equipment, far above any possessed by even the best women composers.

Viéra Vinogradova is a pupil of Leonid Nicoláyev and Maximilian Steinberg, of the Leningrad Conservatory. She is an admirable pianist and has played in Russia, Germany, France and the Baltic States. In her own music an engaging verve, a sure technical grasp, a clear-cut thematic line are combined with a feminine delicacy and emotion of individual touch.

* *
*

In spite of his being forever transplanted to the Western World, Alexandre Tcherepnin must not be eliminated from a description of the younger Russian forces. He has lost nothing of either, intensely Russian technical training or purely and passionately Russian ideology.

His spiritual self bears a striking likeness to that of Liadov's; it exhales a bewitching softness and stillness of an Oriental prince-thinker. His music is that of a hermit. It has a spiced, a stifling undertone of the cell and the hot-house; it cries for wind and riotous sunbeams. But in the delicately and unostentatiously sharp sonority of Tcherepnin's tonal address, in his forms, conceived by a mind of unusual intelligence, there is a relief from the shouting in our ears, beloved tonal game of our day.

Tcherepnin is too prolific and facile. But even this fault has a redeeming touch: creative honesty keeps him from an obvious manufacturing of newness.

However, of his numerous works the *Quintet,* op. 44, contains pages of temperamental might coupled with sparks of unusual formal and rhythmic thought. His *Symphony,* op. 43, is always

276

remembered by that nobly whimsical two-part *melopée* of the horn and trumpet, which opens the second movement. His *Georgian Rhapsody* for cello and orchestra is full of extraordinary detail, such as using only the rhythmic frames of Caucasian folk songs and building his own, composed themes over those rhythmic lines.

Tcherepnin's remarkable technical ideas, such as his *intrapoint* (punctum intra punctum), voices drawn from within the theme and used as contrapositions; his interesting harmonic system based on a nine-step scale of a distinctly Eurasian nature, as well as his adherence to Asia, the motherland of self-contemplation, disturb interestingly the soft charm of this musician, so unusual and yet so Russian.

The pious professors of the Court Chapel in Saint Petersburgh, who mothered Nicolai Berezowsky, another gifted expatriate, would scarcely recognize their former student. From a typical adherent of the Russian academic school and worshiper of Glazunov, Berezowsky has developed, during his two decades of very active life in America, into a thorough modern musician, capable of using every fine point of contemporary craft.

277

It is, perhaps a pity that the excellent artistic qualities of this typical Slavic nature, are sturdier than his racial expression. For his three symphonies and numerous chamber works reveal a sensitive musical nature and an innate craft both elegant and resourceful, which could have served a wider aim, than a still newer form for well-groomed eclectic art.

As to Vladimir Dukelsky, author of several symphonies and ballets of international reputation, his strange creative existence is split and confused by periodical re-incarnations into Vernon Duke, composer of music-hall "hits".

His drama is three-fold. Very Russian, he is forced to be a cosmopolite. Conservative by nature, he is forced to comply with the up-to-date. But his worst struggle is that of Vladimir Dukelsky with Vernon Duke. Incidentally, such a drama was also George Gershwin's.

I do not think that these musical Jekyll-Hydes are so by choice, that they swim in either channel at will, with cool deliberation. After all, real creative passion, like sexual urge, is strong and irresistible, sweeps everything before it, certainly the temptation of material gains cropping up in the lighter musical fields.

No, such duality must come from some basic crack in the inmost corner of the creative being, from a lack of wholeness or oneness in it, not from weakness for worldly goods alone.

But through this odd confusion, a nature finely endowed, subtly intelligent and attractive, lurks in Dukelsky's best pages, in the very early, boyish *Gondla* as well as in the riper cantata *The End of Saint Petersburgh.*

MUSIC OF THE RUSSIAN ORIENT

SOUTHEASTERN Europe or rather the extreme southwestern corner of Asia, has been the birthplace of a most valuable folk-music all but unknown to the Western world. We have scarcely an idea of the remarkable Caucasian melodies—Georgian and Armenian,—nor do we surmise the originality of the Hebrew Georgian chant.

Those who know Caucasian music through the vulgar medium of Oriental orchestras or through amateur presentation by Caucasian students of European universities, are astonished and moved when they encounter a true specimen of Caucasian melody, that of the mountains and villages.

I recall vividly my keen impression of an exquisite air I heard on the mountain of St. David, near Tiflis, the capital of Georgia and of all Transcaucasia. That air, touchingly sung by an Armenian *ashug* (folk-singer) who accompanied himself with a local instrument, was a sort of rhapsody set in strophes, in pure Frigian mode. I still remember its adorable refrain:

There rose in my memory the verse of a Russian poet, Polonsky, addressed to a famed olden time singer of Tiflis:

> Sattar! Sattar! Thy savage plaints,
> Thy guttural, dull cry
> And those trebles of thy *tchianour,*
> They have rent my heart.

A scientific survey of both, the loftier types of Caucasian music and of the other Russian-Oriental musical folk-lore, reveals extraordinary pages of history concerned with the activity of valiant nations and ancient standard-bearers of culture, like the old Georgians and Armenians. As early as the first centuries A.D. these two races formed the vanguard of Christendom and stemmed the ferocious waves of Persians, Arabs and Mongols, barring their march toward the Eastern Roman Empire and Europe.

* *
*

Of the Caucasian folk-songs, the least articulate are those of the Transcaucasian Tartars. The songs of this people are greatly inferior, both melodically and emotionally, to the music of the Tartars of Crimea. This is to be explained by the admixture of the Genoese and Venetian settlers who colonized Crimea in the Middle Ages, intermarried with the Tartars and formed a very beautiful and musical race, the present Tartars of the Crimea.

However, the folk-song of the Transcaucasian or the Azerbeidjan Tartars, debris of musically primitive Mongol tribes originating in middle Asia, though inarticulate melodically, possesses some peculiar rhythmic traits.

It is interesting to note here that the songs of the Volga Tartars and of other Mongol tribes of Eastern Russian and of the Ural Mountains, such as the Bashkirs or the Kalmouks, have a much subtler melodic and emotional content.[1] But what is more important, their ancient primitive polyphony, with its embryos of imitation and unison cadences, and even the melodic structure has un-

---

[1] See S. Rybakov, *Music and Songs of the Ural Moslems*, published by the Academy of Science, Petrograd, 1897, also my *Songs of the Russian Orient*, published by the Universal Edition, Vienna.

doubtedly influenced the folk music of the Great Russians, that is, the racial and tonal source of the art of Glinka, Moussorgski and Rimski-Korsakov.

The songs of Georgia and Armenia present, beyond doubt, the most developed type of Transcaucasian musical folk-lore. Georgia's political sovereignty, culture and written literature date from early Christian times. Georgian music was highly developed at a very early period. While other Christian nations, such as the Byzantine Greeks, for instance, had hardly mastered primitive harmony (the *hysson* or the West European *organum,* with one voice in motion forming the counterpoint to a sustained note), the Georgians had created a veritable three-part folk-polyphony of which the inner voice, highly developed and ornate, was named *modzachili.* A study of ninth, tenth and eleventh century notation shows that musical science and other elements of a solid culture had already come to life. The tenth century, the Georgian Renaissance, epoch of King David the Restorer, witnessed a methodical gathering of the religious chants of Georgia by Saint Michael Modrekili, one of the mighty builders of Georgian music. Another great age follows, that of cruel

Queen Tamara and of her troubadour, the greatest Georgian poet, Shota Rustaveli, author of the poem *Legend of the Leopard's Skin,* the national epic of Georgia.

Then an endless era of bloody invasions by the Mongolians and Genghis-Khan, Persians and Turks set in. Finally, during the nineteenth century, Russia forced Georgia to a union and to an assimilation of Russian culture. Beginning only with the present epoch have Georgian musicians tried to save their native songs from oblivion, to publish and to develop them into works of art.

* *

*

Among the most interesting Georgian tribal songs are those of the *Huri* tribe of Western Georgia situated near the southeastern shores of the Black Sea, and the *Svan* melodies sung by the inhabitants of Svanetia, the high mountain plains of Eastern Georgia which are buried in snows and inaccessible most of the year. The *Huri* songs possess a richness of intonation, a most original and savage, natural three-part polyphony with fantastic and sudden inner pedals, in the form of whimsical ostinatos.

The *Svan* airs are even more austere and barbaric. Voices of a belligerent and half-pagan tribe, always at war with their feudal princes and with their neighbors, Circassians and Ossiétins, these songs have a unique heroic gravity of utterance. Even their funeral dirges end in a warlike hymn named *Zari*, sung by two male choruses. One of their most original songs, *O Sabréla Namkhsur Djatchvlian* is an echo of their struggle with the oppressor, a Moslem prince, Islam Dadeshkeliani, of the fifteenth century. The pure Hypodoric structure of the song, its rhythm, also the accompaniment entrusted to a folk-string instrument named *chunir*, are as curious as are the words:

"Woe to me, the unhappy Namkhsur Djatchvlian! I live in the valley of Ladrari; Prince Islam presses hard upon me. I have lost my children; I have taken refuge behind steep rocks. . . . Saddle my steed! I shall mount my old cat and ride unto far countries."

* *

*

Armenian religious chants have been known since the fifth century A.D. These chants named *shar* (an ancient Semitic word corresponding to the Hebrew *shir*—song) were gathered into ecclesiastical collections named *charakan* or *charaknotz* by Fathers of the Armenian Church, Saint Saak and Saint Mesrop and by the famous Armenian historian, Moses of Choren. This compiling lasted from the fifth to the eighth century; the collection corresponds to the publication of the Gregorian antiphonaries by the Western church. The ancient Armenian chant, a sort of ornate recitative or cantillation, was sung in the former manner of the old Western church, by following special signs or neumes placed over the sacred text. The Armenians name their neumes *khaz*.

This cantillation was carefully deciphered and printed in the form of musical notes by the Patriarch-Catholicoss Kevork IV, head of the Armenian church and nation, in the nineteenth century. These chants were later harmonized by Makar Ekmalian and, together with newly collected and cultivated folk-songs of the Caucasian and Turkish Armenians, form the basis of Armenian national music. Of the new Armenian composers, the monk, Father Komitas Vardapet, a former choirmaster of the Patriarch's residence in Etchmiadzin,

286

and a musician of extraordinary subtlety, has harmonized and developed some of the most ravishing of Armenian folk-songs. He has handled them in a manner and with a mastery not surpassed even in Rimski-Korsakov's and Liadov's famous harmonization of Russian folk-songs, nor in Ravel's similar work with Hebrew and Greek songs, nor in Manuel de Falla's transcription of Spanish folk-airs.[2]

The Armenian folk-songs belong to three main melodic and rhythmic types. The most elementary of the dance-song type is often built on the banal Oriental scale, Frigian with the augmented third. The love and wedding songs have a more developed form and melodic line; the finer kind is often a Hypodoric modal structure. Yet the loftiest and best preserved specimen of old Armenian folk-song is to be found in the isolated mountaineer settlements near Ararat, on the lake of Van, in the district Kochb near Erivan, and in other such remote repositories of original Armenian melos.

Among the tribes of Transcaucasia we find an-

[2] Père Komitas' collections are published in Paris by the Armenian Folk-Song Society.

287

other extraordinary ethnic unit, a creator or rather "curator" of a most original religious music. The Georgian Jewish tribe, which in all probability filtered through Asia Minor after the Babylonian and other invasions of Palestine, has preserved the beautiful heroic Hebrew of the Bible. In every other way they have assimilated the usages of the Georgians, their dress, habits of life, even their physical traits. But the domestic music, dance and wedding tunes in some measure, and the religious music particularly, has kept intact its utterly individual and ancient melodic line. It has kept its modal structure, Hypodoric and Lydian, often penthatonic, and also its short diapason. The cantillation of the Bible by the Georgian Jews contains fragments of extraordinary beauty: such is the cantillation of the "Songs of Songs" of King Solomon.[3]

The folk-song of the Russian Orient with its melodic and structural freshness, with its seminal power, should have become a basis of a new musical culture. Some of these songs have been yeast in

[3] This chant, as well as other Georgian and Armenian songs of rare beauty, form part of my *Songs of the Russian Orient*, published by the Universal Edition, Vienna.

the growth of Russian music. They have served such immense creative spirits, as Glinka in his *Ruslan and Ludmila* (in the exquisite Ratmir aria, for instance), and Moussorgski, in his vigorous cantata, *Joshua, the Son of Nun,* based on a Jewish chassidic melody. Balakireff, Rimski-Korsakov, Borodin, Rubinstein—all have found a creative impetus in the many songs of the Russian Oriental tribes. It is evident that no race exists but whose folk-song can be transmuted into a jewel of cultured art.

However, scientific deductions remain to be drawn from the history and the analysis of the musical folk-lore created by the "minor" races of Russia. A close study would be eminently profitable for musical science. Most stubborn conventions, even the foundation of European musical æsthetics, so much of it now under fire by the new music, could be shaken.

* *

*

I. First of all, one finds certain striking resemblances in the structure of these folk-songs of peoples which, at a first glance, seem to have no racial relationship, no community of ideas, no close intercourse, nor historical bonds of culture.

A large number of Georgian folk-songs, such as the traditional religious chants of Georgia, consist of a *natural polyphony,* which differs from the ordinary, non-polyphonic structure of Oriental songs. These chants often close with unison cadences, as in the Greater-Russian songs. (See *Benedice Animam Meam.*)

The embryos of polyphony and the unison cadences found in the songs of some of the Mongol tribes of the Ural Mountains, of which I have already spoken, form a most interesting link between the Great Russian and the Georgian music. But, of course, early Western influences must be also considered.

Another meaningful circumstance is a similarity which exists between some inferior types of the folk-music of the Orient—for example, between the Jewish wedding melodies constructed on the popular Oriental scale (Phrygian, with the major third) and the Armenian melodies beloved by the folk-orchestras of Transcaucasia and their folk-singers, the *ashugs.*

I will cite an example of this kind, taken from the collection of Armenian folk-songs compiled by A. Ter-Ghévondian and Spiridon Mélikian, contemporary Armenian composers.

This resemblance, as in the first case, may be explained by a certain *neutralization of melody,* that deforms in a vulgar way the *wandering* type of Oriental song beloved of these peoples. From similar causes the same poetic motive or narration is found in a neutralized form in such divergent sources as the Hindoo book of tales, *Kalila and Dimna,* Petronius' *Cœna Trimalchionis,* and the Russian folk-tales of the sixteenth century.

Still more surprising and not easily accounted for, is the similarity noted between the purer and evidently more ancient type of Armenian song, and the traditional religious melody of the Jews. Compare, for instance, the well-known synagogue song *Kol Nidré* with certain Armenian religious chants.

But most striking is the fact, that several of the beautiful specimens of Armenian folk-song are

291

constructed in the same manner as the most perfect type of Jewish song, on the Hypodorian scale, which was equally a favorite with other ancient peoples.

The solution of these riddles is possibly to be found in an analysis of the ancient psalmody, Scriptural chants and neumes, that have been employed by the Hebrews and the Armenians since ancient times.

Then, we must investigate the question in connection with the whole problem of Semitic culture. The famous authority on Caucasian race subjects, Dr. N. Marr, President of the Academy of Material Culture in Leningrad, considers the folksongs and religious chants of Transcaucasia to be connected with the religious cult of the ancient Orient, and not to have derived from Aryan or Semitic sources, but from the so-called Japhetic one, that particular race which has bequeathed to humanity so many marvelous monuments. Dr. Marr holds that Armenians, Celts and also the ancient Scythians belong to the Japhetic race.

In any case, a comparative analysis of the origins of Armenian and Oriental Semitic music may to a certain extent be enlightening. I am of the opinion, formed after a tour of Syria and Palestine, that Armenian songs contain elements of a purely Arab and Arabo-Persian origin. One sees at a glance that the Caucasian songs contain definite characteristics of Arab melody and rhythm. Here the Arabian antecedents are as evident as the lexic roots of some Caucasian family names. (Amilachvari, a princely Georgian name, is nothing but the Arabic *amir al achvar,* master of the horse, corresponding to the Western *connétable,* constable, that is, count of the stable.) Just as the Ural-Mongol and Caucasian Mongol link may explain points of similarity in some of the Great Russian and Georgian folk-harmonies, so a most unexpected link, though one of unmistakable origin, is to be found which elucidates the similarity of the Armenian and Hebrew songs. I recall the poignant Mozarabic chants. One still hears a metamorphosis of them in the Cathedral of Toledo or in that extraordinary Visigoth Toledan chapel, Christo la Veja, with its ancient Templar breath.

All this indeed signifies an Arab source common to Armenian and Jewish song of the neutralized Oriental type. It may not include the most ancient kind of Hebrew melody. The cantillation of the Bible whose modal and even melodic structure, often pentatonic, is more archaic and dates to very early sources, is rather itself the source of early Christian music.

II. Further observation of the music of the southern Russian peoples and of the Caucasians, upsets the notions of natural polyphony and of the natural scales, that have been gradually fostered by European musical history, and which conceivably influenced the Western aural instinct.

The most admirable phenomenon of this kind is the Georgian folk-song. Some of the Georgian folk-songs present a natural three-part harmony, the progressions of which often consist of consecutive fifths and triads. Below is a very characteristic folk-dance obtained by the composer Dimitri Arakichwili from among the *Ratchines,* inhabitants of Imeretia, in Western Georgia.

The words of this dance-song are curious. "Digori and Bassiani (two villages) are full of *tcherkesski* and *bourki* (Circassian costumes and overcoats). The river Quedroula has discharged its waters and carried away the mountains and valleys; it has swept away the cart-house and the barn with its grain."

"I would not be the River, if I did not destroy everything. Behold, I have demolished the mill; have ground the wheat a little."

The Girl laments: "Now, behold! What has come to me! My beloved comes and I have nothing but *tchadi* (a sort of maize-bread) to offer him."

In many of the old airs this three-part harmony of the Georgian song is developed into a real polyphonic structure, with peculiar inner pedals and ostinatos. It often gravitates to a "dissonant" tonic composed of a fourth and a major second that plays the part of the basic triad: an extraordinary anticipation of some modern harmonic concepts. Sometimes the voices, particularly the middle one, grow so whimsical and independent, that they achieve a veritable heterophony.

It is curious to see the old Georgian ecclesiastical music, which appears to have had a singularly austere harmonic structure, consisting of frank successions of fifths and triads. Here is an example from a collection of another Georgian musician, Zachariah Paliashvilli.

"Benedice Animam Meam, Domine" (*Georgian*)

To explain the marked difference between the harmonic basis adopted by this race of Christians and the principles of European harmony, is difficult. One may, however, find something of an explanation in the peculiarities of Georgian history. Georgia, which has seen much and undergone much, was a cauldron ever boiling with war. A ceaseless collision between the various cultures of interior Asia, Greek, Armenian, Arabo-Persian, was in progress and kept Georgia inapproachable, like the fires built by Wotan around Brunhilda.

Thus it may have been that the vague, musical-metaphysical ideas postulated by the Pythagoreans, their monstrous classification of intervals and the interdiction of successions of diatonic thirds and sixths, the ancient source of European harmonic concepts, remained a pious tradition in isolated ancient Georgia, when that country was developing its own culture, later on.

III. The scales peculiar to the music of the Oriental peoples of Russia are also extraordinary. One finds abundant application of all kinds of *mixed* tonalities. The most remarkable in this sense are the melodies, called *Chassidic,* of the Russian Israelites. These melodies, beloved by the Jewish masses, pertain to the Chassidim sect, who have a special doctrine of piety and believe that the world of melody and the world of repentance are closely related.

The best specimens of this Chassidic melody are mainly built in the Phrygian tonality, with the major third, or in the Hypodorian mode, with sudden slips into major passages.

One may observe the same fantastic scales in the wedding dances of the Israelites who inhabit Podolia, a region of Southern Russia, and in some of the beautiful specimens of Hebrew religious melody, as in the chant *Omar rabbi Elozor* (And rabbi

Eléazare said), discovered in a Jewish synagogue in Lithuania.

—"And rabbi Eléazare said, and rabbi Chanina said: Wise men and learned men increase the peace of the World."

"*Omar Rabbi Elozor*" (*Lithuanian-Hebrew*)

And again, we find the same "mixed" scales in some of the ancient Spanish church melodies of Arab origin, as well as in Armenian ecclesiastical music.

These whimsical scales are composed of ordinary minor and Æolian or other passages, mingled with abrupt majors. Such peculiarities mark also certain Georgian songs.

298

Refrain of a Georgian Song, District of Tiflis.

* *
*

All these facts are highly important in the elucidation of the origin of the European tonal system. They are necessary to explain the nature of the dominant scales which have been grafted on the ear of civilized Europe, through the tonal leveling accomplished by the Sebastian Bach era.

It is quite possible that the real supremacy should be attributed to those mixed scales; they might have been shaped after the purest and most ancient melodic formations.

Possibly, our Western scales present nothing but fragments or mutilations of the former; perhaps they are but artificial alterations of a dogmatic character. At any rate, in analyzing the remnants and the transmutations of the ancient, aboriginal chants and scales, we form some idea of the pre-Christian racial musical language of our common ancestors, just as from a study of the ancient tablets of the Hittites, Elamites and Summerites and of their *Ursprache*, we elucidate many dark points of our own language and usages.

RUSSIAN BALLET, ITS HEIRS AND NEW OPERA

THE pure dance-impulse, "movement for its own sake," has been isolated and made the driving force in the art of dance by the vigorous craft of Rudolf von Laban and Mary Wigman. But even their fresh reasoning has not entirely cleared the dance-platform of a heterogenous, grotesque blend, at times drastically anti-choric,[1] that prevailed in the later stages of the Russian Ballet.

True, to some extent the Choric Theater of von Laban with its revival of mass-movement and Mary Wigman's *Totenmal* itself, are a rebound of dynamic pictorialism, one of the later stages of the Russian ballet. To be exact, the *Totenmal* is a re-echo of Natalie Gontcharova's massed and propelled black-and-white of the Paris production of *Noces*.

---

[1] I shall use the term "choric" for everything pertaining to the pure dance impulse or dance motion.

301

The art of Mary Wigman and some late flare-ups of Russian choric dynamism, such as Lifar's choreography for *Le Fils Prodigue*,[2] has helped to fashion the new American dance headed by such brilliant artists as Martha Graham and Doris Humphrey. In his valuable book on dance John Martin says justly that "Graham is unquestionably our greatest dancer and Humphrey our finest composer, . . . and together with Charles Weidman, who is in a field apart, they constitute the principal shaping forces" in the American choric art.[3] I would certainly add the fine ensemble directed by Lincoln Kirstein.

The Russian ballet where all these fresh springs originate, is itself a compressed scheme of dance-history. But one must re-study the remote sources of the art and also, revalue the Russian ballet itself, if its modern sequels and negations are to be defined.

* *

*

Let us trace the changes brought about by the interference of sound, rhythm and the spoken word

[2] Serge Lifar is an eminent Russian Ballet master and author of an authoritative book on the dance.

[3] John Martin: *America Dancing* (Dodge).

with the primeval dance-impulse or dance-posture. These mutations belong to the ritual, the classical and the dramatic phases of dance.

The first flicker of music—a melodic outcry, a beat of the tom-tom—pointed the ritual gesture of primitive man and increased the expressive strength of his dance-motion. But also, this first drop of music distorted the choric idiom; it dislocated the free flow of the pure choric motion.

The long era of interpretive dance was thus ushered in.

The chaotic early ritual stage is followed by the folk-dance, an issue of the growing rule of crystallized rhythm. In this new form, dance is but plastic counterpart of rhythm. The visible frame of rhythm oscillates in the old folk-dance which provided after a while the basis for the stage medley called ballet. During a certain period the exterior of ballet wore a quasi-Hellenic or Renaissance drapery—it was called classical on this score. A detail of no importance.

Technical virtuosity is, of course, a by-product of the classical dance. *Fouettés, pirouettes, batements* mean but choric dress for variations discoverable in the rhythmic texture of music made into

303

dance. Paul Valery's profound description of classical dance as man's effort "to evolve termless renovation from himself to elude uniformity," is here very apt.

The classical dance-idiom has never left the Russian ballet; not even in its late, music-hall phase. *Sylphides,* that pure thought of Fokine's genius, is, indeed, the perfect embodiment of the classical idiom. Yet it was not missing even belatedly, in certain passages of Prokofiev-Lifar's *Le Fils Prodigue,* no matter how violently circus defaced the ballet, in the latest Diaghileff productions.

The glowing mid-history of the Russian ballet mirrors the invasions, dramatic, pictorial and literary, flowing from without the dance. This stage, sometimes called the romantic ballet or the ballet of action, might be more exactly described as extra-choric.

It fell to a rare choric gift put to wrong use, to Isadora Duncan, to mother this new current. Full to the brim of choric sensibility but a born improviser misled by personal musical passions and false dogma—Delsarte's among others—Duncan lost sight of the body as the creative source of a new art of its own. She flung herself into the orgy of interpretive dance. Thus she led dance history along a wrong avenue, and for a long time.

Still, not for a moment should the radiant genius of Isadora Duncan be forgotten, nor the tremendous import of her art in dance history. I subscribe heartily to the admirable description of Duncan in Lincoln Kirstein's fine history of the dance.[4]

Invoked by Isadora Duncan, the pictorial and interpretive tendency helped to throw the Russian ballet into an all-embracing, loosely knit synthetic theater in which pure dance forms appeared only casually. Even *Petroushka* is but an alloy of silent drama, folk dance and costume effect.

One must say, however, that fortunately the Russian ballet was influenced also by the dynamic undertones of the Duncan school, by its choric impetus. Thus the outspoken *danse d'action* found itself ingrained in Russian choreography.

No matter what may be wrong with that motley of drama, tableaux vivants and pantomimic conversation, a *spectacle de luxe* cemented by dance, the irresistible creations of the Russian ballet, the

[4] Lincoln Kirstein: *Dance* (Putnam). See also Mr. Kirstein's summary of dance history in his article on ballet in Oscar Thompson's magnificent *International Cyclopedia of Music* (Dodd-Mead).

great Fokine's *Polovetzki Dances* and *Petroushka*, Massine's *Good Humored Ladies*, choreography of brilliant wit and imagination, breathed vitality of an organic type. That was the best, the Russians were predestined to create.

* *

*

The dressing of dance motion with music and fixed rhythm transformed ritual gesticulation into folk-dance and then, into classical ballet. In the same way, a tempering of the dance impulse with things extra-choric, spoken word, description and drama, has transformed the classical into the pictorial, dramatic ballet.

In his illuminating book on Stravinsky, Boris de Schloezer strives to show that the unity of *Petroushka*, perhaps, the most vigorous creation of the dramatic ballet, hinges on an application of the purely instrumental form of the sonata. The introductory Carnival-scene is an allegro, the scene at the Moor's—an andante, the Ballerina's entrance —a scherzo and the closing Carnival and Petroushka's death—a rondo finale.

At a close scrutiny of *Petroushka's* structure

one observes, however, that its unity is only accentuated, not created by its concise and simple musical scheme. It is the clarity and efficiency of *Petroushka's* dramatic nucleus, the visual, easily grasped collision that binds the characters, the details and the choreographic weaving into a telling whole.

But gradually the unity and clarity of collision in the dramatic ballet have faded. Already in *Sacre* these traits degenerate into an anecdotal dramatization of the sacrificial rite, pagan brutality, etc. Of course, remembering how such theatrical rubbish as the book of Mozart's *Zauberflöte* was made eternal, music endeavors to vitalize into oneness the multicolored amalgam of *Sacre*. Still, all the superb tonal invention poured into this gigantic mold has not succeeded; the image and the form crack and are passing.

The final failure of the Russian ballet has come through not realizing the mission of our day: to fight the domination of music and of other extra-choreographic forces; to turn to the absolute dance element, and to evolve new forms from that base. Instead, the Russian ballet tried to find a new cement for its forms in the frenzied tonal dynamism of the present day. They sought new choreographic building material in the gymnasium, the circus and the music hall. It is only just to mention that Diaghileff having an uncanny sense of fashion's weather, swerved, with rare flexibility and with no loss of time, to the course opened by Jean Cocteau and Darius Milhaud in *Le Bœuf sur le Toit*. That first consecration of the circus-inspired and circus-fashioned ballet was a very important advent of the music-hall era in choreography. Begun with Satie's *Parade* and closed with Prokofiev's *Le fils prodigue*, this tail end of the Russian procession broke up the dramatic-pictorial form. It eclipsed choric stalemate, the "Ptolemaic" dance, and just as usefully as jazz, it has destroyed the "Ptolemaic" dance æsthetics of the Western world, their petrified canons and habits.

*   *

*

The tortuous history of the Russian ballet, tremendous in its variety of invention, of changing dogmas and tendencies, has gradually crystallized the conception of the new, autonomous dance.

We have realized the difference between plastic gesture, that surmises plot and scenery, and choric gesture, precise and self-sufficient.

We have grasped the necessity to isolate the choreo-action and to liberate it from the yoke of tonal expression and drama. Choric personality has taken the place of dramatic personality as center of the ballet. From now on, only choric, dance logic and impulse, are intended to shape the dance motive, as well as the dance development. The choreo-form or even its slenderest arabesque, strives to be more than a translation of a tonal or dramatic move. The ideas and work of Rudolf von Laban and Mary Wigman fell upon us like fruit that had ripened.

Speaking of the new—or as he calls it—abstract dance, meaning by this, purified dance, Richard Hammond points to its kinship with the classical ballet: "Though the abstract dance of today has stylization, and is based on the initial thesis of dance for the dance, yet in certain ways it has developed away from its predecessor of antiquity, the classical ballet. While the latter tended toward complexity and elaboration, the abstract dance is a study in economy. While the former

309

was a gesture of elegance, the latter is a means of expression, though devoid of the robust emotional "outlet of romanticism." [5]

Yet it is too soon to say that the new dance, conscious as it is of its aim and destiny, has actually purged itself from all the sins of the Russians. One of the characteristic and strong traits of Mary Wigman's art is its intense and peculiar orientalism. Its new decorative vein is in itself a link between her conceptions and the Russian ballet. But the fascination is irresistible in such a beautiful dance-thought as *Zeremonielle Gestalt* (Ceremonial Image), no matter how much the new choreographic logic may condemn it.

Certainly much of Mary Wigman's dance motion is derived from a space cognizance. The contrasts of pure movement are drawn from the various registers of the acting body, in the *Drehtanz*, for example. But an imposing part of her dance is propelled also by emotive, musical and rhythmic impulse; for instance, *Spanish Dance* or *The Dance of Suffering*. The dance-stretto and coda of *Sommerlicher Tanz* (Summer's Dance) is

[5] Richard Hammond: "Music and the Dance Theatre," *Modern Music*, Volume VII, 2.

also distinctly a tone-form conception. Sometimes her motion-scheme seems to be a plastic-pictorial improvisation, a display of a plastical *clavilux* that emits line and color for the sake of a pictorial whirl. The new ballet's lapses into emotive, interpretive and pictorial channels may be found to be less casual than they appear.

Mary Wigman still finds it necessary to ignite her dance with a musical spark, be it a lightly traced *ostinato* or a primitive rhythmo-melodic design given to percussion. This suggests that, perhaps, rhythm condemns the dance to be eternally wedded to music, at least in crystallized dance forms. It is clear, however, that undiluted dance motion, emancipated from music, has not yet transcended the aboriginal borders of its own element, has not yet found its way to vast form-building from within its material. As long as the dance incorporates an incentive essentially tonal, such as a rhythmo-melodic line, the new ballet must abandon the vision of a purely choric structure.

The best and most original achievements of Mary Wigman, such as *Festive Rhythm* and *Ceremonial Image* show that perhaps, when the interpretive link between dance and music is replaced by functional parallelism, the union of tone and dance motion may yield new, vital forms. I believe such new interrelation to be the germ of the future ballet; already it is active in the present dance.

＊　　＊

＊

Of all tonal ingredients rhythm alone has the power to secure for the tone its domination of the dance. The larger aspects of music have come to a position of supremacy only in the interpretive and subjective ballet. Only in the *ballet d'action* has the music's æsthetic level acquired importance. In folk-dance or in classical ballet the audible frame of rhythm, to be materialized in dance, is the important factor, not the quality of the music or its psychological content. And the new ballet is reverting to this former state.

But in spite of the new dance conception, the tone, the word, the image still continue in power. Their corrosive strength forces upon the ballet the very same dilemmas and collisions, as those in opera throughout its history. These dilemmas will probably exist *ad secula seculorum.*

Either music or dance can in some measure resist the corrosion menaced by the sheer tonal points of the spoken word, of its rhythm and accent.

Between the two basic elements of the dance language, which Rudolf von Laban juxtaposes with such clarity, as *zeitrythmisch* and *raumrythmisch,*[6] it is the latter, the space-rhythmic element that provides the dance with the strength to resist the extrachoric pressure. I mean by this, tonal content coming from either the music or the spoken, or even the non-audible word, the verbal image. But it is the word's psychological import that carries the power to radically shatter the tone-structure, as well as the dance-structure.

The picture of the gradual infiltration of the word and of its psychological weight in operatic music, prompts us to appraise the stability of the dance form and to speculate as to its future. The absorption by music of the ever increasing verbal material (verbal accent, verbal image, declamatory recitative, dramatic narration) in the operas of Gluck, Verdi, Wagner and Strauss, has proved definitely, that such absorption must be counter-

[6] Rudolf von Laban: "Tanzcomposition und Schrifttanz" (*Schrifttanz,* October, 1928).

acted by an increasingly dynamic stage. Aware
of all the Wagner pitfalls, aware of the static
essence of the word forced into a musical mold,
Strauss resorts to dance in *Electra*, Alban Berg
dynamizes *Wozzeck* by clading its crisp narrative
in instrumental formal armor, Malipiero groups
his tonal material in each scene of *Torneo
Notturno* around a rigid musical form as a center
of tension.[7] When menaced by disintegration and
stagnancy arising from narration, the ballet senses
a similar urge to fortify itself with a dynamic
form borrowed from instrumental music. The
reason for *Petroushka's* sonata structure is evident.

Of all these expedients, Strauss' use of the dance
in *Electra* is probably the most sagacious. In these
choric moments enhanced by the dark glow and
magnificent fury of the music, Strauss' sense of the
stage triumphs where Wagner's so often fails.
With uncanny judgment Strauss expands moments
transformable into vocal music and contracts

[7] One of the most triumphant and brilliant pages of modern
music drama, where intense verbal material is actually burned up
by true theatrical music full of dramatic motion, is to be found
in the extraordinary opera *Jürg Jenatch* of Heinrich Kaminski. Its
remarkable performance in Dresden under Fritz Busch cannot be
forgotten.

those resenting vocal dress. He tempers the latter
moments with mimo-plastic action.

*　　*

*

Opera-ballet looms as the form of the impending synthetic theater. Not only Strauss, but Verdi
and even Mozart realized—perhaps only unconsciously—that word and image are not elements
naturally fit for transversion into music. The replacing of a musical narrative or a declamatory
recitative by dance is dictated by correct stage
instinct.

This interweaving of ballet and opera in new
art is not accidental. Nor are the parallel lines of
their history and fate. The source of this deep
interdependence lies in the basic convention of each
of these forms of art.

In plain words, this basic convention is that situations which could not be "sung" in life, are sung
in opera; situations which could not be "danced"
in life, are danced in ballet. Opera and ballet being each a facet of the theatre, the chief power of
conviction lies in their visual essence. This is why
their means are interchangeable, why the increasing

315

demands for visual truth and life-like illusion, demands spurred by the motion-picture, will force a re-integration of dance in opera.

Because of these new forces in the theatre, notably the motion-picture technique, the vitality of the basic convention of opera is lowered to a vanishing point. The lyrical momentum alone keeps opera from falling to pieces. In spite of its vast deserts of inane dialogue and obscure, deadly narrative that means nothing on the stage, *Die Walküre* still lives because of the lyrical pillars of the Siegmund-Sieglinde passions in the opening scenes and the Wotan-Brunhilde poignant farewell of the closing.

But present opera will not be long in withering away unless a new and more vital liquid be poured into the arteries of operatic formula.

The essence of true opera is lyrical drama. Even action, to say nothing of narrative, dialogue and other remplissage, serves here only as a bridge between emotional situations. These alone are *naturally* transmutable into music. The basic convention in opera can not, indeed, be abolished but its padding can be eliminated; transitional and descriptive music can be given visual strength. Thus opera will be re-vitalized, even saved.

In the future opera, danced narrative conveying the dramatic links of the book with infinitely greater efficiency, will replace sung narrative. Danced dialogue will be heir to sung dialogue, and the rest of operatic remplissage will be disposed of in the same way.

Thus the new, the integrated opera-ballet will come to life as the summit of both, operatic and dance-history.

* *

*

The ballet of the future, as well as the coming operatic forms, will set a new relationship between its music, and the verbal material and imagery intertwined in the book. This relationship will be, as I have intimated earlier, that of functional parallelism.

All trace of the old interpretive dependency will disappear. The dramatic logic, unity and development in the new opera, as well as the choric logic, choric unity and development in the new ballet, will leave their musical counterpart autonomous, self-centered and self-dependent, in a special way.

The music of the future ballet and opera will indeed flow along the line of action, choric or dramatic, yet it will remain as effective, self-sufficient and self-circumscribed, as if it were absolute music of an instrumental form.

Then for the first time, the law of formal self-dependency, imperative for any music, will have its full and beneficial sway in opera and in ballet alike. The development of a choreographic motive will become immune from tonal interference. Functional co-existence of music with the new opera and the new ballet will thus be established.

PART IV

THE NEW ART OF CONDUCTING

THE NEW ART OF CONDUCTING

LIKE singing, the art of conducting belongs to a dark domain of performance. The mechanism and resources of either are still vaguely understood and not at all systematized.

The absence of a scientific theory aggravates a dimness in the understanding of conducting by the layman, the professional musician and sometimes by the conductor himself. We are still unable to define precisely what part in the rendition is due to the conductor's craft and what to the competence of the players.

It may occur, that having in his hands a flexible orchestra, able reader of old and new repertory, a bold and technically clever conductor, externally energetic and aided by the right measure of *cabotinage,* will acquire the reputation of a valuable and inspired leader, possibly that of a great one, when being mediocre, even ignorant as a musician.

One finds confusion and incertitude as to the very qualities and their measure, necessary for conducting. Equilibrium is rare. Often one requisite dominates to the detriment of others. Sometimes an excellent performing gift and a fine general musicianship is coupled with a lack of the technical and physical qualities indispensable to a leader. All his attention is then absorbed by his struggle with the technical problems of leadership; his interpretive plans can be realized only in part and casually. Then again, the reverse may be true: a great technical gift united with mediocre performing talent and an inferior type of musical mentality. Many a celebrated man has belonged to this type.

To measure justly the artistry of a conductor, his basic qualities and faults, and to assure oneself of even the sheer necessity of his office, one must be present at his rehearsals. There alone one can fully estimate his faculties, his competence, his plan of performance, his ability for realizing his designs, his share in the performance. The rehearsal, even more than a carefully analyzed reading, gives answer to the often intelligent questioning of whether or not a conductor is an actual necessity.

Of course, this could be questioned only in our day of virtuoso orchestras. The description of orchestral conditions by Berlioz and his priceless portrait of a conducting ignoramus, can not be forgotten. The picture of rehearsing in the times of Leopold Damrosch and of the old New York Symphony Society of the eighties, by the venerable dean of the American conductors, Walter Damrosch, in his book *My Musical Life*, leaves no doubt of a sore need of a competent conductor in those times.

In an attack on this picturesque and today deified figure Nicolas Slonimsky, himself a gifted and highly competent orchestra leader, asks why a quintet or an octet do not require a conductor, whereas one seems to be indispensable to an orchestra.

"A good prompter," says Mr. Slonimsky, "is as necessary as he is harmless. But when he mounts the stage and begins to play the magician, and, by the aid of a deaf-and-dumb alphabet, dispenses lines that are Shakespeare's, acknowledging the praise that is destined for the actors, as if they were trained seals, then he must be branded as an impostor and denounced as such, even if tradition has sanctioned his farcical presumption." [1]

[1] Nicolas Slonimsky: "The Art of Conducting an Orchestra," *Plain Talk*, December, 1929.

The question arises manifestly because of the well known types, the mediocre drill-master and audacious *cabotin*. No doubt, a gifted, inspired and well-equipped concert-master or even a council of three or four authoritative members of the orchestra might devise infinitely subtler performing schemes, and might even energize their ensemble far more efficiently than a conducting mediocrity. Possibly, a living metronome is not more useful for the rhythmic unity of the orchestra and for economy in rehearsing than a mechanical metronome, a "robot." [2] But how is one to replace a Toscanini or a Furtwängler, a Klemperer or a Mengelberg? A Scherchen, a Stokowski or a Bruno Walter?

*   *

*

The paramount confusion in the domain of conducting and the dimness of its mechanism result from a failure to evolve all the consequences hidden in the basic fact of orchestral directing. The conductor has in his hands an instrument not only

[2] In his early stages the conductor was but a loud and obnoxious metronome. Schünemann in his *Geschichte des Dirigierens* quotes complaints by the Parisians of the brutality of the loud time-beating by the Italian opera conductor. They likened his beat to the hack of a woodchopper.

of gigantic size—the size in itself demands a special technic of handling—but also one of *a double nature* and composed of heterogeneous elements. This apparatus is first an ensemble of physical elements, the various instruments in the hands of the players, and then, an ensemble of spiritual instruments, the players themselves, with their individual emotions, tastes, individual rhythmic sense and reactions.

The theory of conducting amounts to the deducting and systematizing of all the consequences resulting from the central fact, that of the orchestra's being an infinitely complex psycho-physical contrivance. In this way one embraces all points of the new art of conducting, since the new technique of orchestra leading, practically though unconsciously, is guided by a grasp of this pivotal fact of orchestral action.

A scientific theory of conducting does not yet exist. There is no trace of one in the well-known treatises on conducting by Berlioz, Wagner or Weingartner. These contain either precious though disconnected remarks on the interpretation of classical works or criticism of some particular conductor. The recently published admirable

Lehrbuch des Dirigierens by Hermann Scherchen, a conductor of outstanding talent and knowledge, has purely practical aims, notably that of instructing a leader how to work out the orchestral sonority. The excellent *Technic of the Baton* by Albert Stoessel,[3] one of the leading American conductors, serves mainly practical ends also.

The ground principles of the art of conducting which I shall now strive to present, have been deducted from psychological reasoning, as well as from an observation of those leading modern masters of orchestra whose art combines subtle technical instinct with an intelligent system. Among these I would name first Arthur Nikisch, the father of the new art of conducting.

* *

*

The complex power of the conductor unfolds a triple aspect:

   a) The government of the rhythmic ensemble of the orchestra.

   b) A working out and handling of its sonority.

   c) A guiding of the spiritual ensemble of the

[3] Published by Carl Fischer, New York.

326

orchestra, its collective soul, forcing it to materialize the leader's general conception of the work and his plan of performance.

THE RHYTHMIC ENSEMBLE

Our visual field embraces not only objects on which our visual axis focuses, but includes also things placed somewhat outside the focus of vision. The latter objects are perceived by our lateral sight.

His direct vision the orchestra musician uses for the music on his desk. He focuses on that his conscious attention, reads the notes and reproduces them on his instrument. He achieves the literal performance of the musical work. But owing to the lateral vision directed by subconscious attention, he adapts himself to the movement and gesture of the conductor. Through the half-conscious attention and through other subconscious psychic forces, the orchestra musician perceives the intentions of the conductor, intimated by his facial and bodily movement.

If the musicians should focus their conscious attention on the conductor's gestures, try in this manner to gather his design, the literal performance of the work, that is the reproducing of the musical signs, would become impossible. The unity of the orchestral mass would immediately decompose. The individual rhythmic sensitiveness, each trait of individual perception of each instrumentalist, would begin then to count. Then the orchestra would have ceased to be a performing entity and would have become an assembly of individual performers, feeling the music, judging the leader's intention and responding to it each in his own way.

There are exceptions, however, to the principle of subconscious attention. In certain cases the transfer of that submerged attention to the conscious mind is a necessity. If the orchestra ensemble is shaken by a lack of skill in its leader or by accident, the instrumentalists are forced to restore the unity themselves. They consciously observe the conductor's gesture to find out what is wrong. Again should the instrumentalists know their part by memory, then their conscious scrutiny, no longer occupying itself with literal performance, is focused on the leader and follows his movement. Sometimes, in rhythmically dangerous passages or in those requiring exceptional unity of ensemble, the musicians read their music somewhat ahead, and this permits them to observe consciously the conductor's gesture. This often occurs when the orchestra accompanies a soloist.

The following experiment will clarify the special rôle of the subconscious perception. At the end of the introduction of the *Oberon* overture, the divided violas sustain *piano* a second which the full orchestra breaks up suddenly with a short, cutting *forte*.

Oversustain this second somewhat, in order to stress the instrumentalists' anxiety of waiting, thus over-exciting their attention. Then indicate the *fortissimo* re-entrance of the full orchestral *tutti* not with the habitual downbeat but with a brisk jerk of the wrist toward the orchestra, a sort of swift rejecting gesture. Such a dry and cutting movement of the conductor will provoke, under the circumstances, an immediate and unanimous reaction from the orchestra, and we shall have obtained a perfectly concise and neat chord. The

329

longer we sustain the violas' second, the shorter and more sudden is the leader's gesture, the more perfect is the ensemble of the orchestral response. This comes from the fact that the rapidity of gesture, which finally releases the tension produced by oversustaining the violas, hinders the orchestra to realize consciously what is happening. For an instant the conductor's jerk levels the psychology of the instrumentalists to one and the same state.

Such a collective attention of the orchestra, which completely neutralizes the individual perception of the musicians, is the only condition capable of yielding a response of perfect unity from the orchestral ensemble. I still recall after many years, how such a remarkable conductor as old Ernest Schuch of Dresden, could never obtain that fulminating, clear-cut response from the orchestra, which master-technicians of a thoroughly modern type such as Kleiber, Koussevitzki, Molinari or Fritz Reiner achieve in that *Oberon* passage using a swift jerk of the right hand. Schuch indicated that chord in the routine way and aggravated this mistake by not forgoing the upbeat, here most evidently harmful.

Another passage, of slightly different rhythmic

nature, also requiring a brisk lateral gesture of the wrist to get the ideal chord-sweep, is to be found in the following example from Strauss' *Till Eulenspiegel*.

The instinctively wise desire of the conductor to get an automatic, subconscious and united response to his gesture, is the root of one of the most remarkable discoveries in the new art of conducting. I speak of Nikisch's method of indicating the entrance of orchestra chords somewhat, an infinitesimal fraction, ahead of the metric time. This proceeding lashes the subconscious attention and the rhythmic sense of the instrumentalist and secures an extraordinary unity of ensemble when applied masterfully. In cases like choral singing *a capella*, entries ushered in this manner, require real bravery on the conductor's part, and also a great firmness of gesture, especially in *forte*, as singers are instinctively inclined to try out their tone before they emit it with assurance.

331

* *

*

In order that the subconscious attention might have full sway, it is necessary that the movement of the conductor be perceived by the orchestra with the least possible engagement of their conscious effort. The perception must then be a will-less one, effected with all possible ease. To economize the psychic strength of the orchestra, is imperative. The proper rôle of the conscious attention is concern for the higher, interpretive part of the performance.

An effortless grasp of the director's action is possible only when his rhythm-setting gesture emanates from a certain fixed and single center, a focus, so to speak, radiating rhythm. Such a center should be permitted to revolve in but very narrow limits, so that the instrumentalists may have it always within their lateral visual field and perceive it without strain.

The center of the rhythmic radiation is the wrist of the leader's right hand. From the technical point of view, there is nothing more disconcerting, and also nothing more disagreeable to the spectator, than a conductor who continually marks rhythm with both hands or one who paces his podium, forcing his musicians to waste their psychic energy on superfluous watching.

It is significant that great conductors, such as Nikisch, Toscanini, Mengelberg, Muck, all stand immovable on their podium.

The rhythm being marked by the right wrist, its movement must be confined to a triangle or a rhombus with the sharp angle pointed to the focus, where the initial downbeat originates. The right hand alone is the legitimate organ of rhythm; the left must be considered chiefly a signifier for shading.

As the rhythmic focus of conducting must deplace itself as little as possible, and the expense of attention be reduced to a minimum, the latter normally addressed to a reading of the notes, it is evident that the gesture which generates rhythm, should not be over-large. The entries of the instruments should therefore be indicated not by a jerk of the body or by a large gesture of the right hand but by a slight sign from the left hand or from the head, or even better, by a glance. One never forgets the incomparable ease and grace of Nikisch's or Toscanini's indicating of the entries. Showing the entries must by no means upset the right hand and detract it from its principal rôle, directing of the ensemble's rhythmic life.

From this point of view, it seems that the baton has a special value, and it is scarcely wise to abolish the use of it. The gesture of a batonless hand grows less concise. It loses the neatness of rhythmic punctuation which the movement from the wrist transmits to the baton-point with such clarity. The ensemble feels the absence of the baton at once, particularly when sharply rhythmic music is played. One can, of course, obtain excellent results in ensemble directing without a baton, but at an additional demand on the orchestra's attention, wasteful and consequently harmful.

One of my boyhood reminiscences of Safonov, the famous batonless Russian conductor and one time director of the New York Philharmonic, is the uncertain, toppling unison of the triplet string figuration in the *Saltarello* of Mendelssohn's *Italian Symphony*. Safonov was a rare musician; his piano and ensemble playing always breathed a stern precision. The rhythmic confusion in that performance of the *Saltarello* can be accounted for by nothing but the absence of a concise focus of conducting caused by abolition of the baton.

Of course, it would be absurd to demand that the orchestra leader follow the described technical rules blindly. Under stress of emotion he might indicate a simple entry with a large, violent, generally inappropriate gesture of the right hand. His temperament might induce him, now and then, to mark the rhythm with his left hand and thus lead temporarily the conscious attention of the players from the rightful center, the wrist of the right hand.

The picture of a conductor who never permits himself a deviation from the rules, is indeed dreary. There are maestros who from principle never use the left hand; it hangs at the side like a horsewhip. After all, a conductor may be permitted any liberty provided he observe the rule of the single focus of rhythm centered in the right wrist, and the rule of a minimum consummation of the instrumentalists' attention. For the less energy they waste on grasping the rhythmic signs of the conductor holding the ensemble's unity, the greater is the reserve of the players' attention directed to the interpretation, the more perfect is their obedience to the performing plan of the *chef d'orchestre.*

Under a conductor who masters such a clear technique of the rhythm, it is easy to play. The old flutist Fürstenau who played under Wagner told Weingartner: "When Wagner was at the desk, the instrumentalists lost the impression that they are conducted." [4] The modern technic of conducting has its origin in the short and concise gesture of Wagner. However, only orchestra players accustomed to performing under leaders, who possess the modern technic of their art, can appreciate the value of such directing. Musicians who work under the habitual type of orchestra director, under a "time-beater" (*Taktschläger*), often complain of an incertitude which they feel under some of the great conductors owing to the scantness of their gesture. Nikisch himself, with his flawless technique, did not escape reproach of this sort.

The art of conducting is therefore a modern *chironomy* adapted to the direction of rhythm, just as the ancient chironomy used in the direction of choruses in the early Christian era, indicated to the singers the melodic line. It follows that the other

[4] Felix Weingartner: *Ueber das Dirigieren.*

means of a leader's action, his posture, facial expression, gestures reflecting his emotion, should be applied solely to the details of the performance.

Only conductors of a primitive type, technically uncouth, try to interfere everywhere, to show everything with their stick: the entries, the shades and the general conception. They understand nothing of conducting the phrasing and the dynamics of a work. These time-beaters do not see that in the following passage from Tchaikovsky's *Romeo and Juliette* overture the conductor should

be able to combine in his gesture two rhythmic flows running parallel. With light, scarcely perceptible, strokes of his right wrist he must rule the regular rhythm of the phrase, the even flow of its figuration, while a brighter, more conspicuous gesture of the same hand should mark the capricious rhythm of the chord-jerks, according to the scheme below (the dash indicates the main beat, the sign ‿ shows the weak times, and arrows point to the up-and-down beats evoking the wind-instrument chords).

The time-beaters are not aware of the axiom that the leader's gesture must reflect the spirit, the rhythmic life of a work, not its arithmetic. These nervous chord-jerks of the woodwind will fall with precision and unity into their right position, if indicated an instant ahead of the time-beats flashed by the string figuration. After the first few beats the main rhythm need not be conducted at all; it will run flawlessly by itself, owing to the rhythmic energy accumulated by the flow of the string figures.

*   *

*

The ruling of the orchestra's rhythmic ensemble has problems of subtler order. A leader not conscious of them, is quite helpless. I speak of handling the fermatas (holds) and of the application of the special upbeat preceding the attack.

One finds conductors who do not know how to

release a fermata according to the occasion. Should one release the fermata, cut it off with one separate gesture, pause and then continue, or should one combine the gesture of release with the downbeat starting the renewed flow of music? There are directors who do not even suspect that a kind of fermata exists which should never be severed from the continuation. Not realizing a necessity to economize the gesture and consequently, the orchestra's attention, with the cutting off the fermata, they also lower their right hand; they must therefore lift it again for the consequent upbeat. The gesture is unnecessary, drags the pause, and is particularly disagreeable and futile in fermatas sustained piano.

I vividly recall how complex and mysterious seemed the technical problems to be settled, when, at the dawn of my own annals, I was to conduct Beethoven's *Fifth Symphony.*

Was it necessary to release all the fermatas of the opening section or only some of them? And which ones? Should one mark the end of a fermata only when it separates opposed musical thought, or in other cases as well? Does not the particular charm of the non-released fermata consist just in the suddenness with which the new musical idea emerges? Is it necessary, by releasing the fermata to underline once more the moment that had been already stressed by the fermata itself? Certainly I would not choose to release the fermata at the coda-end in the *allegro* of the *Fifth Symphony,* and I would hesitate to mark the end of the fermatas at the opening.

Confusion reigns also in managing the special upbeat, that right wrist gesture in the form of a hook which precedes the regular stroke, the start of the orchestral flow.

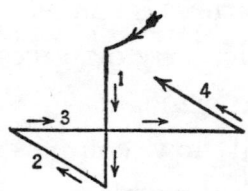

Many directors are not quite aware of the fact that this attack-upbeat is applied in two definite cases only.

The attack-upbeat originated in the necessity to allow the chorus or the wind-instruments to draw their breath before entrance. Then it became a method to indicate the rhythm of the music to be performed. These two strokes, the attack-upbeat plus the downstroke, are sufficient for a precise grasp of the rhythm.

But the *Taktschläger* does not realize that if, for example, the music begins with a rest, however small, this compels a dispensing with the attack-upbeat. A regular downbeat, free from any addition, can alone insure unity of ensemble in the entering chord. The opening bars of Strauss' *Don Juan* will be best ushered in by such a gesture:

With due respect for Albert Stoessel's observation and judgment, I cannot agree with the statement in his excellent manual,[5] that a full measured, rhythmically correct attack-upbeat is always useful and even necessary. I am of the opinion that such an upbeat in an orchestral *forte* detracts from the energy and from the enthusiasm of the entrance. It is certainly harmful in the case, I have described, of a short pause preceding the entering

[5] Albert Stoessel: *The Technic of the Baton*, Carl Fischer, New York.

chord. Mr. Stoessel's proposed full length upbeat may at times be useful in the case of an orchestral *piano* or in a *cantilena*. But after all, a conductor should coordinate the scope and intensity of his attack-upbeat with the dynamic shade and the orchestral color of the entering chord.

It is difficult to exhaust the details, more or less important. An apt application of detail depends on the technical talent, the orchestral instinct and the experience of the leader, as well as on an ensemble of qualities indispensable to a ruler of orchestral rhythmic life. These might be enumerated as first, a faithful sense of rhythm, a faculty for maintaining the rhythm taken and for modifying it at will and in right measure, when necessary; second, a flawless memory for tempos and an instinct for the right movement, in other words, a capacity for determining without fault the only inherent tempo of the given piece; third, natural technical facilities, such as a flexible and well developed wrist, a certain pliability of body, etc.

I have not mentioned here the hearing, as a keen analytical listening and auditory perception are indispensable only to the rehearsing and the handling of the orchestral sonority, and not to the directing of the rhythmic ensemble.

A memory for tempo and an instinct for the true *melos* of a given work, are of prime importance. We appreciate these gifts when we hear such perfect rhythmic plans as the glorious readings of the G-major symphony of Haydn or Ravel's *Daphnis* under Toscanini, of the *Second Symphony* of Brahms under Furthwängler, of the B-minor Suite of Bach under Mengelberg or of Mozart's E-flat major symphony under Bruno Walter.

As to bodily characteristics, even the stature of the conductor has a certain consequence. Excessive tallness is rather a hindrance than otherwise, for with a tall leader the focus of rhythm is placed too high, the gestures acquire a broad radius, in accord with the stature. This throws additional stress on the subconscious attention of the instrumentalists. Assuredly, there are outstanding conductors who overcome the handicap of height, such as Karl Muck, Furthwängler, Fritz Busch, Stokowski, Rodzinski, Goossens. However, the general impression that great conductors are usually short, finds support in the examples of

Nikisch and Toscanini, of Mahler and Mengelberg or for that matter in Wagner, himself a great master of orchestra leading.

ORCHESTRAL SONORITY

The working out and the control of orchestral sonority, a meeting of its requirements, is a very special domain in the labors of a director. It partakes of the same nature as that of any virtuoso's exercise of his instrument. But unfortunately conducting has not as yet established definite methods to guide this work. Its *Gradus ad Parnassum* or *Schule der Gelaüfigkeit* do not yet exist. However, the magnificent chapter *Orchesterkunde* devoted to the working out of the orchestral sonority in Hermann Scherchen's most valuable *Lehrbuch des Dirigierens* is a true beginning of a future *Gradus ad Parnassum* for conducting. Strauss' edition and supplements to Berlioz's *Instrumentation* contains admirable remarks on bowing and embouchure, invaluable to a conductor.

Before setting himself to work with his orchestra, the leader must be in possession of not only a rhythmic plan of the performance, a full chart of the main rhythmic movements in the composition, but he must also have a plan for its sonority to aid him in the working out of the sheer sound of the orchestral ensemble. He should not fail to know in advance, to hear clearly in imagination how the piece should resound, and he must be sure of how to obtain the desired sonority.

The treatment of the orchestral sonority and its control present a double aspect. One observes first an ensemble of means definitely aiming at cohesion and equilibrium within the various groups forming the orchestral mass. Then the balance and true tonal color of the whole ensemble has to be established. Systematic and general labor is not sufficient to accomplish this. Each composition has its special exigencies. The orchestral sonority of a work may be well conceived by the composer in his day, yet its actual equilibrium may demand modification for present-time performance; even the scoring may need change. This may be caused by a difference in the technique and composition of the orchestra, variances due to the time of birth of the piece and the present period. To revise some of the orchestration or to effect changes, so modifying the equilibrium within some of the instrumental groups and underlining certain shades or designs, is sometimes a necessity.

Thus, in some of Beethoven's symphonies a sustained note of a woodwind instrument or even its solo is too feeble to penetrate the dense chord of the tremendous string group of our day. In the canon of the Allegretto of the Seventh Symphony, for instance, the strings would surely strangle the clarinet part if we were to follow Beethoven's shading. It is necessary then either to alter the shading, or to double the woodwind, or to diminish the number of strings. Of these alternatives the doubling of the woodwind is a rather brutal proceeding, and it marred performances of Beethoven's symphonies by even such a great master as Gustav Mahler. The only flaw of Mengelberg's beautiful reading of Bach's B-minor Suite is the performing of the flute part by a unison of several flutes, instead of decreasing the string mass. On the other hand, it is a joy to hear the greatly diminished string section whenever an early classical work is played under Toscanini. Who could forget the divinely proportioned tonal balance, the matchless style and sonority of the orchestra in

Toscanini's performance of Mozart's g-minor or Beethoven's First Symphony?

* *

*

Systematic work on orchestral sonority begins with the tuning of the orchestra and a correcting of the intonation of various groups and instruments. Scherchen advises that a tuning fork be set in the orchestra room, so that the tuning may be done thoroughly, and before the rehearsal. Still this does not entirely free the conductor from the work of controlling the orchestral intonation which is being upset continually.

The conductor must obtain a neatness in the melodic design and a balance of the various groups in the orchestral chord. He must secure a harmonic clarity of the latter. To this end the bass of the instrumental chord should be made distinctly transparent and yet it must not overshadow other voices. When the composer's intentions require it, the orchestra leader must be able to screen or to submerge secondary designs and sonorities, such as pedal points supporting the flux of changing harmonies, polyphonic voices of the subordinate kind, etc. The conductor must also control

347

the uniform and conscientious bowing of the strings and the embouchure of the wind instruments. However, the very usefulness of uniform bowing is doubted by Richard Strauss in his remarks in *Instrumentationslehre* by Berlioz-Strauss. Scherchen's book points to many important details of string playing. He opposes, for instance, accentuation with the fingers to emphasis with the bow. Scherchen's remarks are very significant in regard to the rhythmic subtleties demanded by our modern composers, subtleties that require an especially clear articulation.

This part of the director's labor can be justly appraised only at the rehearsals. Of course, one guesses at that special effort when one hears at the concert the divine, elfin alertness of the wind-embouchures in Mendelssohn's Scherzo from the *Midsummer Night's Dream* under Toscanini, whose woodwind always plays with the precision, lightness and articulation of string instruments. One surmises the work on intonation and balance when one listens to the shining and warm sonority of the brass chords closing Strauss's *Heldenleben* under Mengelberg.

I have had the privilege of listening to the rehearsals of such world-known leaders and masters of rehearsing as Wilhelm Furthwängler, a conductor of remarkable genius, and of Willem Mengelberg, Artur Bodanzky, Adrian Boult, Pièrre Monteux, Leopold Stokowski, Alexandre Siloti, an admirable master of rehearsing, and among the outstanding younger forces, those of Otto Klemperer, Fritz Busch, Rodzinski, Fritz Reiner, Hermann Scherchen, Eugene Goossens, Barbirolli, Nicolas Slonimsky, Vladimir Golschman, Hans Lange, Alfred Wallenstein.

I mention especially those at whose rehearsals one can measure the height of the modern demand on orchestral sonority. Among all these admirable artists, Mengelberg is perhaps the most persistent and uncompromising. It is a delight to see him curb the players' resistance, to make the strings play a *spiccato a punto d'arco* when they would so gladly slide into the lesser effort of a *staccato* played by the middle of the bow; to make them sound a real *martellato* which they would so readily replace by a lukewarm *detaché*.

The effort of the conductor always meets with that well-known psychic resistance on the part of the instrumentalists. An inertia of inborn habits, inclinations, and an inertia of attention, feeds such resistance. Regulation of the performing habits of the orchestra and a struggle with the retard in the transmission of his intention, is a part of the director's problem.

Every conductor knows, for instance, how the natural inertia of the orchestral mass manifests itself in a tendency to play all music in a neutral *mezzo forte*, for this requires the least effort from the players. The conductor is compelled to exert real pressure to get his instrumentalists to execute a veritable *forte*, a real *piano* and to obtain the gradual, true *crescendo* and *diminuendo*. The instinctive tendency of the ensemble to play every *calando* also as *diminuendo*, and to add to an *accellerando* some degree of *crescendo*, is always to be combated.

An Italian sociologist has ingeniously shown in a treatise on mass-psychology that the decisions of an assembly or a parliament, composed even of talented intellectuals, must inevitably be mediocre and banal. For the particular taste, the individual talent is levelled and smothered in the resultant of common instinct and habit which gains supremacy in any mass-assembly. This explains why any orchestra, even one composed of gifted and cultured players, if abandoned to its own performing sense, would shade, for instance, the beginning of the development section in the first movement of Beethoven's Seventh Symphony, according to the well-known banal scheme:

> *piano-poco crescendo ed accellerando;*
> *piu forte et piu allegro; diminuendo e*
> *rallentando, meno allegro, etc.*

The quoted passage from Tchaikovsky's *Romeo and Juliette* presents excellent material to illustrate a method of combating the retard of the orchestal mass. The brass chords should be indicated by short strokes of the wrist marked somewhat ahead of time. Nikisch conducted them so; the response of the instrumentalists comes then at the right moment with astounding precision.

The strings are naturally less inert. With them the tendency to retard their response to the conductor's gesture is less manifest than with the wind-group. But there are cases when short strokes of the wrist somewhat anticipating the beat, would also yield good results, in directing string players. In the *Adagio* of the Emperor-concerto

351

of Beethoven, the strings double the harmonies of
the piano part with chords pizzicato.

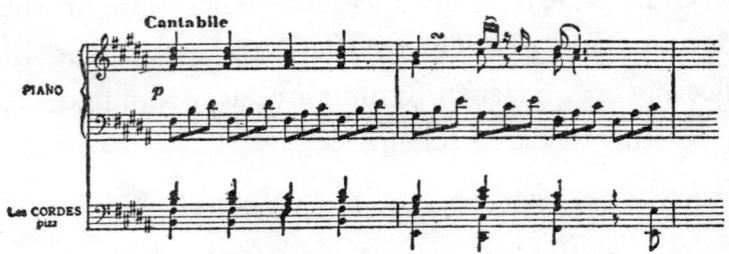

The conductor has to follow not only all the
expressive deviations of the pianist, but he is also
to obtain a perfect cohesion of the pizzicato chords
and their flawless dropping at the proper instant.
The slightest incertitude would be felt immediately in this transparent web. The best way to
achieve a perfect ensemble is to indicate the
pizzicato chords with dry, brief strokes preceding
by a smallest fraction of time the accentuation of
the pianist.

This advice suggests but one of countless proceedings which instinct and experience point out.
Being purely theoretical in this survey, I cannot
delve deeper into the field of controlling the
orchestral sonority. In the chapter *Orchesterkunde* of Hermann Scherchen's book, one will
find a wealth of facts, of fine advice and sugges-

tions, pertaining to this phase of the conductor's art.

INTERPRETATION

The manning of the rhythmic ensemble and of the orchestral sonority lies in the elementary sphere of orchestral leading. Its superior domain embraces ways and means to achieve unity of plan, to animate the performance and to bring out the true character of the composition which the conductor senses.

This is, of course, the task of every interpreter, but the special character of the instrument handled by an orchestra leader, confronts us with some peculiar problems of execution.

The gesture of the conductor and his pose should be addressed solely to the instrumentalists. These are justified only when, and as long as they are useful to the orchestra. The mimoplastic art of the directing musician is only similar to, not identical with that of an actor. Drama is differently addressed. Both the gesture and attitude of a conductor are basically wrong when they act on the public directly, and so transform listeners into spectators.

Grace, elegance in the leader's gesticulation and attitude are legitimate when necessary for the performance. A concise gesture, gracefully executed, will evoke an automatically exact and elegant orchestral response. A plastic movement of the conductor, æsthetically significant, will achieve the desired shade and detail with magic fidelity. But if the conductor, even remotely, half-consciously, addresses himself to the audience as spectators, his authority loses at once some of its power, and the performance suffers even technically. The orchestra's habitual state of subconscious, automatic and faithful transmission, is upset. A sensitive listener perceives immediately a subtle incoordination between the conductor's gesture and the orchestral response; a blemish is apparent in the spiritual ensemble of the orchestra.

They are eminently mistaken, those conductors who think to hypnotize their listeners with other proceedings than that of addressing themselves to the orchestra. Many more or less unconsciously pose. They mean to follow Nikisch, whose gesture and attitude, however, had always technical significance.

A conductor begins where he ceases to watch his

own gestures or to revel in them, just as an orator begins where the man ceases to listen to himself. Otherwise they are misguided actors addressing the wrong audience. Conductors of bad taste do not or do not wish to understand the true rôle of their mimoplastic medium and the principle of its application. The "touch," the *toucher* of the *chef d'orchestre,* that is, the inner nature of his gesture, must be such as to bear on nothing but the mere regulation of the orchestral performance. The rôle of the conductor must be confined, in the brilliant definition of Dr. Isaac Goldberg, "to visible editing of music."

In no task is the conductor's regulating rôle observed with such clarity, as in his guiding of the orchestral accompaniment to soloists, and nowhere is a leader's over-directing more absurd. Here the conductor's movement should reach the minimum so as not to hinder the orchestra in listening to the soloist. Only in this way can a perfect contact between soloist and accompaniment be achieved. Generally speaking, the skill of orchestral accompaniment is a touch-stone for a conductor's technical mastery.

From the preceding study of gesture and its

action on the subconscious mind of the instrumentalists, we may draw the following inference:

a) The movement of the director must conserve the orchestra's energy so that at a needed moment all its power may be summoned. In this respect monotony of gesture is especially harmful.

The abuse of large and expressive gesticulation which certain orchestra leaders bring to the verge of hysterical exaggeration, exhausts quickly the psychic strength and the enthusiasm of the players. They are likely to be found non-responsive, emotionally paralyzed just when a special effort—a particularly powerful sonority, an emotion of supreme potence—is demanded of them. Again, monotony of short gesture modeled after a badly understood Nikisch or Muck, dulls the intentness of the instrumentalists and their responsiveness to demands by the leader for subtle shade and detail. Only a wisely diversified gesticulation, when it is also restrained and centered, is capable of keeping the ensemble's attention watchful without fatiguing it.

b) The conductor must constantly be aware of the fact that his gesture is his natural instrument of action on the subconscious mind of his players, and that the word, the address to their conscious sphere, is but a secondary means of communication. The latter, however, may be useful when judicious. I often recall the exquisite manner in which the Petrograd Orchestra played that noble string music from Tchaikovsky's *Romeo and Juliette*, the section following the second theme, after Nikisch had remarked at the rehearsal: "This music should rustle gently like foliage of the platanum trees over the heads of Romeo and Juliette, in the Verona gardens." Yet Nikisch, following his admirable instinct, talked to the orchestra sparingly; he knew the harm of lecturing at rehearsals.

*　*

*

A union of all the qualities demanded for an orchestra leader is rare. One meets combinations of very diversified traits, at times contradictory, even. Therefore, what follows must be considered as schematic. The main interpretive characteristics requisite for orchestral leadership, are isolated for closer scrutiny.

Conductors of an inferior type usually lack self-control. They are constantly in a state of feverish agitation, sometimes simulated, and this is often mistaken for temperament. Their interpretation consists of a wandering through primitive sequences of orchestral crescendos and diminuendos, in an abuse of *piano subito*, in a setting up of orchestral climaxes at random, by instinct. Now and then such leaders intuitively find a happy detail but their execution is mainly haphazard improvisation. They abuse shading, are apt to lose themselves in detail. Weingartner calls them wittily *Tempo rubato-Dirigenten*. Absence of a general plan for performance delivers them to the path of "least resistance," facile and banal schemes, habits of the trade. Many great works are buried under a thick layer of habitual temperamental platitudes of performance.

The opposite type is not more valuable. Now it is Apollo who reigns instead of Dionysius. The interpretation is studied, cerebral and sometimes artificially impassive. This type of conductor cultivates an external self-possession exaggerated at times to artificial grandeur, a pomposity often coupled with an admiring of his own technical ease. A Narcissus of this kind substitutes studied impassiveness for artistic restraint.

One should apply the general rule "to govern means to foresee" to the superior sphere of orchestra leading, just as methodically, as it is applied when creating a plan for directing the rhythmic ensemble or for handling the orchestral sonority.

In conductors of a superior type one finds a close union of the dynamic, passionate forces with the intellectual element. The latter molds the execution into concise form, brings the essence of the composition into relief and co-ordinates the various plans for performance, those for rhythm, tone-color, etc., with the conception of the whole.

The Apollonian principle,—plan, control, consciousness,—and the Dionysian element,—temperament, intuition,—in the elevated type of a conductor, stand in inverse relationship to those in the inferior type. Caprice and intuition may govern details of an interpretation of a supreme nature; improvising may find a place there. But the general form, in great reading, an idea of the work as a whole, is preconceived. Such a formal conception may also be considered as springing from intuition, but it is ingrained in the interpretation by the Apollonian forces of the leader, no matter how often impulse may generate detail.

Passion, impetus, exaltation do not upset, nor confuse a conductor of this type. They elevate, illuminate his faculties to the highest degree; a fiery creation of detail would be incapable of dissipating his vision of the whole. These leaders have digested the advice of genius given by Flaubert to a friend: *"Méfiez vous de l'inspiration."* Do not trust to inspiration!

These qualities acquire a special significance in the interpretation of modern works. Intricacy and the coloristic display in present-day composition are apt to lure the conductor into an overdressed kind of rendition, overabundant in detail and gaudy. Today more than ever, unity demands a preconceived executive plan. To counteract by a simplicity of general conception the richness and multiplicity of detail, is now imperative.

* *

*

No executive artist's nature harmonizes so completely the Apollonian and Dionysian elements as that of Toscanini's.

His exceptional gifts alone, the memory and the hearing of a Mozart, and an incomparable mastery of the orchestra rising from union of power and lucidity that mark his genius, would in themselves entitle him to the cognomen given to Orlando di Lasso: *Princeps Musicæ*. But, of course, it is the superior order of his musical instinct, his inborn artistic sagacity and an intense æsthetic individuality that create for him a unique place in music.

There are still people who compare him to his disadvantage with the masters of the romantic and coloristic school, with Nikisch, Furthwängler or Mengelberg. Some do not realize that Toscanini's nature is priestly and Hellenic to the loftiest degree. Great priest that he is, he reaches out for nothing but the soul of the work to be rekindled by him. He sacrifices everything,—color, brilliance, sonority, emotion too direct and crudely manifest, to the pure thought-substance, to the spiritual line of the music, he is projecting.

Toscanini's executive genius is best embodied in his extraordinary *touch* that illuminates the vibrant contour and the very kernel of the composition. Toscanini is the creator's trusted mouthpiece, devoted and honest to a martyr's degree. He is faithful to everything that the music breathes, to its inner dynamics, its true rhythmic pulse, its spiritual *cachet*. Not only his conscious self but the remotest recess of his instinct, loathes all that smacks of overemphasis, the perfumery, the visible or imperceptible *cabotinage* that saturate the inflated ego of today's deified conductor-emperor.

His mastery of ensemble surpasses even Nikisch's in its delicacy, in its elfin agility and radiance of spirit.

One marvels at the range of his interpretive grasp. It embraces the perfection of style in his reading of Mozart, the volcanic, flaming *credo* in his reading of the *Ninth Symphony,* the lofty intensity of his Wagner renditions which Lawrence Gilman describes so justly as "unendurable in their beauty." Then one recalls the noble engraving in his recreation of Ravel's *Daphnis,* the torrential sound orgy evoked in Honegger's *Pacific,* the light and radiant silhouette of his *Till Eulenspiegel,* and one is subjugated by this protean clairvoyance. Traits in general predilections or in his technique, may have some affinity with the masters of the past, but in purely tonal taste he is entirely a musician of our day, just as much so as a Hindemith, a Milhaud or a Prokofiev. His very aversion for adorning music, for inflating it with meaning, with extra-musical content, for emotionalizing what is but pure line and form, is the aversion of a today's musician. He is bewitched by the very flesh of music, by its sonority and rhythmic flux; their plan and balance entrance him. In this he is a true neo-classic musician, both Hellenic and modern.

To analyze the technique of Toscanini is difficult as it is at times exceptionally personal and complex. His gesture, in the past uniformly large and violent, the typical trait of an Italian master accustomed to the directing of great theatrical ensembles, is still used liberally, especially in orchestral *tutti*. His leonine manner is occasionally opposed to that carefully restrained movement of the wrist established by Nikisch, which dominates the modern school of conducting. At times, an incredible attention is demanded from the orchestra by Toscanini's gesture, in the execution, for example, of the orchestral *recitativo* that opens the finale of the *Ninth Symphony*. But we must bow before a superhuman will that achieves everything it desires, and with any means it may choose.

* *

*

In the preceding *exposé* I have undertaken a defining with all possible precision of the art of conducting. I have undertaken to circumscribe rigorously each of the three orders of proceeding, carried by the art. I have shown that conducting comprises the direction of the rhythmic life of the orchestral ensemble, a control of the latter's sonority, and an unfoldment of the plan and spirit of the work.

A conductor is therefore a very peculiar complex of artists. He is all in one:

a psychophysical metronome;

a pedagogue amalgamated with a virtuoso handling a gigantic instrument;

a mime, but one whose gesture is for the orchestra only.

THE COMPOSER AND THE CRITIC

A POSTLUDE

THE drama of the critic is that his court has no cases.

He sits in judgment at the table of art and is condemned to a ceaseless review of mediocrity. Nothing really happens in this gray flow of week-days. That is why the critic is ever lying in wait anxious for any glitter of genius. The fresh case of Sibelius, a regional luminary created first prince of the blood overnight, mocks us only too readily.

It is a vicious slander to say that the critic knows no enthusiasm.

* *
*

And now, to our quarrel.

The "litigation" between the critic, on the one hand, and Mozart, the fantastic pauper, Beethoven, the deaf madman, and Wagner, the arrogant man-ufacturer of "music of the future," is long over.

But there is an invisible standing contention between the critic and the composer, his contemporary.

I am not in the least interested in discussing a shallow type of attitude in either composer or critic, nor a shallow brand of their relationship. I refuse to consider the banal kind of critic who plays Jupiter in a sour disposition, or the humorless composer who sees himself as a focal point in the universe, and each compilation of his an event in history. Even a Whistler has no business to ask his critic "not to stray about blindly in his brother's flowerbeds and bruise himself."

The fact is that there is no relationship between the composer as such, and the critic. Their *rancunes* and their differences—almost entirely back stage—arise from confusion in understanding, more than from bad temper.

The composer and the critic have nothing in common as to either, mental position or stage of action. The composer is a creative and dyonisian power. Instinct, invisible promptings of his peculiar æsthetics, contradicting emotional truths living in the same soul, are his law. The critic is mainly a reasoning force. As such he is bound to seek yardsticks of judgment, consistency, a clear and centered source of the creator's visions.

In his habitual attitude toward the critic, the composer is, however, not an iota different from the tenor or other opera heroes or the concertizing fiddler.

He rarely realizes that the critic is solely an appointed agent of the public and has nothing to do with the composer. As a juror acting for the public and its instructor in the arts, the critic is simply out of the composer's reach and grievance.

And when the clear-thinking Oscar Thompson sees the critic's task as "holding up a mirror to what has been composed," [1] I take the liberty of adding: "by public commission."

Toward composers the critic should feel like Gilbert (Sullivan's grim *alter ego*) among clergymen, "like a lion who fell into a den full of Daniels." Among composers the critic is an alien body in entirely unrelated environs. The composer's feeling for the congregation of critics should be the same, interested but unrelated.

True, the critic, being practically the main source of information on the composer, is under

---

[1] Oscar Thompson: *Practical Musical Criticism* (Witmark).

obligation to bring him out in a useful way. But again, this is an obligation to the public, not to the composer. To the composer as such he owes nothing.

It follows, however, that while it is the inalienable right of the critic to be the protagonist or the antagonist of the composer, his ecstatic and unpaid press agent, so to speak, or his detractor, there is one thing the critic may not do. He may not be silent, ambiguous or cryptic on the work he is appointed to appraise. He must speak and enlighten; he owes this to the public.

* *

*

How broad are the critic's right and domain, anyhow?

In antiquity the critic was a servant of religion and the state—Cato, the Censor, looking after the *mores* of Rome; the *Gaonim,* Fathers of the Synagogue (in the first centuries A. D.) forbidding the playing on the *irus*; Saint Clement of Alexandria forbidding the flute because King David had not used it; later Savonarola fighting the "vanities."

Their position was exactly the same as that of

today's critic. They were agents of the public, but with this variance of mission. Their business was to see whether art built or destroyed. But the critic of our day has no such aim.

In spite of all attempts to turn the art of our day back to the civic and social directives of antiquity and make it again the handmaid of worship, but with new gods to kneel before, criticism today is more than ever a branch of free art, or science, or both. Its aim does not and must not be concerned with anything but the dissecting of facts of an *æsthetic* order and the defining of their true meaning.

This does not, however, exclude the personal and emotional element in judgment, if only because some hidden emotion is always spread at the bottom of our reasoning.

Oscar Wilde thought Keats a great poet, and Carlyle styled him "a dead jack-ass sprinkled with rose water," and each could surely write a strongly reasoned book to evolve his admiration or aversion.

In his excellent volume on orchestration Cecil Forsyth calls the second theme in Tchaikovski's *Francesca da Rimini,* the famous clarinet solo, "an exquisite melody." And I have always disliked

369

this flat tune, square, utterly prosaic, without grace and warmth. I could write reams on its pseudo-Russian style, ludicrous as a portrayal of Francesca's loveable Latin silhouette.

Of course, there is no such thing as objective criticism in that margin of appraisal which lies beyond the dissection of the physical and technical body of a piece of art. The peculiar usefulness of criticism lies in its subjective nature. The personal response is what we want, in addition to measurement taken of the musical fact.

Criticism is, indeed, science when it means dissection, but it is art, and one of deep human nature, where intuition and enthusiasm come in. The critic is, or should be, an ecstatic doctor as well as a warrior. How nobly is this duty put in Spinoza's saying that a wise man *"de humana impotentia non nisi parce loqui curabit at largiter de humane virtute seu potentia"*—is one who encourages improvement rather than forever damning the faults!

Alas, we critics are not saints, and our criticism is at its weakest when it would be "constructive." One must say, however, that obdurate professional negativeness in a critic is sign of a lack of sensibility and of an inferiority complex as well.

370

* *

*

Having thus made my stand clear it seems that the relationship between the composer and the critic is so simple and so slight that it is exhausted before they ever come into a related position. It seems that these "litigants" by misundersanding have really no point of contact: that the discussion that comes up epidemically—"Does the composer need the critic," "Must the critic serve the composer" etc., is a part of that airless futility which the French call so aptly *minauder dans le vide,*— making faces in an empty space.

The situation has, however, its intricacies.

The critic does not need the composer, that is, the contemporary, in the same sense as the public does not need him—and never did. It is the living composer who strives to create a demand for his work and thus imposes his music on his fellow man, which is quite right, of course. Only a weakling with little to say, an impotent schemer, a false genius can fail to force the world to listen to the address which a real creator is born to deliver.

But the composer, as it happens, needs not only

his listener but also *a* critic (not *the* critic, mind you).

For the very reason that a man cannot hear his own true voice and needs to be advised on the matter, the composer drops with one side of his being into the line of people who are served by the critic as public appraiser and instructor in the arts. An artist of real size listens to any criticism with cool keenness. He sifts it and puts it to good use even if a judgment be ignorant or malevolent.

Criticism, no matter how warped by personal notion, is a springboard for perfection. This truism is a bromide, but one ever good to take.

Any spiteful comment driven by personal malevolence is often a greater help to a craftsman than the mediocre gilded neutrality of "constructive criticism," just as the lash spurs the lazy knave better than the Ten Commandments.

Because I, too, have acted at times as critic, because I have not spared my fellow-composer and have never concealed even a most drastic opinion —I felt I owed the truth as I saw it—I wish to take the liberty of quoting some illuminating examples from my own experience with the bitter drink of the condemned. I have in mind some remarks made years ago concerning my own composition, comment lost in banality, inaccuracy and personal vilification.

In a criticism of an early orchestral piece of mine, amidst mockery at my "cosmic" stand or faith, with the inescapable ʃ"wagoner and the star" dragged in for good measure, amidst statements more ignorant than disparaging concerning my orchestration, I found a line dictated by instinct and by a noble if unconscious sense of responsibility, a note on the wrong way I was said to have built my climaxes.

I did not realize at the time that this remark as well as the angry words of another critic "Lazare, Lazare, wake up" [2] very properly censoring the over-contemplative, stagnant strain in my younger music, would forever cure me of the Russian academic torpor of my artistic infancy and would play an outstanding part in my later composition.

No one objects to a composer's foaming or fulminating at a critic; it is in the natural order of things. But detachment, sense of humor and a

[2] In *The Port of New York* by Paul Rosenfeld whose aversions are as honest and eloquent as his infatuations.

good ear for criticism are something the composer would not wish to be deprived of.

The real or even the imaginary foe's camp is the best place to learn.

* *

*

The judgment or the final verdict of the critic, is after all, an issue of one single man's taste and reasoning. And as any other individual, the critic can never withstand the impact of even artificially sustained glamour, propaganda and publicity for any old firm manufacturing music, even when, as in Stravinsky's case, it has run dry. Nor can the critic, a son of his day and a victim of his personal passions, keep his reasoning whole and balance his judgment as the collective judgment of mankind does—history, I mean.

This is why the wisest always shelter themselves from the outcry of wounded artists by insisting that their verdict is, of necessity, that of one man.

The eminent London music critic and thinker Frank Howes varies this point with finesse:

"The critic forms a scale of values, his own merely and not necessarily endorsed by others, but

374

still an organized and considered scale. His judgment may still be an opinion but it is considered opinion." [3]

In the light of these facts what remains of those mutinies and rebellions of the third of our century just passed?

In an age reeking with composers by propaganda, with the pressure of publicity and firms of a dazzling rénommée that have contrived to glitter long enough to keep it up still longer, even though their glitter is false and their pith rotten, even in such an age the collective opinion of mankind still refuses to be bedevilled.

And let this be a consolation to the composer.

Not the current criticism, the long line of opinions of him, remains in the memory of the world, but tangible things about him, facts. The actual worth of the composer, his lasting influence hinges on the impress he leaves on the form of art, the lines and furrows inbedded by him in the eternal mold of music.

Nothing else matters. He is a fool who tries to matter in art in any other way.

[3] Frank Howes: *A Key to the Art of Music* (Thomas Y. Crowell Co., New York, 1937).

INDEX

INDEX

Haydn, 5, 42, 43
Hebrew music, racial influence, 118; of the Russian Orient, 280, 288, 291-294, 297-298
Hebrew-American composers, 152-162
Heine, 249
Heinsheimer, Hans, quoted, 4 n.
Henderson, W. J., quoted, 159
Henry, Leigh, quoted, 141, 159, 207
Hindemith, Paul, *Daemon*, x, 8, 44, 67, 69, 74, 89, 130; *Marien-Lieder*, 44; *Neues zum Tage*, 44, 66, 69; *Die Junge Magd; Landsknecht's Trinklied*, 130, 165
Historical and prophetic aspects of tonal language, 84-114
Hoërée, Arthur, quoted, 54
Honegger, *Pacific*, 23, 26, 46, 62, 362
Hopkins, E. W., cited, 96 n.
Howard, John Tasker, 148 n.
Howes, Frank, quoted, 375
Human voice the font of music, 76, 80
Humphrey, Doris, 302
Hungarians, racial influence, 118; music, 141
Huri songs, 284

Impressionism, 112
Infra-atonality, 30
Irish melodies, 122, 123
Ives, Charles, 151, 166, 167, 170; genius and works, 173-175

Jacobi, Frederick, 152, 161; *Piano concerto; Second Quartet*, 177-178
James, Henry, quoted, 162
James, William, quoted, 105
Jazz, 18, 34, 40, 48-50, 69, 89, 122, 123
Jemnitz, Alexander, cited, 137 n.
Jews, racial influence, 118; *see also* Hebrew
Josten, Werner, *Concerto Sacro*, 177

Kevork, iv, 286
Kirstein, Lincoln, 302, 305
Kleiber, Erich, 330
Klemperer, Otto, 324
Kodaly, 141
Koechlin, Charles, 60
Koussevitzki, 330

Noises, inborn, 25
"Non-relativity" in orchestra, 35
Nordoff, Paul, works, 186-187

Oberon overture, conducting the, 329
Objectivist dogma, 58-68, 72
Opera-ballet, 315-317; opera, essence of, 315-317; future opera, 317-318
Orchestra, sound mimicking, 21; sway of old principle over, 33; salient features, 34; disintegrated by pressure of market, 44; as reflection of a cosmos-inspired era, 106; new art of conducting, 321-364; rhythmic ensemble, 327-344; sonority, 344-353; spiritual ensemble, interpretation, 353-357; conductors, 357-363
Orchestral *tutti*, 20, 33
Organic musical creations, 107, 108
Oriental music, 139, 244, 280-300
Originality, 16
Ornstein, Leo, 155, 156
Ostinato, 74

Palestrina *Sicut Cervus*, 78
Paliashvilli, Zachariah, 296
Paoli, Domenico de, cited, 52 n.
Percussion, use of, 37
Pétit, Raymond, quoted, 252 n.
Petrograd school, 223, 225, 238-243
Pisk, Paul, quoted, 73 n.
Piston, Walter, works, 177
Pizzetti, 134, 135; *Phoedra*, 135
Poe, Edgar Allan, 16
Polovinkin, Liév, 270, 274
Polyphony, 13, 36, 78
Polytonality, 19, x
Porter, Quincy, works, 177
Prokofiev, Serge, ix, 9, 118, 119, 167, 223, 225, 245; *Shout*, 51, 252; *Scythian Suite*, 119, 251; genius and works, 250-253; *Le fils prodigue*, 252, 302, 304, 308; *Ugly Duckling*, xi
Ptolemaism, musical, 49

Race, controlling force of, and revolution, 117-124; influences of, in America, 149; racial flow of music, 76, 81, 86-90
Rachmaninov, 224, 245, *Second concerto*, 196

INDEX

388

INDEX

Tonal language, technical and moral aspects, 3-83; historical and prophetic aspects, 84-114
Tonality, synthetic, 28
Tone, *see* Sound
Tonmalerei, 23
Toscanini, 134, 324, 333, 343, 344, 346, 348, 360-362
Tropuses, 72
Tutti, orchestral, 20, 33
Twelve-tone harmony, 38

Universal tonal language, 81, 86
Upbeat, attack—, 338, 340, 341

Valéry, Paul, quoted, 27, 65, 304
Vallas, Léon, quoted, 103; book on Debussy, xxi n.
Veprik, Alexandre, 270, 273
Vigny, Alfred de, quoted, 4
Villa-Lobos, works, 191-192
Vinogradova, Viéra, 275
Von Laban, Rudolf, 301, 309, 313
Von Webern, 73 n.; *Five Orchestral Pieces,* 34, 38, 47
Vuillermoz, Emil, quoted, 19, 33

Wagenaar, Bernard, 178
Wagner, 14, 19, 42, 57, 75, 78, 79, 87, 104, 134; *Parcifal,* xviii, 93, 95, 103, 104, 106, 109; *Tannhaüser,* 107; *Faust Ouverture,* 109; *Walküre,* 201, 204, 315; as conductor, 325, 336, 344
Wallenstein, Alfred, 349
Walter, Bruno, 324, 343
Weingartner, 325, 358
Wellesz, Egon, cited, 34 n.
Western racial music, 82, 86, 97, 99
Whistler, quoted, 366
Whithorne, Emerson, 152, 166, 167
Whitman, Walt, 105, 124
Wigman, Mary, genius and works, 301, 309-311
Wilde, Oscar, quoted, viii, 57, 369
Williams, Vaughan, ix; *Fantasia on a theme of Tallis,* xxv; genius and work, 209-210; *London Symphony,* 210
Wolf, Hugo, xvii

Yasser, Joseph, 29, 80, 90